D1606241

Umberto Eco is Italy's most famous living intellectual, known among academics for his literary and cultural theories, and to an enormous international audience through his novels, *The Name of the Rose, Foucault's Pendulum* and *The Island of the Day Before*. *Umberto Eco and the Open Text* is the first comprehensive study in English of Eco's work. In clear and accessible language, Peter Bondanella considers not only Eco's most famous texts, but also many occasional essays not yet translated into English. Tracing Eco's intellectual development from early studies in medieval aesthetics to seminal works on popular culture, postmodern fiction, and semiotic theory, he shows how Eco's own fiction grows out of his literary and cultural theories. Bondanella cites all texts in English, and provides a full bibliography of works by and about Eco.

Umberto Eco
and the open text

Umberto Eco
and the open text

Semiotics, fiction, popular culture

Peter Bondanella

Indiana University

Published by the Press Syndicate of the University of Cambridge
The Pitt Building, Trumpington Street, Cambridge CB2 IRP
40 West 20th Street, New York, NY 10011-4211, USA
10 Stamford Road, Oakleigh, Melbourne 3166, Australia

© Cambridge University Press 1997

First published 1997

Printed in Great Britain at the University Press, Cambridge

A catalogue record for this book is available from the British Library

Library of Congress cataloguing in publication data
Bondanella, Peter E., 1943–
Umberto Eco and the open text: semiotics, fiction, popular
culture / Peter Bondanella.
p. cm.
Includes bibliographical references.
ISBN 0 521 44200 1 (hardback)
1. Eco, Umberto – Criticism and interpretation. 2. Semiotics and
literature. I. Title.
PQ4865.C6Z58 1997
853'.914–dc20 96-3099 CIP

ISBN 0 521 44200 1 hardback

VN

For
Lynn Luciano
In Memoriam

Contents

Contents

Preface

Umberto Eco is probably Italy's most famous living intellectual figure. A significant portion of his critical works has been translated into English, not to mention countless other languages, even though that portion is but a small fraction of the mass of work he has produced in a wide variety of fields. While it is his literary and cultural theory, particularly associated with semiotics (a field to which he has made major contributions since the mid-1960s) which has established Eco's reputation as a major European intellectual, capable of comparison to such thinkers as Foucault, Lacan, Althusser, Derrida, or Barthes, Eco has a second and even broader international audience created by the extraordinary success of three widely read novels: *The Name of the Rose* (made into a major motion picture starring Sean Connery); *Foucault's Pendulum*; and *The Island of the Day Before.*

Given Eco's fame, it is surprising that numerous English-language books on him and his works are not already available. Dozens of books each year appear in English focusing upon other major European literary or cultural theorists, but readers searching for reliable information about Eco's intellectual development must be satisfied to peruse specialized scholarly journals or to glance through the all-too-brief critical introductions or translators' comments included in several English translations of his major works. The fact that French is the foreign language and culture most familiar to English or

American academics (especially those interested in literary theory or cultural studies) undoubtedly helps in part to explain this strange oversight. But this is only a partially satisfactory explanation, since it is regrettably the case that most French theory is read by English or American academics in translation, rather than in the original language. Too often, Anglo-Saxon academics have been inattentive to truly innovative developments in Italy for reasons that are often simply parochial; while medievalists and Renaissance specialists feel they cannot ignore Italy's contributions in literature, art, music, and culture, all too often contemporary scholars of literature in the English-speaking world have not looked to Italy for many years for original critical perspectives. In fairness, it must be noted that the recent appearance of a number of English translations of Eco's early books on aesthetics and popular culture will no doubt focus attention upon his entire career now that representative selections from every stage in his career are available in English. Nevertheless, a reader without some knowledge of Italian and lacking a firm grounding in Italian literature, culture, and history will find approaching Eco's works sometimes a difficult task, given the scope of his interests and the depth of his erudition.

The purpose of *Umberto Eco and the Open Text: Semiotics, Fiction, Popular Culture* is to provide a reliable, thought-provoking, but necessarily brief account of Umberto Eco's intellectual development and major theoretical contributions during the past four decades. It is my hope that the results will satisfy specialists in Italian studies, literary theory, and semiotics, but the book is also designed for what I trust is an even larger group of people, the educated but non-academic readers who still care about critical discourse on literature and contemporary culture. In short, this book defines as its model reader the same model reader Umberto Eco examines in his theoretical essays on narrative theory.

A complete bibliography of Eco's works would require a separate book by itself. Moreover, the massive quantity of Eco's writings is further complicated by the author's polyglot nature and his sometimes bewildering habit of publishing numerous variants of a single article or book in a variety of languages, making small and sometimes imperceptible but nevertheless important revisions each time. Lately, Eco has begun to compose articles and books in languages other than Italian, so that the "original" may well be written in a foreign tongue while the "translation" appears in his native language. Moreover, as Eco's international reputation has grown and grown in the aftermath of the appearance of his three novels, writings from other periods have been reprinted in numerous Italian editions (usually with modifications or revisions and new prefaces) or in translations which may sometimes differ from the Italian originals. In this study, I have cited English editions of Eco's writings whenever available, although my own assessment of Eco has been based upon the Italian texts. Any of Eco's works that have not yet appeared in English and to which I refer have been translated, if cited in my study, by me and will be so noted in the footnotes. In every instance that an English translation is employed, I have also provided a reference to the most current Italian edition.

Perhaps more than any single individual, Umberto Eco embodies the postmodern sensibility: his own work has made major contributions to the definition of what the term "postmodern" signifies, and his own personal habits as a writer seem to deny the uniqueness of individual artistic creation (the ultimate goal of literary modernism), and propose, instead, a continuous "work in progress" that constitutes his entire bibliography, an ever-evolving and highly sophisticated collection of original theories, heuristic ideas, amusing observations, and incisive vignettes that paint an unforgettable portrait of contemporary popular culture and provide a means of understanding the very cultural milieux that have produced Eco and his works.

In this study, I have decided to concentrate upon Eco's major books. For the most part, I shall deal with Eco's many hundreds of articles, essays, book reviews, and interviews primarily only when they are collected, as they periodically have been, and published as a book. Furthermore, in discussing Eco's novels, I shall focus not only upon their literary merits (which are considerable) but also upon their status (less often acknowledged) as implicit treatments of the nature of literary discourse, practical demonstrations of key philosophical concepts first expounded in his "serious" theoretical works, and highly self-conscious reflections of how Eco defines the mutual dependency between "high" culture and "mass" or "popular" culture in the postmodern world. It is my belief that Eco's move from semiotic theory to fiction represents a step forward, not a betrayal of "pure" theory but, rather, a fascinating experiment combining theory with practice that could have been successfully achieved by very few academic thinkers of his generation. Such a transition can hardly be said to imply a theoretical failure on Eco's part or a flaw in semiotics, since it was precisely Eco's immersion in structuralist and semiotic theory that allowed him, first, to understand the mechanisms underlying narrative fiction and, then, to become one of the century's most original and popular practitioners of postmodernist storytelling.

Eco's intellectual career moves through a remarkable series of intellectual developments. He intended to write a traditional thesis on Thomist aesthetics but eventually produced a rejection of the Crocean aesthetics that constituted modern Italy's most original contribution to twentieth-century philosophy. A precocious reader of James Joyce in an Italy that ignored the Irish novelist at the time, Eco, influenced not only by Joyce but also by communications theory and structuralist thought, then produced a post-Crocean aesthetics founded upon the concept of the "open work." Subsequent essays collected in a number of influential anthologies on popular culture emphasized the search for a methodology that could deal simultaneously with both the high culture literature of Dante as well as the comic strips of a Charles Schulz or the spy novels of an Ian Fleming. Eco's interest in exploring general theories about culture led him toward semiotics, the science of signs, and he was responsible, in part, for popularizing this new methodology and for turning the theory of semiotics toward a reappraisal of the American philosopher Charles Peirce, making Peirce's key ideas the cornerstone of his own semiotic theories. A major shift in Eco's career occurred when he turned from theory to practice, producing three major novels, the first of which, *The Name of the Rose*, reached astronomical sales figures never before even imagined by an Italian or European author in the world market. His fascination with demonstrating through concrete examples of prose fiction many of the theoretical concepts that had always attracted his attention (the role of the reader, the place of tradition in literature, various narrative strategies producing diverse effects, the philosophical status of textual interpretation, etc.) marks Eco's post-modernist stance as a novelist who simultaneously addresses a number of different audiences. It is this marriage of practice and theory that has characterized the latter part of Eco's intellectual career.

If Eco's career has been characterized by a complicated odyssey from Thomist aesthetics to postmodern fiction, the man behind the works has remained a constant. Eco's writings on semiotics, popular culture, and literary theory, as well as his fiction, all celebrate intellectual tolerance and an open-minded fascination with new ideas, while their author delights in polemical debates with his interlocutors and employs his rapier wit and ironic sense of humor in a prose style that has earned him the respect of readers in many different cultures.

I am indebted to critical comments on the manuscript supplied by a number of friends, colleagues, and students. I would like to thank the anonymous reader for Cambridge University Press who provided a critical eye to this manuscript that I found extremely useful. Katharina Brett, the Cambridge editor who originally dealt with me on this project, was a joy to work with, and Linda Bree was a perfect editor when the manuscript actually reached the press. I owe special thanks to Julia Conaway Bondanella, Jody Shiffman, and Matei Calinescu for reading parts of the manuscript and offering their useful advice at various stages of its composition. I am also grateful for the encourage-ment and advice of my colleagues Willis Barnstone, Bruce Cole, Harry Geduld, and David Hertz. Tom Sebeok, the founder of the program in semiotics at Indiana University, bears some responsibility for my interest in Umberto Eco (although none of the blame for any errors I might have made here): he was primarily responsible for inviting Eco to Indiana University on numerous occasions, having many of his works translated and published by our university press (on some of which he was a collaborator with Eco), and for nominating Eco for an honorary degree from Indiana University. Finally, Umberto Eco himself was kind enough to read the final manuscript and to provide detailed corrections about matters of fact concerning his life and the history of the publication of his works, information that has helped me to avoid the many errors of fact that plague almst all discussion of Eco's life in print in Italian reference works. Obviously, a critical biography of Eco written with full access to his own archives would be an important project for the future. In his reading of my manuscript, Eco scrupulously avoided ever attempt-ing to have me modify my own interpretations of his career, confirming the opinion that any reader may form of him from his own works, in which he constantly defends intellectual curiosity and a tolerance and respect for the views of others.

This book is dedicated to a dear, departed friend who met Umberto Eco several times in Bloomington under very amusing circumstances.

Bloomington, Indiana
Rome, Italy

1996

one

§

Umberto Eco's intellectual origins: medieval aesthetics, publishing, and mass media

Umberto Eco was born on 5 January 1932 in the city of Alessandria in the Piedmont region of Italy. Alessandria in the nineteenth century had become best known for the location of the most important factory of the Borsalino company, Italy's premier maker of hats.[1] According to the accounts of his childhood that have come down to us after he reached international fame (accounts, therefore, which may be somewhat tinged by hagiography), Eco was a precocious young student who excelled in cartoons, parodies, and intellectual games. Apparently he composed a parody of Dante in hendecasyllabic verse entitled *La diacqua commedia* (The Divine Water Comedy), purporting to narrate events in his family as if he were the *sommo poeta*.[2] After completing his *maturità classica* at the Liceo Plana, Eco began his university education, enrolling at the University of Turin, where he completed his degree in philosophy with Professor Luigi Pareyson in 1954.

[1] For Eco's account of his birthplace and its inhabitants, see "Miracle of San Baudolino," *Architectural Digest*, January 1994, pp. 24–32, now reprinted in Umberto Eco, *How to Travel with a Salmon & Other Essays*, trans. William Weaver (New York: Harcourt Brace Jovanovich, 1994), pp. 234–48; for the original, see Eco, *Il secondo diario minimo* (Milan: Bompiani, 1992), pp. 329–39.

[2] The reminiscences of two childhood friends (Gianni Coscia and Giovanni Massola), as well as reports on Eco's life between the time he left Alessandria and the completion of his university education, may be found in Francesca Pansa and Anna Vinci, *Effetto Eco*, Preface by Jacques Le Goff (Arricia: Nuova Edizioni del Gallo, 1990), pp. 1–65.

Even before the publication of his thesis, however, Umberto Eco had begun to make a name for himself, even if not initially in the fields of cultural and literary theory. In 1951, a young man named Mario Rossi was elected president of the Gioventù Italiana di Azione Cattolica (the GIAC), the youth group of the Catholic Church. At this early stage in his life, Eco was a militant Catholic intellectual, working closely with a man and a movement attempting to transcend the heavily conservative religious, social, and cultural policies represented by the then reigning pontiff, Pius XII. Eco worked with Rossi in Rome, writing for *Gioventù cattolica* (the publication of GIAC) and attempting to push the church into the direction that would reflect the more liberal policies of the French clergy of the period. When Pius XII forced Rossi's resignation from the direction of Azione Cattolica on 18 March 1954, Eco left the organization as well, and his resignation began a long period (1954–60) characterized by an avoidance of any practical political activity.

The Italian literary world in the immediate postwar period was predominantly shaped by remnants of prewar Crocean idealism, even though the Marxist literary theories of Georg Lukács and Antonio Gramsci would soon constitute a counterweight to Croce's intellectual hegemony. But neither early Marxist criticism nor Crocean idealism paid serious attention to what we may today label the manifestations of "popular" or "mass" culture in literature. In sharp contrast to this contempt for popular culture on both the right and the left, in an early article in *Gioventù cattolica* (17 January 1954), Eco declared with the self-assurance of youth: "If we went to dig through the library of a famous man, of a man of culture, or a scientist, perhaps we would discover there a series of detective novels. The detective novel is not only a youthful sin; it is a perpetual temptation."[3] This

---

[3] Cited in Pansa, *Effetto Eco*, p. 23. The Italian name for the detective, mystery or "whodunit" novel is *un giallo*, referring to the traditionally yellow covers used by the publishing house of Arnoldo Mondadori, the company that introduced in 1929 what was essentially a foreign literary genre to Italy. The fact that Eco's literary fame is due to his best-selling mystery novel is only one of the many aspects of his career that sets him

early remark about the importance of the mystery or detective novel – the kind of popular literary genre so many of the mature theorist's essays would do so much to explain in successive decades – may be taken as an initial declaration of critical independence from the predominant schools of criticism in Italy at the time, all of which took themselves terribly seriously and were concerned primarily with "high" culture.

While not so well known outside of Italy as Rome, Florence, and Venice, Turin in Piedmont and Milan in Lombardy in the 1950s were exciting intellectual environments in which to live.[4] Milan was the financial and publishing capital of an Italy poised on the brink of what would later be described as the "economic miracle." It was also the home of a significant portion of the Italian avant-garde in art, music, and literature. Turin, the center of the automobile industry and the Fiat Corporation, would lead the mechanization of Italy and thereby ushered into the postwar period not only a consumer society but also an enormous internal migration which eventually turned Turin into the largest "southern" Italian city in the nation. Turin's intellectuals were also reshaping the definition of Italian culture. At the city's university, Norberto Bobbio (1901–) held the Chair of Philosophy of Law after 1948 and began a long series of books, usually printed by Turin's major publishing house, Einaudi, critical of Italy's idealist heritage and focusing upon a number of pressing practical political problems. Giovanni Getto (1913–) came to the university's Department of Italian Literature in 1948. While initially identified with a form of historical criticism indebted to Crocean models, Getto would

apart from his countrymen. For a summary of the history of the *giallo* in Italy, see Benedetta Bini, "Il poliziesco" in Alberto Asor Rosa, ed., *Letteratura italiana – storia e geografia: l'età contemporanea* (Turin: Einaudi, 1989), III: 999–1026.

[4] Umberto Eco's university career will eventually become linked to the city of Bologna, but his early intellectual and editorial connections have closer ties to either Turin or Milan. For lengthy and enlightening discussions of the role Turin and Milan played in the postwar period in Italy, see Marziano Guglielminetti and Giuseppe Zaccaria, "Torino" and Folco Portinari, "Milano" in Alberto Asor Rosa, ed., *Letteratura italiana – storia e geografia: l'età contemporanea*, III: 77–129 and 221–88.

eventually work to introduce Italian scholars to the structuralist analysis of literary texts. Eco befriended one of Getto's star pupils, Edoardo Sanguineti (1930–), who would later become one of the key figures in the literary movement called Gruppo 63. Eco's writings on aesthetics culminating in the publication of *Opera aperta* (*The Open Work*, 1962) reflected, in many respects, the concerns of this avantgarde movement. Sanguineti would eventually become one of the most caustic and unforgiving reviewers of Eco's best-selling fiction. In philosophy, Nicola Abbagnano (1901–) had begun opening Italian philosophy to the foreign influences of European existentialism (Sartre, Heidegger) and away from Crocean idealism. Luigi Pareyson (1918–91), an influential theorist of aesthetics who had come to the University of Turin from Pavia in 1952 and with whom Eco would write his thesis on the aesthetics of St. Thomas Aquinas, devoted his major works to a new theory of aesthetics and historical studies of existentialism, all of which constituted a reaction against Crocean idealism.[5]

In literature, Cesare Pavese (1908–50) had just committed suicide after an unhappy love affair with an American actress, but his editorial work at Einaudi had already begun to shape the Italian literature of the postwar period, especially with a series of translations from American literature. Nineteenth- and twentieth-century American writers became popular and were instrumental in offering stylistic models diametrically opposed to the highly rhetorical prose of Gabriele d'Annunzio, the most popular Italian writer of the prewar period. Pavese had written his own thesis on the poetry of Walt Whitman at the University of Turin in 1930 at a time when such

[5] Pareyson's major works include: *La filosofia dell'esistenza e Karl Jaspers* (Naples: Loffredo, 1940); *Studi sull'esistenzialismo* (Florence: Sansoni, 1943); *Estetica: teoria della formatività* (Turin: Edizioni di filosofia, 1954; rpt. Milan: Bompiani, 1989); and *Teoria dell'arte* (Milan: Marzorati, 1965). Pareyson not only helped introduce European existentialism to Italy but also was important in the spread of Heidegger and hermeneutics. His assistant, Gianni Vattimo (1936–), a classmate of Eco's at the University of Turin, replaced Pareyson in the chair of philosophy at Turin after serving as his assistant for many years.

studies were not common, and he eventually translated such American classics as Melville's *Moby Dick*, Steinbeck's *Of Mice and Men*, and novels by Faulkner, Gertrude Stein, John Dos Passos, Sherwood Anderson, and Sinclair Lewis. Perhaps equally influential and certainly a longer-lasting influence upon the Turin literary scene was Elio Vittorini (1908–66), like Pavese another early enthusiast of American literature and an editor at Einaudi. From 1945 until 1947, Vittorini edited the weekly cultural magazine *Il Politecnico*, a publication that engaged in lively debates with the official publications of the Italian Communist Party over the proper direction for postwar Italian culture. Vittorini would direct a number of Einaudi's book series and edited, with Italo Calvino, Einaudi's important literary review, *Il Menabò di letteratura*, which first appeared in 1959 and in which Eco would eventually publish an important essay entitled "Del modo di formare come impegno sulla realtà" (Form as Social Commitment), a piece eventually worked into the second edition of *The Open Work* in 1967. And, of course, there was the increasingly important presence of Italo Calvino (1923–85), editor at Einaudi from 1947 until 1983, whose literary fame had been originally launched at Einaudi by Cesare Pavese with the publication of *Il sentiero dei nidi di ragno* (*The Path to the Nest of Spiders*, 1947). Finally, while less important to Eco's formation, mention should also be made of other major literary figures from Turin such as Primo Levi (1919–87), Carlo Levi (1902–77), and Natalia Ginzburg (1916–91), many of whose most influential literary works first appeared with the Einaudi imprimatur.

Northern Italy was therefore an intellectually exciting place. Between Turin and Milan, Eco's twin points of reference, old modes of thinking were tested, modified, and rethought in a number of literary and cultural fields as Italian society itself was transformed into a modern, consumer-oriented society characterized by an emerging popular or mass culture that the dominant prewar elites, staunch defenders of "high" culture, preferred to ignore. Umberto Eco would take advantage of access to such cultural changes by plunging directly into one crucial expression of this new mass culture – the upstart medium of television. Immediately after completing his doctorate in 1954, Eco took a position with the Milanese television studio of the RAI, the Italian state network that at the time exercised a monopoly within the peninsula over all means of mass communication. It was at the RAI that Eco met Furio Colombo (1931–), a journalist who became a life-long friend and would eventually direct the Italian government's cultural institute in New York. At the RAI, Eco also befriended Luciano Berio (1925–), whose avant-garde music would play a major role in formulating the theories Eco introduces in *The Open Work*. Eco's television experience was therefore crucial in a number of respects. Besides making a number of personal contacts that would influence the rest of his professional and private life, he was thrown pell-mell from the rarefied atmosphere of the Italian university, a cathedral devoted to the often monastic pursuit of learning, into the everyday world of popular culture. His work covered a wide variety of fields, from cultural programs to book reviews, children's shows, and dramatic reconstructions of historical events. A version of the popular American program "You Are There" was one of the projects upon which he collaborated. Like its American counterpart, the Italian program was devoted to imaginary interviews with important histori- cal figures at a crucial moment in the past, and the series had a primarily didactic purpose. Everything was broadcast live in an era before video tape, and the entire industry still had the improvisational atmosphere of a new toy that must certainly have constituted its major attraction. Such an experience would later bear fruit in some of Eco's most thought-provoking essays on popular and mass culture phenom- ena in the 1970s, his so-called "semiotic" period. And his years in Turin, surrounded by the intellectual ferment the city boasted during the 1950s, represent a fundamental stage in Eco's early development, during which time he moved beyond his essentially academic back- ground into a wider, broader, and far more suggestive framework for his theoretical writings.

Eco published several important essays in the 1950s, but his original ideas and theories about the nature of the contemporary avant-garde and the "open work" would first see the light in journals of relatively limited diffusion before eventually being turned into book-length essays in the early 1960s. As we might expect from a promising young intellectual with a voracious memory and prodigious appetite for erudition, Eco's doctoral thesis, defended in 1954 and published in 1956, was devoted to what is even for well-educated readers (except for fans of James Joyce) an esoteric subject: the aesthetic theories of St. Thomas Aquinas. The first edition was entitled *Il problema estetico in San Tommaso*. In a second edition, which contained a number of stylistic modifications and an important new conclusion written during the time Eco was heavily influenced by structuralist theory, the title is modified to *Il problema estetico in Tommaso d'Aquino*. Thus, as Eco's thinking evolved, the learned doctor of the Catholic Church lost his saintly title. Yet, Eco's treatment of Aquinas' aesthetic theories argues paradoxically for the increased relevance of Scholastic philosophy for twentieth-century methodology. Shortly thereafter in 1959, Eco published a far briefer synopsis of his aesthetic theories which nevertheless embodied most of the ideas in the more erudite volume devoted to Scholastic aesthetics, "Sviluppo dell'estetica medievale" (The Development of Medieval Aesthetics) which would later appear in English in 1986 as *Art and Beauty in the Middle Ages*. In the following year, an enlarged and revised version of the English edition was published in Italy as *Arte e bellezza nell'estetica medievale*. The two works can be discussed together without doing too much damage to Eco's arguments, since the shorter essay recapitulates, for the most part, conclusions argued with more subtlety and far more attention to detail in the longer work.

Eco himself points out the defects of the first edition of the work on Aquinas in his preface to the second edition of 1970: "it is a typically youthful work, with all the faults that this implies: a convoluted style, a tendency to equate the readable with the unscientific, the headstrong insistence of a young scholar upon technical-sounding phrases instead of plain language, and an overblown apparatus whose purpose, often enough, was merely to show that the writer had read everything he could find on the subject."[6] More important than his honest appraisal of his stylistic pretensions is Eco's acknowledgment that when the work was begun in 1952, the writer himself was a practicing Catholic working in the militant ranks of Azione Cattolica. By the time Eco completed the study and published his findings, he had set aside both Thomistic metaphysics and a religious outlook on life for a more secular attitude.

Yet, in both the first and second editions of the study, Eco emphasizes the continuing relevance of the methodology he evolved in his study of Aquinas, even going so far as to quote in his second preface of 1970 a statement on methodology in the first edition:

> I believe that a philosopher's significance appears most fully when he is placed in his own time, considered as a representative of his period, and when his ideas are seen as part of a problematic peculiar to that period. His greatness consists in his ability to encompass the spiritual temper of his age . . . And what we can learn from him is above all the lesson of his humanity, which is also a lesson in method in a somewhat wider and deeper sense of that term than is usual.[7]

In the preface to *Art and Beauty in the Middle Ages*, Eco is even more blunt about rejecting the typical flaws of young Italian scholars ("tortured syntax as a respectable symptom of wisdom and maturity"), while accepting the basic opinions expressed in the essay: "maybe in this small book I tell my story with the clumsiness of a young scholar, but I tell a story in which I still believe."[8]

---

[6] *The Aesthetics of Thomas Aquinas*, translated by Hugh Bredin (Cambridge: Harvard University Press, 1988), p. vii; for the original Italian, see Umberto Eco, *Il problema estetico in Tommaso d'Aquino* (Milan: Bompiani, 1982), p. 5.

[7] *The Aesthetics*, p. viii; *Il problema estetico*, pp. 6–7.

[8] Umberto Eco, *Art and Beauty in the Middle Ages*, translated by Hugh Bredin (New Haven: Yale University Press, 1986), p. ix.

Few readers interested in Eco's literary or cultural theory will become passionately involved in discussions of medieval aesthetics, although readers familiar with his best-selling novels will not find Eco's medieval erudition surprising. Yet, it is necessary to grasp what Eco means by the evolution of his critical method in his work on Scholastic aesthetics in order to understand his approach throughout his intellectual career. A fundamental characteristic of Eco's scholarship here and in his later theoretical writing – his impressive linguistic abilities – literally leaps out at the reader on every page. Today, anxious young scholars seeking tenure busily cite Derrida, Foucault, Lacan, and Gramsci at every turn in English translation. Few possess the ability to read such theorists, or the numerous literary works such theorists analyze, in the language in which either the theory or the literary works first appeared. In contrast, Eco's mastery of medieval Latin and his facile command of major European languages cannot fail to impress. Eco brings such erudition and energetic research to bear upon all his projects, and his academic persona seems to hark back to an earlier tradition of nineteenth-century philological scholarship usually identified with Germanic academics, such as Auerbach, Curtius, and Spitzer, and which in Italy found its most felicitous expression in Benedetto Croce, Eco's theoretical *bête noire*. In Eco's case, the felicitous combination of such Teutonic linguistic prowess and erudition avoids the arrogant pedantry too often associated with the lesser exponents of such learning and is lightened by his celebrated sense of humor, a quality not often associated with the German philological tradition.

Without Eco's linguistic preparation and his generally impressive erudition, his methodology would fail to function, for its major goal, in the author's own words, is to "explain and clarify every term and every concept in the original texts in the light of the historical circumstances to which they belonged," remaining "genuinely faithful to Aquinas," and returning him to "his own" time and "his authentic visage." When Eco applied his own methodology to

Aquinas, he discovered that "his truth" was no longer Eco's truth.[9] Umberto Eco's philosophical method thus begins with true "faithfulness" to a literary text, which involves thorough preparation in languages other than his own. As Eco has become a popular figure with the publication of his novels, his mastery of English and French (in which he gives lectures, writes original articles, and composes entire books, as well as assisting in the translation of his many works) has always represented one of his trump cards in introducing his ideas directly into various academic and cultural communities around the globe.

Historically, Eco faced two major stumbling-blocks to an understanding of Aquinas' aesthetic theories. In the first place, there were the neo-Thomist or neo-Scholastic scholars who approached Aquinas as a doctor of the church. A doctor of the church could not, in principle, err. When Eco speaks of learning the lesson of Aquinas' "humanity," he implicitly rejects the elevation of this thinker, or any thinker, to such a privileged position. Understanding a mind from the past involves clearing our own minds of any contemporary ideology and allowing the past to speak in its own language, with its own technical terms, and with its own ideology. Such a language should always be considered not as eternal or revealed "Truth" but, rather, as a historically circumscribed "truth," one of many possible "truths." Accepting the claims of the church that Aquinas was an infallible philosopher would, Eco believed, preclude any historical understanding of his role in the development of a medieval aesthetic.

Perhaps even more of an ideological or intellectual obstacle to Eco's historical methodology was the Crocean idealism that then dominated and had dominated Italian criticism even before the beginning of the Second World War. In fact, Eco begins his study of Aquinas with a discussion and critique of Benedetto Croce's negative assessment of medieval aesthetics contained in a review of Nelson Sella's *Estetica musicale in San Tommaso*, which Croce had published in his review, *La critica*, in 1931:

[9] *The Aesthetics*, pp. vii–viii; *Il problema estetico*, p. 6.

The essential thing is that the problems of aesthetics were not the object of any genuine interest, either to the Middle Ages in general, or to St. Thomas in particular . . . For this reason, studies of the aesthetics of St. Thomas and other medieval philosophers make dull and unhelpful reading when (as is usually the case) they lack the restraint and good taste that characterize Sella's work.[10]

Croce's dismissal of Scholastic aesthetics provides Eco with the target all young and ambitious academics love to attack when justifying a new book on an old and seemingly worn-out topic – that of the Master in error. The aesthetic theories Croce propounded made it impossible for the Neapolitan theorist to come to grips with the kinds of problems that fascinated Eco. The foundation of Croce's aesthetic theory was the belief that art derived from pure intuition. Furthermore, Croce believed that all art is an expression of the artist's emotion and is therefore ultimately "lyrical" – the intuition of an image. Therefore, for Croce, writing the history of either a literary genre or a period style, as well as working on projects involving comparative literature, were, in theoretical terms, fruitless endeavors. The critic's task consisted primarily in the identification, interpretation, and assessment of the lyrical, uniquely "poetic" moments in literary texts. Such moments are not only original, creative moments, but they are also only expressed through individual, concrete images. In Croce's theory, there is of necessity a strict organic unity between form and content. Croce rejected any type of rhetorical, generic, or formal theory stressing historical development over time rather than the concrete, unique character of an individual work of art. Ultimately, in his later essays on aesthetics, Croce even went so far as to affirm that a critic's primary task was to distinguish between "poetry" and "non-poetry" in a work, and Croce defined "non-poetry" as all elements not reflecting the perfectly achieved expression of the lyrical essence of art.

Eco is perhaps one of the few Italian scholars in the postwar period to share the kind of erudition and linguistic ability Benedetto Croce

---

[10] *The Aesthetics*, p. 1; *Il problema estetico*, p. 15.

enjoyed. Yet Eco rejected Croce's aesthetic theory because it denied any historical development and any diachronic instability. For Croce, poetic moments in Dante, Shakespeare, or Ariosto existed in a timeless realm of completely achieved lyrical expressions that had little or nothing to do with the historical periods they reflected. In fact, Croce's ahistorical aesthetics suffered from the same fatal flaw that Eco will finally discover embedded in the aesthetics of Aquinas.

Influenced by Pareyson's own aesthetic theories, which rejected Croce's emphasis upon art as idealistic vision or as the expression of lyricism, Eco preferred to see art, following Pareyson, as *form* and to replace the Crocean concept of "expression" with that of "production" as a forming action.[11] His exhaustive analysis of numerous classical sources for medieval aesthetics, as well as almost every pertinent Scholastic statement on the subject, led him to a long treatment of the definition of beauty contained in Aquinas' *Summa Theologiae* (I, 4, 4, *objectio* 4): "Beauty, however, has to do with knowledge, for we call those things beautiful which please us when they are seen" (*visa placent*).[12] Eco analyzed beauty as a transcendental category in Aquinas in great detail, along with the formal criteria for beauty (proportion, integrity, clarity). He concluded that "form is the cause and origin of the aesthetic," thereby refuting Croce's emphasis on *liricità* and affirming the lessons learned from his master Pareyson.[13] A chapter dealing with concrete Scholastic aesthetic problems – the beauty of the Son of God, the beauty of mankind, the beauty of music – leads to a discussion of three different types of medieval symbolism (metaphysical symbolism, universal allegory, and the differences between scriptural and poetic allegory) that will have a bearing on Eco's future

[11] Eco discusses Pareyson's ideas in an essay included in the English edition of *The Open Work*, trans. Anna Cancogni with an intro. by David Robey (Cambridge: Harvard University Press, 1989), "Form and Interpretation in Luigi Pareyson's Aesthetics," pp. 158–66 (the original essay appeared in *Lettere italiane*). This essay was not included in either the original Italian edition of *Opera aperta* or in subsequent Italian reprintings of that book.

[12] *The Aesthetics*, p. 35; *Il problema estetico*, p. 54.

[13] *The Aesthetics*, p. 121; *Il problema estetico*, p. 153.

works on semiotics, hermeticism, and meaning. Ultimately, the crucial lesson derived from Eco's book on Aquinas was his realization that the Scholastic definition of beauty as a transcendental is ultimately contradicted by the fact that beauty is defined with the key phrase *visa placent*: beautiful things *please us when they are seen*. A subjective condition for beauty is in direct contradiction with its status as a transcendental.

As mentioned in the preface, Eco's works are frequently revised or modified in subsequent editions or translations. Additions, deletions, revisions, as well as explanatory prefaces or conclusions, may be added to the original edition to reflect the constant evolution of the author's thinking. Eco's treatment of his own written work as an evolving artefact and not an immutably fixed, ideal form parallels the lesson Eco learned from the internal contradictions he unearthed in Aquinas' magnificent philosophical system. When he first completed the study of Aquinas, Eco himself was "as yet too much of a Scholastic" and still believed that the discovery of internal contradiction, in a work of philosophy, required the repudiation of an entire philosophical system.

By the time Eco had written his second preface, however, and had published his own original study of contemporary aesthetics, *The Open Work*, he had already encountered the works of the major European structuralist theorists. Eco had come to realize that "every system has a contradiction within itself":

> a system *must* have a contradiction to undermine it, for a system is a structural model which arrests reality for an instant and tries to make it intelligible. But this arrest, necessary for communication, impoverishes the real instead of enriching it. The model is of value only if it stimulates an advance to a new level of understanding of reality, a level on which it then seems inadequate.[14]

As a result of this insight, it became possible for Eco not only to view Scholastic aesthetics in its proper historical context and with its own

---

[14] *The Aesthetics*, pp. x–xi; *Il problema estetico*, p. 11.

terminology, but also to judge it by its own criteria of consistency and not by criteria produced by the present. Because of this perspective, his erudite analysis of Scholastic aesthetics still makes interesting reading almost four decades after its first appearance. But even more enlightening for the student of Eco's future cultural and literary theory are the lessons, outlined in his additional preface and conclusion of 1970, that Eco applied to theory in general. For a by-product of his study of Aquinas and medieval Scholasticism was the revelation that the then popular structuralism resembled Scholasticism in some of its more negative aspects. The ideological goal of Scholasticism, to demonstrate that "reality could be construed as a motionless system of relations, fully intelligible and not subject to further change," is not, for Eco, dissimilar from the approach of structuralist theory, which also avoided dialectical contradiction and a sense of diachronicity, stressing synchronicity instead.[15] Eco discerned other less negative parallels between Scholasticism and structuralism, however. Both claimed to be interdisciplinary discourses. Both boasted a universal logic. Both sought to reduce all human sciences to a single master science (to linguistics, in the case of structuralism). Both frequently proceeded by way of binary divisions, dominated by the synchrony that characterizes their approaches to reality.[16] Ultimately, Eco suggests that Aquinas actually invented the structuralist model, for his Scholastic view of reality was a structure made up of relations among what Eco calls "full" elements (that is, substantial forms), while the structuralist system is a structure made up of relations among "empty" values, or values defined solely by their difference from other values. As a result, Eco concluded that the explanatory model of Aquinas, "when emptied of its content, was the same as the structuralist model. That is, it offered the same possibility of conceiving of a compound as a system of values."[17]

---

[15] *The Aesthetics.*, p. xi; *Il problema estetico*, p. 11.

[16] *The Aesthetics.*, pp. 216–17; *Il problema estetico*, pp. 258–59.

[17] *The Aesthetics*, p. 219; *Il problema estetico*, p. 261.

Eco's treatise on the aesthetics of Aquinas had limited its scope to a narrow focus upon a specific problem in one branch of philosophy, aesthetics. With the evolution of his views on aesthetics, however, embodied in the new 1970 preface and conclusion to his studies of Scholasticism, Eco added a new historical or ideological dimension to his earlier book. As he notes, no system of thought as well organized as that of Aquinas collapses solely because of apparently *logical* or internal inconsistencies. Such systems arise "as a response to specific social, political, and cultural questions and to solicitations which are implicit in the relations of production and are mediated through the superstructure"; the failure of a philosophy results from a breakdown in "something *outside* it."[18] Aquinas' image of an immutable reality was "mystificatory," Eco believed, since the facts around him in the dynamically changing society of medieval Italy contradicted the Scholastic search for essences. In the eyes of experience, science, and especially the new vernacular literature of Dante, Petrarca, and Boccaccio (together with the new merchant class they represented), such essences had already changed drastically and immutably: "the Thomistic model expressed the ideology of a system of relations of production, and a system of political relations, which they, the new men, were beginning to annul."[19] Eco concludes that *all* systems of thought attempting to rationalize individual historical relations at a particular moment in historical time are of "equal value" and that every philosophy's claim – "This is how things really are!" – represents "an act of mystification."[20]

Eco's remarks in his 1970 preface and conclusion are themselves demonstrations of the idea they express, for such views certainly mirror his interest in Marxist theory after 1968. His reference to "relations of production" and other similar Marxist terminology suggest that he, too, has absorbed new ideas from his milieu that were

[18] *The Aesthetics.*, pp. 209–10; *Il problema estetico*, p. 251.
[19] *The Aesthetics*, p. 213; *Il problema estetico*, p. 254.
[20] *The Aesthetics*, p. 215; *Il problema estetico*, p. 257.

not as influential when Eco first published his study of Aquinas. But the conclusion Eco draws from his retrospective assessment of his work on medieval aesthetics avoids the far more revolutionary conclusions many of his university colleagues drew during that troubled period in Italy. Eco was attracted by the parallel between Scholasticism and structuralism as a valid reason to study past aesthetic theories. The impact of Scholasticism upon modernist poetics in writers such as James Joyce, and upon the literary theorists of the Chicago School or the New Critics, provided additional incentives. Only a few years later, Eco himself would devote many pages to a study of Joyce within the context of his own aesthetics in *The Open Work*. Ultimately, however, Eco justified studying the Scholastics not for philosophical, historical, or intellectual reasons but for what ultimately represents an aesthetic and a moral impulse:

> Anyone who makes use of the thinking of the past is enriched by an experience which is organic and complete, and is enabled subsequently to reconsider the world from a higher level of wisdom. However malformed and misplaced the tower which he has clambered up, he will see a larger vista; and not necessarily behind him. As Bernard of Chartres remarked, with a genial, imperious, and spurious humility, we are dwarfs standing on the shoulders of giants.[21]

Few readers of Eco's treatise on medieval aesthetics could have imagined that its author would eventually produce a best-selling novel replete with medieval erudition, untranslated Latin phrases, and puns of all kinds. And in truth, concentration upon Eco's early career with an eye only on his studies of Scholastic aesthetics would do Eco's personality and the wide range of his interests a great injustice and would never prepare us for the humor of his future works, as well as his irreverent attitude toward clerics and theorists in general. To anticipate fully the mixture of humor and erudition that

---

[21] *The Aesthetics*, p. 222; *Il problema estetico*, p. 264.

will characterize Eco's entire career, we must make at least brief mention of a little pamphlet called *Filosofi in libertà*. The title can be rendered into English as either "Philosophers in Freedom" or perhaps "Liberated Philosophers," if the phrase "in libertà" also makes reference to the Futurist motto "parole in libertà" or "words in freedom." In this work, Eco treats the history of philosophy in cartoons and verse, from the pre-Socratics to the present day. His goal is to "liberate" philosophy from its overly serious character and to apply laughter to its sometimes all-too-ponderous posturing. The book was first published under the Joycean pseudonym of Dedalus in a small volume limited to 550 copies by Marianne Abbagnano. It was issued again in 1959 in another 500 copies and subsequently a third time in 300 copies in 1989. This semi-serious narration of the development of philosophy soon became a collector's item and was included by popular demand in Eco's *Il secondo diario minimo* (*How to Travel with a Salmon & Other Essays*, 1992).[22]

Fifteen cartoons, not dissimilar from those in daily newspapers, illustrate a humorous trip through the pre-Socratics, Aristotle, Saint Anselm, Abelard, Aquinas, Nicholas of Cusa, Roger Bacon, René Descartes, Spinoza, Vico, Kant, Schopenhauer, Hegel, Marx, Nietzsche, Croce, Gentile, Boutroux, Bergson, Dewey, Husserl, and a number of existentialists and ordinary language philosophers. The cartoons capture Eco's talent for puns and for his subversive, irreverent sense of humor. In one of them, for instance, Abelard (famous for the emasculation he suffered as a result of his love affair with Heloise) is addressed by a friar with a single question: "Vir?" ("Man?") and like a good medieval debater, Abelard responds: "Sic et non" ("Yes and no"). In another, at the ticket counter of the train station, Nietzsche asks for "un biglietto di andata e eterno ritorno." Here Eco plays upon the Italian expression for "round-trip ticket"

---

[22] See *Il secondo diario minimo*, pp. 201–43, for the complete text and Eco's explanation of the work's history. The partial English translation, *How to Travel With a Salmon*, does not include *Filosofi in libertà*.

("un biglietto di andata e ritorno"), adding the adjective "eternal" in a reference to Nietzsche's notion of the "eternal return." In a third cartoon, Giovanni Gentile, a philosopher associated with a form of idealism expounded in his *Teoria generale dello spirito come atto puro* (*The Theory of Mind as Pure Act*, first published in 1916) is shown at a confessional, describing his philosophical "sin" to a priest: ". . . and then I committed a pure act . . ." Gentile's confession refers both to the philosopher's major book and puns upon the Italian euphemism for masturbation ("atti impuri" or "impure acts"). The rest of this collection continues in much the same vein.

Of course, no student of Eco's works would equate this bit of goliardic verse and collection of cartoons with the scholarly achievement represented by Eco's two major books on medieval aesthetics. But Umberto Eco and all his theories cannot be understood without some notion of his sense of humor, his love for word-punning, and his ingenious linguistic games. These qualities reflect a mentality that permeates *The Name of the Rose*, an entire novel centered on a villainous monk who fears the redemptive power of laughter. Laughter, Eco always reminds his reader, is an activity that is proper only to man. And it is ultimately Eco's sense of humor that prompts him to apply serious analytical tools usually identified with "high" culture to phenomena generally associated with "low-brow" mass culture, such as cartoons, advertising, television programs, James Bond novels, and Superman comics. The alternation, or, more accurately, the contemporaneous composition, of erudite and theoretical writings, on the one hand, and less weighty, apparently frivolous books, on the other, will characterize each important phase of Eco's career. Eco's combination of theory, learning, and erudition with humor, parody, and pastiche constitutes one of the fundamental traits of his way of theorizing about literature, culture (both "high" and "low"), and the world around him.

two

§

The Open Work, Misreadings, and modernist aesthetics

Umberto Eco's treatises on medieval and Scholastic aesthetics reflect the esoteric and rarefied atmosphere of an Italian university, an erudition he satirizes in his parody of the history of philosophy. With his subsequent publications in the early 1960s – *The Open Work* and *Misreadings* – Eco continues his pattern of alternating a learned and erudite work with a parody and pastiche of the same subject-matter, but his cultural and critical theory now encompasses theoretical positions associated with the Italian avant-garde. During the same period, after working with the Turin television studio of the RAI from 1954 until 1958, Eco abandoned this post for an even more eventful career collaborating with Bompiani, a major Italian publishing house centered in Milan. From 1959 until the present day, Eco has played a major role at Bompiani, not only as the house's most profitable novelist but also as a major influence upon its editorial policy. While Eco's role at Bompiani was originally to direct a philosophical collection, *Idee nuove* (New Ideas), he was brought into the press for his familiarity with innovative theories from a wide variety of fields, and he continues to this day as an editor of several collections dealing with the fields of sociology and semiotics. By Valentino Bompiani's own testimony, it was Eco's parody of the history of philosophy in verse that first brought the young intellectual to the publisher's attention, not his more learned tomes on Scholastic aesthetics.[1]

It is also in this period that Eco took the first tentative steps in what eventually became a brilliant academic career. After obtaining the *libera docenza* in aesthetics in 1961, he began offering seminars and courses at the universities of Turin and Milan in 1962. In 1966, he received the Chair of Visual Communications at the Faculty of Architecture of the University of Florence, and this position would later be followed by his move in 1971 to the University of Bologna, where he joined a new and experimental faculty – DAMS – Discipline dell'arte, della musica e dello spettacolo (DAMS: Disciplines of Visual and Performing Arts and Music) – and eventually was awarded Italy's first chair in semiotics. DAMS had been founded by a classical Greek scholar named Benedetto Marzullo to respond to the need for specialization in fields not covered by traditional academic departments, in particular mass communication. In 1993, Eco moved from DAMS to a new doctoral program called Scienze della Comunicazione (Sciences of Communication), a program of which he is the *presidente* (Chairman or Director). He retains his Chair of Semiotics in both programs. Eco's international success as a best-selling novelist has not changed his commitment to the academic life, and he is universally regarded by both students and colleagues alike at the University of Bologna as one of the institution's most conscientious and charismatic lecturers.

Eco's links to the artistic and intellectual avant-garde of contemporary Italy[2] in Milan and other cities in Italy (Rome, Bologna, Genoa, Palermo, Florence) led to the publication of his first controversial work, *The Open Work*. Eco's close connection to the European

---

[1] For Bompiani's comments on Eco's arrival at the Bompiani publishing firm, see Pansa and Vinci, *Effetto Eco*, pp. 57–59.

[2] The best consideration of the Italian neo-avant-garde in English is Christopher Wagstaff, "The Neo-avantgarde," in *Writers & Society in Contemporary Italy: A Collection of Essays*, ed. Michael Caesar and Peter Hainsworth (New York: St. Martin's Press, 1984), pp. 35–61, to which this discussion is indebted.

avant-garde came about through his collaboration on a number of influential journals or "little magazines," as well as his relationship to a particular movement, the Gruppo 63, which itself stemmed from collaboration on such literary reviews. The first and most influential journal to shape Eco's theoretical thinking was *Il verri*, a literary magazine founded in Milan in 1956 by Luciano Anceschi (1911–) and others. The journal was moved to Bologna in 1973 after Eco himself joined the university in that city and continues to be published there today. Besides Eco and Anceschi, other key figures associated with this journal were Edoardo Sanguineti, Antonio Porta (the pseudonym of Leo Paolazzi, 1935–89), Nanni Balestrini (1935–), and Alfredo Giuliani (1924–), all poets and writers directly engaged in the activities of what eventually became Gruppo 63. Balestrini, Giuliani, Porta, and Sanguineti were all included in an important collection of experimental poetry, *I novissimi*, that Einaudi published in 1961. Two other magazines may be linked to the avant-garde and Eco's participation in it. The first review was *Marcatré*, a publication lasting from 1963 until 1972 that published many of the writers associated with *Il verri* and Gruppo 63. *Marcatré* included the participation of two men who wrote on aesthetics, contributing writings that have played a part in the birth of a postmodern sensibility, the kind of aesthetic taste with which Eco would later be identified through his novels and essays on mass culture. The first was Gillo Dorfles (1910–), a professor of aesthetics at the University of Milan from 1960 to the present, best known for provocative and humorous treatments of mass culture phenomena – in particular an anthology entitled *Kitsch: The World of Bad Taste*.[3] The second was Paolo Portoghesi (1931–), an architectural theorist whose ideas have become influential in formulating contemporary theories of postmodernism.[4] Both Dorfles and Portoghesi undoubtedly shared

---

[3] New York: University Books, 1969.

[4] For a consideration of postmodernism, see Matei Calinescu's *Five Faces of Modernity: Modernism, Avant-garde, Decadence, Kitsch, Postmodernism*, 2nd rev. ed. (Durham: Duke University Press, 1987); or Thomas Docherty, ed., *Postmodernism: A Reader* (New York: Columbia University Press, 1993), which contains an excerpt from Portoghesi's

Eco's precocious interest in extending the traditional discipline of aesthetics to include both popular culture and postmodernist phenomena, such as postmodern architecture. The second review was *Quindici*, a short-lived periodical (June 1967 until July 1969) that collapsed because of internal editorial problems arising from divergent political views on its editorial board. The board included not only Eco, Porta, and Sanguineti but also Renato Barilli (1935–), a student of Anceschi who had earlier collaborated on *Il verri* and had been part of Gruppo 63. Barilli is currently one of Eco's colleagues at the University of Bologna.[5] It was the demise of *Quindici* in 1969 that marked the definitive death of the Italian neo-avant-garde and of Gruppo 63 by "hara-kiri" or "suicide," as Eco himself put it in a survey article on Gruppo 63 included in the English translation of *The Open Work*.[6]

In its broad, ecumenical, cultural outlook, the avant-garde associated in particular with *Il verri* looked abroad for theoretical models that would open up Italian culture to a variety of new and often imported ideas. For example, it was during this period, and in part due to the influence of neo-avant-garde theorists, that such intellectual currents as structuralism, Russian formalism, the Frankfurt school, Brechtian theater, semiotics, American New Criticism, myth and archetypal criticism, the *nouveau roman*, phenomenology, and existentialism were all introduced into Italian intellectual life. The academic circles Eco frequented were particularly attracted by structuralism and semiotics. In some respects, the neo-avant-garde followed its better-known antecedent, the pre-fascist Futurist avant-garde, in its rejection of conventional poetic language, as well as taking an active

definition of postmodernism. Portoghesi's works in English translation include *After Modern Architecture* (New York: Rizzoli, 1982); and *Postmodern, the Architecture of the Post-Industrial Society* (New York: Rizzoli, 1983).

[5] Barilli has written a number of major critical works on Italian literature and aesthetics, some of which are available in English translation: *Art Nouveau* (London: P. Hamlyn, 1969); *Rhetoric* (Minneapolis: University of Minnesota Press, 1989); and *A Course on Aesthetics* (Minneapolis: University of Minnesota Press, 1993).

[6] "The Death of the Gruppo 63," in *The Open Work*, p. 249. This essay was not included in the original Italian edition or subsequent Italian editions of *Opera aperta*.

interest in contemporary political problems. But whereas the Futur-
ists embraced a nationalistic and proto-fascist political stance, the
intellectuals and poets associated with the neo-avant-garde and
Gruppo 63 were fundamentally leftists – but "respectable" leftists
with close ties to the most important Italian universities and publishing firms. As Eco has commented: "since we started out from a
position of power, it ought to be pretty clear that we hardly ran any
risk."[7] But their success in opening up Italian society to a sometimes
bewildering variety of non-provincial outside cultural influences
should not go unappreciated.

The appearance of *The Open Work* in 1962 certainly owed a debt to
the intellectual ferment that the neo-avant-garde produced within
Italian culture. Eco's book quickly became a *caso* in Italy (selling some
tens of thousands of copies) and was frequently seen as the theoretical
manifesto of the poets and literati making up the neo-avant-garde.
However, the book – originally entitled "Form and Indeterminacy in
Contemporary Poetics", an academic title judiciously replaced by the
far more memorable title it now possesses by Eco's astute publisher
Valentino Bompiani – cannot actually be described as a manifesto of
Gruppo 63, even though Eco belonged to the group and its ideas on
aesthetics often paralleled his own. In fact, many of the concepts
developed in *The Open Work* are just as closely connected to Eco's
earlier work in medieval aesthetics as they are to the neo-avant-garde.
This medieval intellectual linkage is less obvious from a reading of the
English translation of *The Open Work*, which has been greatly
abbreviated, omitting the entire second section of the book drawing a
parallel between the medieval world view and the writings of James
Joyce, Eco's most important example of what he defined as an "open"
literary work. What was originally a single book when it first
appeared in Italian became eventually, in both Italian and English,
two separate books: one section, *The Open Work*, contained a general
aesthetics of modernism; the second part, rendered into English as

---

[7] Eco, "The Death of the Gruppo 63," in *The Open Work*, p. 239.

The Aesthetics of Chaosmos: The Middle Ages of James Joyce, was eventually transformed into a monograph on Eco's favorite novelist.

The original Italian book presented an imposing obstacle to readers whose aesthetic theories were rooted in Romantic idealism or the aesthetic theories of Benedetto Croce. Once again, as in Eco's analyses of Scholastic aesthetics, the ultimate target of Eco's revisionary ideas was Benedetto Croce. The very notion of "culture" held by most Italian intellectuals when the book appeared was antithetical to Eco's approach. "Serious" scholars were expected to spend their lives analyzing "high" culture, the "great works" produced by "masters." Such obviously philistine products of mass or popular culture as television, cartoons, or even the cinema were not considered worthy of reflective attention, let alone a prominent place in a book dedicated to contemporary aesthetic theory. Yet, Eco proposed that the defining boundaries of contemporary poetics should be set by considering products of popular or mass culture, the artistic theories of the avant-garde, and illustrations from works of high modernism, such as *Finnegans Wake*, a work only grudgingly accepted in Italy by intellectuals but scarcely read by a wide public at the time. In fact, *Ulysses* was translated into Italian only in 1960, and *Finnegans Wake* had yet to appear in a complete translation when Eco's book was published in Italy. In *The Open Work*, therefore, Eco automatically alienated Crocean critics as well as numerous representatives of the official intellectual elite who were simply not prepared to deal with an aesthetic dominated by an incomprehensible English novel they were unable to read. The hostile review of Eco's book by the poet Eugenio Montale, who attacked Eco's work on several grounds in an essay published on 29 July 1962, is most revealing in this regard, since Montale can hardly be suspected of philistine tendencies. In only a single sentence, and with a thinly disguised sarcastic tone, Montale undermined Eco's original interpretation of Calder's mobiles (the "moving art" to which Montale referred) and implied that real cockroaches scampering around a kitchen floor were as "open" as the more famous insect immortalized by Kafka's classic tale, "The Metamorphosis":

> I am completely convinced that everything in the world is connec-
> ted; and that moreover even the cockroaches of Capogrossi, placed
> under the rubric of moving art, can possess the undeserved honor of
> figuring next to the works of Kafka, which are also open as a result of
> their countless meanings.[8]

Montale simply refused to treat Eco's views seriously. He then
continued in much the same vein, disparaging the clearly leftist tenor
of *The Open Work*, insofar as Eco's theories on contemporary
aesthetics claimed to demonstrate that the "open" work was an
accurate reflection of twentieth-century "alienation." Montale refers
to Eco as one of a group of young men who are "more or less
Marxists, or rather, if I beg your pardon, Marxians," who

> look with complete confidence toward the advent of a society in
> which science and industry, united, create new values and destroy
> forever the archaic face of nature, substituting in its place a landscape
> of machines, the perfect background for a man who is finally
> "integrated."[9]

A few years later after the French translation of *The Open Work*
appeared, no less a figure than Claude Lévi-Strauss would continue
such harsh attacks, affirming that Eco's book

> defends a formula that I absolutely cannot accept. What makes a
> work of art a work is not its being open but its being closed. A work
> of art is an object endowed with precise properties and [it possesses],
> as it were, the rigidity of a crystal.[10]

So strongly ingrained were notions of linking artistic merit with
closure and an artist's intentions that Eco's aesthetics thus angered

---

[8] Eugenio Montale, "Opere aperte," in *Auto da fé* (Milan: Il saggiatore, 1966), p. 197 (author's translation).

[9] *Ibid.*, p. 199 (author's translation).

[10] Paolo Caruso, ed., *Conversazioni con Claude Lévi-Strauss, Michel Foucault, Jacques Lacan* (Milan: Mursia, 1969), p. 81 (the original interview was first published in *Paese Sera* on 20 January 1967, author's translation).

not only Crocean idealists but also intellectuals such as Montale or
Lévi-Strauss, both normally representatives of progressive points of
view. Yet, while Eco's aesthetic theory is resolutely anti-Crocean,
intriguing affinities between the two thinkers do exist. Croce's
aesthetics contrasted *poesia* to *non-poesia*. Thus, the successful expression of an artistic intuition in a moment of *liricità* – for example, the
greatest dramatic moments in Dante's epic poetry – were defined as
"poetic," while what Croce considered non-artistic material in that
same poem, such as Dante's views on theology, would be called
"non-poetry." While Eco's aesthetic theories are completely opposed
to those of Croce, Eco sometimes seems to repeat Croce's habit of
grouping works of art into opposing camps, not unlike the distinction
Crocean critics set up between "poetry" and "non-poetry." Thus, Eco
contrasts "closed" or traditional works of art with "open" artistic
works in a variety of fields: music (Luciano Berio, Karlheinz Stockhausen, Henri Pousseur, Pierre Boulez), literature (here the example
of James Joyce occupies what later becomes a separate book), and
sculpture (Alexander Calder, as the creator of "works in motion," is
Eco's strongest example). Of course, neither Croce nor Eco was ever
so naive as to believe any binary grouping of complex works of art
could exhaust their meaning, and such a rhetorical stance was
primarily a polemical one, adopted to strengthen the force of their
argument. It is important to note that Eco does not refer simply to the
ambiguity inherent in any work of art from any historical period. Such
ambiguity, so highly praised by the American New Critics, is insufficient to constitute a truly "open" and modernist work. Joyce's
Finnegans Wake, which moves beyond mere ambiguity toward an
"open" quality, does so in a manner characterized by Eco as
"intentional, explicit, and extreme."[11] In a brief but illuminating

[11] *The Open Work*, p. 39; *Opera aperta: forma e indeterminazione nelle poetiche contemporanee*
(Milan: Bompiani, 1962), p. 78. I cite from this edition and not from subsequent editions
of this work because it contains the original chapters on the poetics of James Joyce. For
a newer edition of this work, see the Bompiani edition of 1993 which omits the chapters
devoted to Joyce.

juxtaposition of Dante's definition of the Holy Trinity in *Paradiso* 33 (lines 124–26) with a brief passage drawn from the fifth chapter of *Finnegans Wake*, Eco employs these two texts to set his notion of the "open" versus the "closed" in aesthetics in relief:

> O Light Eternal fixed in Self alone,
>   known only to Yourself, and knowing Self,
>   You love and glow, knowing and being known!

> From quiqui quinet to michemiche chelet and a jambebatiste to a brulobrulo! It is told in sounds in utter that, in signs so adds to, in universal, in polygluttural, in each auxiliary neutral idiom, sordomutics, florilingua, sheltafocal, flayflutter, a con's cubane, a pro's tutute, strassarab, ereperse and anythongue athall.[12]

According to Eco, Dante – always the orthodox Catholic – intends his verses to explain to his readers the nature of the Trinity, the greatest mystery of the Christian religion. Since the Scholastic fathers have carefully defined this theological phenomenon once and for all time, Dante accepts their orthodox view but employs such a careful integration of rhythm and phonic material that the lines not only "manage to express not just the concept they are supposed to convey, but also the feeling of blissful contemplation that accompanies its comprehension – thus fusing referential and emotional value into an indissociable formal whole."[13]

Dante's lines – despite their brilliance and genius – are essentially "closed" in their referential aspect. In contrast, Joyce's "open" text concerns a mysterious letter found in a dungheap that demands to be deciphered. But it is no less a linguistic mirror of Joyce's literary universe than Dante's definition of the Trinity was a reflection of the

---

[12] I cite the English translation from the English rendering by Mark Musa: *The Divine Comedy Vol. III: Paradiso* (New York: Penguin, 1986), p. 394; Joyce's text is found in *Finnegans Wake* (New York: The Viking Press, 1972), p. 117. Dante's original Italian text is as follows: 'O luce etterna che sola in te sidi / sola t'intendi, e da te intelletta / e intendente te ami e arridi!' (Dante, *La divina commedia: Paradiso*, ed. Daniele Mattalia [Milan: Rizzoli, 1975], p. 648).

[13] *The Open Work*, p. 40; *Opera aperta*, p. 79.

Florentine's world view. However, rather than reflecting a univocal meaning, a "closed" sense as in Dante's poem based upon Scholastic dogma, Joyce's text represents an entirely different order of aesthetics:

> the chaotic character, the polyvalence, the multi-interpretability of this polylingual *chaosmos*, its ambition to reflect the whole of history (Quinet, Michelet) in terms of Vico's cycles ("jambebatiste"), the linguistic eclecticism of its primitive glossary ("polygluttural"), the smug reference to Bruno's torture by fire ("brulobrulo"), the two obscene allusions that join sin and illness in one single root, these are just some of the things this sentence manages to suggest.[14]

Both Dante's tercet and Joyce's sentence are similar in that "an ensemble of denotative and connotative meanings fuse with an ensemble of physical linguistic properties to reproduce an organic form." And both are "open" in the limited sense that they both provide, upon repeated readings, ever renewed and increased aesthetic pleasure. In Dante's case, however, the text provides a "univocal message" whereas in Joyce's text the message is "plurivocal," and this kind of openness results in an "increase in information."[15] The theoretical slant of Eco's aesthetics may be demonstrated by what amounts to a far lesser dependency upon textual criticism in *The Open Work* than was typical of Eco's analysis of Aquinas' philosophy. The two citations amounting to only a few lines from Dante and Joyce are carefully chosen to serve as the basis for a decidedly theoretical, philosophical definition of aesthetics. In fact, Eco subjects very few texts to his scrutiny for formalistic analysis in *The Open Work*. His aesthetic theory has reached such a level of abstraction that his argument could function perfectly well without citations from Dante or Joyce at all. This is not to contend that Eco has not read both works thoroughly and with close attention to detail. On the contrary, in order to produce his essays, Eco demonstrates a masterful grasp of both Dante and Joyce. Now, the academic textual criticism so typical of his

[14] *The Open Work*, p. 41; *Opera aperta*, pp. 79–80.
[15] *The Open Work*, pp. 42–43; *Opera aperta*, pp. 80–81.

early book on Scholastic aesthetics has been subsumed under a far more authoritative and original philosophical voice in *The Open Work*. Besides a rejection of Crocean idealism and a willingness to consider the most typical products of popular culture, such as television, in the same breath with the masterpieces of world literature, another novelty of *The Open Work* was Eco's marked emphasis upon the role of the reader/listener/viewer in the aesthetic experience. Most previous discussions of aesthetics current in Italy emphasized the formal properties of the work of art itself. Eco's recognition that an aesthetic "fact" involved not only an object but an on-looker will become extremely important to the works of his later career. Several chapters of *The Open Work*, in fact, deal with the implications of information theory for aesthetics and poetics, and it was Eco's interest in information theory that would eventually lead him toward structuralism and, ultimately, to semiotics. Eco stresses the fact that both avant-garde literature in general, and the open work in particular, employ disorder to increase information: probability and predictability actually always result in a decrease of information. From the perspective of information theory, conventional or classical art "violated the conventional order of language *within well-defined limits*," while contemporary open works constantly challenge

the initial order by means of an extremely "improbable" form of organization . . . whereas classical art introduced original elements within a linguistic system whose basic laws it substantially respected, contemporary art often manifests its originality by imposing *a new linguistic system* with its own inner laws.[16]

To this point, Eco's theoretical aesthetics seem to suggest that *The Open Work* had little of interest to say about a possible linkage between a work of art and the society which produced it. But, just as Eco had already done in his study of Aquinas and Scholastic aesthetics, he underlines quite clearly in *The Open Work* the crucial role aesthetics

[16] *The Open Work*, p. 60; *Opera aperta*, pp. 104–105.

plays in defining what previous generations of critics might have called the "spirit of the age." Any truly important work of art, such as Dante's *Divine Comedy* or Joyce's novel, must be understood as "epistemological metaphors." Such metaphors represent the "structural resolutions" or "a widespread theoretical consciousness (not of a particular theory so much as of an acquired cultural viewpoint)"; they embody "the repercussion, within formative activity, of certain ideas acquired from contemporary scientific methodologies."[17] For example, an "informal" art emphasizes the possible combinations between work and viewer. Such "informal" work calls into question a number of traditional principles of logic and science – the principle of causality, bivalent logics, univocal relationships, and the principle of contradiction – just as a work such as Joyce's *Finnegans Wake* may be said to embody a perfect linguistic reflection of such contemporary scientific forces as the Einsteinian curved universe, the relativity principle, or the uncertainty principle of quantum physics. Because art serves as an epistemological metaphor, it reflects a way of dealing with the reality of one's historically defined universe. Dante's *Divine Comedy* embodies the essence of Scholastic theology and philosophy just as Alexander Calder's famous mobiles – what Eco calls "works in movement" – expand the very notion of artistic *form*. In like manner, the linguistic polyvalence and the aesthetics of chaosmos in James Joyce's great novels – that is, their form and not their content – reflect an intimate sensitivity to the change in the world view that took place during the nineteenth and the twentieth centuries in physics and mathematics. Eco explains this in a key passage of a chapter entitled "Form as Social Commitment," a section he added to the second edition of *The Open Work* and a statement that marks the direct influence of his teacher Pareyson:

> The real content of a work is the vision of the world expressed in its way of forming (*modo di formare*). Any analysis of the relationship

[17] *The Open Work*, p. 87; *Opera aperta*, p. 137.

between art and the world will have to take place at this level. Art knows the world through its formal structures (which, therefore, can no longer be considered from a purely formalist point of view but must be seen as its true content). Literature is an organization of words that signify different aspects of the world, but the literary work is itself an aspect of the world in the way its words are organized, even when every single word, taken in isolation, has absolutely no meaning, or simply refers to events and relationships between events that may appear to have nothing to do with the world.[18]

This crucial addition to the original edition of The Open Work first appeared as an article ("Del modo di formare come impegno sulla realtà") Eco had been invited to write for Elio Vittorini's journal, Il Menabò di letteratura, in the second of two issues devoted to the relationship between literature and industry. Vittorini had defended the writers associated with the French nouveau roman who had been criticized by leftist critics for ignoring the world of the working classes in general and the factory in particular in their works. Eco continued Vittorini's defense using a more theoretical tone. Writers who simply reflect the "real" world in their content but who continue to employ the literary language or codes of that traditional world merely ✓ reproduce the system of conventional language that buttresses a traditional system of class relationships. Avant-garde authors of "open" works, on the other hand, innovate at the level of artistic form, which is always their ultimate content. When properly analyzed and understood, their works of art, always epistemological metaphors, tell us far more about the true nature of reality than any so-called "realist" literature employing out-moded, traditional, and thoroughly predictable literary conventions linked to the old regime.

In the second half of the original Italian edition of The Open Work, Eco had discussed the implications of the "open" quality of James Joyce's works with great persuasive power. Subsequently issued as a separate edition of criticism and translated into English as The

[18] The Open Work, p. 144 (this material was not included in the Italian edition).

Aesthetics of Chaosmos: The Middle Ages of James Joyce,[19] this slim but impressive volume not only makes an interesting contribution to Joyce studies but also implicitly draws a parallel between Joyce's artistic development and Eco's own career. While Joyce moved from a Catholic, Thomist aesthetics to the modernist aesthetics of the open work, the Irish writer remained so fundamentally marked by the medieval world view that Eco can characterize his entire career as "medievally minded": "If you take away the transcendent God from the symbolic world of the Middle Ages, you have the world of Joyce."[20]

Eco argues that much of the characteristically Joycean style has obvious medieval antecedents in its mania for encyclopedic lists (a trait also evident in Eco's own fiction) and in the *summa*-like quality of both *Ulysses* and *Finnegans Wake*. Joyce's transition from a traditional Catholic, Thomist view of the world to a revolutionary revision of that conventional model in two ground-breaking novels that serve as emblematic "epistemological metaphors" for the modern era also finds a parallel in Eco's own career. Eco's mania for an orderly aesthetic theory began with a study of Scholastic aesthetics but eventually resulted not only in an overall *Theory of Semiotics* in 1976 (in its scope, a book reminiscent of the Thomist *summa*) but also in a popular novel filled with medieval lore. Yet, like Joyce's works, Eco's novel is imbued with a completely non-medieval aesthetics. As Eco remarks, "to me Joyce was the node where the Middle Ages and the avant-garde meet, and the present book is the story and the historical-theoretical foundation of such a paradoxical meeting."[21]

If *The Open Work* represented the erudite, theoretical, and abstract aspect of Eco's literary persona, *Misreadings* reflected the humorous, goliardic, and comic side of Eco's intellect. As Eco's prefaces to both the Italian edition and English translation make clear, the literary

[19] Translated by Ellen Esrock (Cambridge: Harvard University Press, 1989). The material on James Joyce's poetics was originally published in the Italian edition of *Opera aperta* (pp. 215–361).

[20] *Ibid.*, pp. 6, 7 (this material was not printed in the original Italian edition).

[21] *Ibid.*, p. xi (this material was not printed in the original Italian edition).

parodies and pastiches in this collection were originally begun in the avant-garde review *Il verri* in 1959 and were subsequently revised, augmented, and republished many times.[22] Eco himself emphasizes the link of these parodies to the atmosphere characterizing the neo-avant-garde's interest in revolutionizing Italian literary language: "I had a further, deeper reason for adopting pastiche: If the work of the neo-avant-garde consisted in turning inside out the languages of daily life and of literature, the comic and the grotesque should be a part of that program."[23]

The original Italian edition of 1963 contained seventeen different parodies, essays, or imaginary book reviews and editorial comments on manuscripts supposedly submitted to a publisher. Like every other book Eco has written, *Misreadings* has undergone numerous changes between its initial edition and the latest Italian printing or its English translation: only ten of the original seventeen chapters were included in the recent paperback printing of *Diario minimo* in Italy, while five chapters not present in the original edition are now included. The first English translation includes 10 of the original 17 chapters from the 1963 Italian edition, plus 5 sections taken from subsequent editions that are still included in the latest Italian edition. Thus, the printed book we now have available in bookstores represents a substantially revised work from that which appeared in 1963 and contains essays that were written as late as 1972.

The topics parodied in *Misreadings* refer precisely to those crucial philosophical issues Eco and the intellectuals associated with neo-avant-garde magazines, or the publishing firms of Einaudi and Bompiani, did so much to disseminate. Not only do these parodies touch upon the most serious cultural issues of the time, but they also combine humorous considerations of "high" culture subjects with themes from "popular" or "mass" culture. In the latter vein, perhaps

---

[22] *Misreadings*, trans. William Weaver (San Diego: Harcourt Brace, 1993), p. 1; or in Eco, *Diario minimo* (Milan: Bompiani, 1992), p. 7.

[23] *Misreadings*, p. 2 (this material was not printed in the Italian preface).

the most famous of all the essays in the original collection was a piece called "The Phenomenology of Mike Bongiorno," which deals with a quiz-show host who has been a star on Italian television since its inception, usually as the master of ceremonies in programs copied from such American classics as 'Twenty-One" or "The $64,000 Question" ("Lascia o raddoppia" in Italian). While certainly originally intended to be funny, Eco's analysis of the Bongiorno phenomenon, read today with its still biting and sarcastic tone, reflects something of the attitude of the traditional elitist intellectual opposed to popular culture that Eco would later criticize in one of his major works devoted to a typology of twentieth-century intellectuals in 1964. In fact, while the most recent Italian edition of *Diario minimo* contains no reconsideration of the author's attitude toward Bongiorno, the English translation contains something of a mild recantation: "Mike Bongiorno, while unknown to non-Italians, belongs to a familiar, international category; and, personally, I continue to consider him a genius."[24]

Certainly, Bongiorno himself did not consider the original essay a compliment. In a recent interview on Eco, Bongiorno maliciously noted that most of the intellectuals who worked behind the scenes at the television station in Milan and elsewhere were envious of the public success of those, such as himself, who were in the limelight. Moreover, in order to highlight what Bongiorno obviously considers to be intellectual hypocrisy on Eco's part, Bongiorno pointed out a little-known fact – that "among the experts who filled out the little questions for the contestants there was also a young man with fine hopes named Umberto Eco."[25] It is only fair to report that Eco has disputed this account of events in his weekly column for *L'Espresso* and has denied categorically that he ever helped to provide such questions.[26] While most serious discussions of the mass media in Italy

---

[24] *Misreadings*, p. 3 (this material was not printed in the original Italian edition).
[25] Cited in Pansa and Vinci, *Effetto Eco*, p. 44 (author's translation).
[26] Umberto Eco, 'Non ho mai lasciato né raddoppiato. Contributo a una storia della TV," *L'Espresso* 41 (2 June 1995), p. 218.

give a great deal of credit to Eco for having been one of the first to understand its impact upon Italian popular culture, Mike Bongiorno believes that

> in reality, like all the so-called intellectuals of that time, Eco did not understand anything about television. . . . The philosopher did not understand that TV was the true cultural revolution of the century. For him I was only an idiot put there to ask ten questions. Instead, it was all much more complicated. . . . that young man wanted to make himself publicity at my expense. But instead his attack went to my advantage. The public was entirely for me and against the intellectuals like him.[27]

If Bongiorno had employed the terminology Eco's own studies were soon to popularize, he would have called Eco an "apocalyptic" intellectual, the kind of elitist who feels that high culture has been irredeemably destroyed by popular or mass culture, such as Mike Bongiorno's television programs, and that such negative phenomena should be disparaged and ignored.[28] The other side of the coin, one equally dangerous to a comprehensive understanding of contemporary culture, is that of the "integrated" intellectual who sees every aspect of mass media and popular culture as entirely positive. In most cases (perhaps with the exception of his sarcastic treatment of Mike Bongiorno), Eco's position is somewhere in the middle, accepting the challenge of understanding new media without at the same time renouncing his right to criticize or change them.

Eco's expertise as a satirist strikes the reader of these essays even in translation. Some of the literary pieces reflect the fashions and reading tastes of the period. "Nonita" (rendered as "Granita" in English), for example, is a parody of Nabokov's novel *Lolita* and describes the

---

[27] Cited in Pansa and Vinci, *Effetto Eco*, p. 45 (author's translation).
[28] See Eco's *Apocalittici e integrati: comunicazioni di massa e teorie della cultura di massa* (Milan: Bompiani, 1964). For a partial translation, see the recent *Apocalypse Postponed*, edited by Robert Lumley (Bloomington: Indiana University Press, 1994), which is discussed in detail in the next chapter.

obsessive love of a man named Umberto (Eco's first name and a translation of Nabokov's original character's name – Humbert) for older grandmothers, not under-age nymphets. The English term for grandmother, "granny," produces the English title translation "Granita" just as the Italian original "Nonna" had produced the title "Nonita" of the original Italian parody. "Esquisse d'un nouveau chat" reproduces the minutely detailed descriptions of Alain Robbe-Grillet's "new novel" in its portrait of a cat pondering a few paw-steps toward a meal. "My Exagmination Round His Factification for Incamination to Reduplication with Ridecolation of a Portrait of the Artist as Alessandro Manzoni," the title being almost a verbatim copy of a famous collection of essays on Joyce's *Finnegans Wake*, employs various styles of criticism fashionable in the 1960s (New Criticism, symbolic criticism) in overinterpreting the most important Italian novel of the last century, Alessandro Manzoni's *The Betrothed*. In the 1993 preface to *Misreadings*, Eco remarks that recent overinterpretations typical of deconstructionist criticism "read as if inspired by my parody,"[29] a theme that he will also advance in both his second novel, *Foucault's Pendulum*, and in *The Limits of Interpretation*.

Perhaps the most enjoyable of the essays in the collection are the imaginary readers' reports (first published in 1972): "Regretfully, We Are Returning Your . . ."[30] Here, Eco provides us with an insider's insight on the kind of jargon editors might use in rejecting some of the world's great classics. The Bible is described as "action-packed" and full of sex, murder, war, and all sorts of commercial pluses, but the reader is puzzled by the fact that there seem to be a number of

[29] Eco, *Misreadings*, p. 5. In the Italian preface to the recent paperback edition of *Diario minimo*, this explicit attack upon deconstructionist criticism is not included. Instead, Eco discusses how another essay parodying Adorno and the Frankfurt school anticipates a style typical of right-wing or conservative thinking of the recent past (*Diario minimo*, p. 9). In correspondence with me dated 30 January 1996, Eco noted that this Italian preface was reprinted from one of the preceding editions, before deconstruction had become such a controversial critical issue.

[30] See Eco, *Misreadings*, pp. 33–46 for the imaginary readers' reports cited in this discussion; *Diario minimo*, pp. 142–52.

authors and that the rights question is so muddled that they should be settled before drawing up a contract! Homer's *Odyssey* is called "a page turner, all right, not like the author's first book" but the reader wonders if Homer was really the author. Dante's *Divine Comedy* is rejected because if the publisher puts out a book in Florentine dialect, it will have to do the same thing for all the other dialects in Italy. Moreover, this imaginary medieval reader believes the only part of the poem to have real commercial appeal is *Paradiso*, while the *Inferno* is denigrated as "obscure and self-indulgent, with passages of cheap eroticism, violence, and downright crudity." The Marquis de Sade's *Justine* is paradoxically rejected for its intellectual content and its philosophic perspective: "today's audience wants sex, sex, and more sex ... Let's leave the highbrow stuff to Indiana." Indiana is, of course, the American publisher of much of Eco's semiotic or cultural theory. The insertion of a reference to Indiana University Press in 1993 added to the translation of a work originally published in 1963 and revised in 1972 – long before Eco had any relationship to that press or that university – is only one of the most obvious illustrations of how Eco not only intervenes in the translations of his works but also how he feels no compunction about modifying their meaning and even changing their focus as his own thinking evolves over time.

Equally amusing, and reflective of the theoretical approaches to narrative as a combinative process typical of Vladimir Propp, the structuralists, and creative writers such as Italo Calvino or the Oulipo group in France, is a fascinating piece entitled "Make Your Own Movie" which was added to the original 1963 collection in 1972. The essay, in effect, offers an instructional manual on how to employ stereotypical plot elements from the films of art-film directors such as Antonioni, Godard, or Visconti to produce an almost infinite number of narrative possibilities. Eco's parody of narrative as a combinative process defines the basic formula for Antonioni in two terse senten-ces: "An empty lot. She walks away." Any inveterate habitué of art houses in Europe or America will admit that such a simple scene might well exemplify any of Antonioni's mature films, such as *L'avventura*, *L'eclisse*, or *La notte*. By exchanging the basic formula with a choice of similar narrative elements supplied by Eco from alternate lists, the reader can "make" his or her "own movie," in the process generating some 15,741 different film plots that nevertheless remain faithful to Antonioni's style. The original formula ("An empty lot. She walks away.") can thus be expanded to become: "A maze of McDonald's with visibility limited due to the sun's glare. He toys for a long time with an object."[31] While Eco delights the sophisticated film buff with his parody, he has also managed to say something of interest about narrative structure in the European art film with this clever game.

Of greatest interest for Eco's future writings are two parodies of intellectual currents from the 1960s: "Industry and Sexual Repression in a Po Valley Society" and "The End Is at Hand." The first parody is inspired by classic texts from anthropology (Benedict, Mead, Malinowski) and describes a complete reversal of the situation typical of most anthropological research: aborigines from Tasmania (who thank various foundations for travel grants amounting to twenty-four thousand dog's teeth) examine the city of Milan as if they were the developed culture and the Milanese were the savages. What makes the essay so comical is that its imaginary author insists time and again on an intellectual position of objectivity that is completely unjudgmental: "Gathering coconuts by climbing a palm tree with bare feet is not necessarily a form of behavior superior to that of the primitive who travels by jet aircraft and eats fried potatoes from a plastic bag."[32] Yet, Eco's imaginary researcher with his programmatically multiculturalist perspective (to employ the jargon of another generation) succeeds only in creating a totally obscure picture of life in Milan. The researcher finds himself unable to penetrate an immense construction, "ellipsoid in shape, from which an uninterrupted and frightful

[31] *Misreadings*, pp. 145–46; *Diario minimo*, pp. 133–34.
[32] *Misreadings*, p. 71; *Diario minimo*, p. 64.

din is heard" and which is defined as a place where headmen of the tribe permit people in collective feasts to release their constant tension born of repression. What the researcher is describing, of course, is a soccer stadium! Our aborigine anthropologist then detects signs of sexual repression and frustration in the style of the "tribal dancing" typical of Milan evident from certain "obscene details":

> rather than display normally his naked member and swing it in a circle while the onlookers cheer (as one of our youths would do . . .), the male dancer keeps his scrupulously covered (I leave to the reader's imagination how repulsive this practice is even to the most sophisticated observer). Similarly, the female dancer never allows her breasts to be glimpsed, by their concealment thus stimulating desires that can only produce the profoundest frustration.[33]

The same comic send-up of anthropological methodology combined with the key concept of the Russian formalists – "making strange" as a rhetorical ploy – is applied to Adorno and writers of the Frankfurt school in "The End Is at Hand." This essay is an imaginary diatribe directed against the triumph of "mass man" by an ancient Greek writer who embodies the worst features of what Eco will soon call the "apocalyptic" intellectual and who is incensed over the change in classical culture that ushered in what, in our modern view, was the Golden Age of Aristotle, Sophocles, and Herodotus. Aristotle's *Rhetoric* is denounced as an "infamous handbook," "nothing less than a catechism of marketing, a motivational inquiry into what appeals and what doesn't, what's believed and what's rejected," and his *Poetics*, containing Aristotle's famous doctrine of *mimesis*, suddenly becomes the handbook of mass man, who can only enjoy what appears real and what is produced by imitation.[34]

Given Umberto Eco's reputation for erudition, no interpretation of *Misreadings* could successfully argue that Eco takes an anti-intellectual

---

[33] *Misreadings*, pp. 79–80; *Diario minimo*, p. 71.
[34] *Misreadings*, pp. 111, 113; *Diario minimo*, pp. 106, 107.

position in his parodies and pastiches. Quite the opposite. Eco fervently believes in the power of reason but in a middle way between the obscurities and the pedantries of erudition run amok, on the one hand, and a rejection of reason as a guide, on the other. In Eco's view,

> This is parody's mission: it must never be afraid of going too far. If its aim is true, it simply heralds what others will later produce, unblushing, with impassive and assertive gravity.[35]

Eco's *forma mentis* simply cannot imagine isolating the power of the intellect from the equally powerful and subversive force of wit and parody. It is Eco's way of reminding the reader that intellect often produces arrogance and even intolerance, while parody and humor undermine intellectual pretensions and argue for a balanced, tolerant perspective.

[35] *Misreadings*, p. 5; *Diario minimo*, p. 9.

three

§

Cultural theory and popular
culture: from structuralism
to semiotics

The Open Work and *Misreadings* established Umberto Eco's reputation both as a serious theorist of contemporary culture and as a popular writer whose style was colored by a rare sense of humor and subversive wit. While seldom identifying himself completely with any particular political party or platform, Eco had nevertheless emerged as a representative of the cultural left, clearly believing in the necessity of incorporating the aesthetics of popular culture into contemporary intellectual discourse. This belief represented a notion that many of Italy's older intellectuals found to be simply a contradiction in terms: aesthetics, by definition, could deal only with high culture. The fact that Eco believed strongly in the existence of an aesthetics of popular culture and that it should be analyzed seriously (an even more scandalous belief) set his writings apart from traditional literary criticism of the period, still dominated either by old-fashioned Crocean idealism or the newer Marxist literary criticism that all too often envisioned a quite mechanical relationship between superstructure (culture, either high or popular) and substructure (the means of production), between ideology and economics. In formulating his theories on popular culture and presenting a number of influential essays on various aspects of mass-media culture in comic strips, films, and pulp novels, Eco aimed not only at going beyond the older Crocean idealism (which would hardly deign even to recognize the existence of popular culture) but also to navigate carefully between various Marxist points of view (from Lukács to Gramsci), while accepting the basic Marxist premise that culture does, indeed, reflect the ideology of the class with hegemony over society.

Eco would eventually incorporate his analyses of popular culture into a broader theoretical framework, that of semiotics. His identification with semiotic theory begins in 1968, a fateful year for European culture, with *La struttura assente* (*The Absent Structure*, 1968). This book was followed by *Le forme del contenuto* (*The Forms of Content*, 1971); and then by *Trattato di semiotica* (*A Theory of Semiotics*, 1975). Before these three works had appeared in rapid succession, however, Eco entered what he himself has called his "pre-semiotic" period. This extremely interesting phase of his work, from which some of his most famous and most frequently reprinted essays derive, includes writings that first appeared in print between 1955 and the mid-1960s, all collected together in three books. The first of these, *La definizione dell'arte* (*The Definition of Art*), was printed in 1968, but it brings together essays published between 1955 and 1964. As one might expect from a book containing numerous discussions of aesthetic problems, it reflects Eco's debt to Luigi Pareyson even more clearly than his treatises on Scholastic aesthetics or *The Open Work*. One section of this book – "Two Hypotheses about the Death of Art" – is available in English translation as part of the English edition of *The Open Work*.[1] More important for Eco's future development, however, are two volumes of essays devoted almost exclusively to popular culture. The first and most influential, *Apocalittici e integrati: comunicazioni di massa e teorie della cultura di massa* (*Apocalyptic and Integrated Intellectuals: Mass Communications and Theories of Mass Culture*), appeared in 1964 and generated almost as much controversy as *The Open Work*, a book upon whose aesthetic premises *Apocalyptic*

---

[1] See Eco, *The Open Work*, pp. 167–79; for the Italian original, see Eco, *La definizione dell'arte* (Milan: Mursia, 1990), pp. 259–77 (the original essay first appeared in the June 1963 issue of *Il verri*).

and Integrated Intellectuals depends. While no complete English version of this seminal book exists, one chapter entitled "The Structure of Bad Taste" appeared in the 1989 English version of *The Open Work*;[2] another chapter, containing a justly famous analysis of a classic comic-strip hero, "The Myth of Superman," was included in the 1979 English anthology, *The Role of the Reader*.[3] A third important piece from this book, "Lettura di Steve Canyon" ("A Reading of Steve Canyon") has been translated but is not easily available.[4] More recently, a collection of essays entitled *Apocalypse Postponed* appeared which contains only two chapters from the original book – "Apocalyptic and Integrated Intellectuals: Mass Communications and Theories of Mass Culture" and "The World of Charlie Brown" – as well as the prefaces to the original Italian edition of 1964 and subsequent Italian reprints in 1974 and 1977.[5]

A second book crucial to Eco's intellectual development in this pre-semiotic period is *Il superuomo di massa: retorica e ideologia nel romanzo popolare (The Superman of the Masses: Rhetoric and Ideology in*

---

[2] See Eco, *The Open Work*, pp. 180–216; for the original Italian text, see Eco, *Apocalittici e integrati*, pp. 65–129.

[3] See Eco, *The Role of the Reader: Explorations in the Semiotics of Texts* (Bloomington: Indiana University Press, 1979), pp. 107–24; the essay originally appeared in Enrico Castelli, ed., *Demitizzazione e immagine* (Padua: Cedam, 1962) and was then published in the first edition of *Apocalittici e integrati* (see pp. 219–61 of the previously cited Italian edition).

[4] See *Apocalittici e integrati*, pp. 130–83; an English version, "A Reading of Steve Canyon," appears in *Twentieth-Century Studies* (December 1976) and is reprinted in the exhibition catalogue sponsored by London's Institute of Contemporary Art: *Comic Iconoclasm*, ed. Sheena Wagstaff (London: Institute of Contemporary Arts, 1988), pp. 20–25.

[5] In order to avoid confusion between the Italian original and the English translation with a similar name but very different contents, I shall use the literal translation of the Italian original – *Apocalyptic and Integrated Intellectuals* – to refer to the original Italian edition, while the English-language collection of essays from this and other Italian originals – *Apocalypse Postponed* – refers only to the English anthology. In addition to materials from the original *Apocalyptic and Integrated Intellectuals*, *Apocalypse Postponed* contains several brief articles from Eco's weekly column in the news magazine *L'Espresso*; one essay from a 1973 collection, *Il costume di casa: evidenze e misteri dell'ideologia italiana* (Milan: Bompiani, 1973); one essay from a 1977 collection, *Dalla periferia dell'impero* (Milan: Bompiani); two essays from the 1983 collection, *Sette anni di desiderio* (Milan: Bompiani). The original Italian essay collections contain, for the most part, articles from Eco's weekly column.

the Popular Novel). Best seen as a companion volume to *Apocalyptic and Integrated Intellectuals*, *The Superman of the Masses* finally appeared in book form in 1976, followed by a second revised edition two years later. Its contents, however, had previously appeared as essays in various periodicals as early as 1965. Two of its chapters are included in the 1979 English collection, *The Role of the Reader*: "Rhetoric and Ideology in Sue's *Les Mystères de Paris*," and "Narrative Structures in Fleming."[6] Like the influential essay on Superman, that on spy-novelist Ian Fleming has been widely reprinted. Eco was already celebrated in his native country for his perceptive insight into the fledgling popular culture of Italy, but it is paradoxical that his international reputation as a theorist of popular culture would eventually rest primarily not upon his Italian expertise but, instead, upon the highly positive reception of essays on American comic-strip characters (Superman, Steve Canyon, Charlie Brown) or the English literary character, James Bond.

In several prefaces added in 1974 and 1977 to *Apocalyptic and Integrated Intellectuals*, Eco discusses the origin of this book and a number of negative reviews by important European intellectuals. Eugenio Montale's sarcastic review of Eco's earlier *The Open Work* had rejected Eco's notion that an "open" work was an accurate reflection of contemporary alienation, had called Eco's position more "Marxian" than "Marxist," and had scoffed at Eco's suggestion that in the future, man might be finally "integrated." In spite of the fact that Valentino Bompiani imposed the ultimate title of *Apocalyptic and Integrated Intellectuals* upon a reluctant Eco, it is also likely that Eco invented the juxtaposition between apocalyptic and integrated intellectuals in direct response to Montale's review of *The Open Work*.

In fact, Eco admits that many reviewers who criticized the

---

[6] See Eco, *The Role of the Reader*, pp. 125–72; the original essay on Sue first appeared as a preface to the Italian edition of Sue's novel (Milan: Sugar, 1965), while the famous essay on Fleming's James Bond novels – by Eco's own testimony, the most frequently anthologized, translated, and cited of all his works – first appeared in a volume edited by Eco and Oreste del Buono entitled *Il caso Bond* (Milan: Bompiani, 1965).

"hotchpotch" character of *Apocalyptic and Integrated Intellectuals* were correct. The book was actually born from a completely self-interested and practical concern, Eco's desire to apply for what he calls "an absurdly named university chair: Pedagogy and Psychology of Mass Communication."[7] In order to have a chance at the chair, Eco needed a book that would deal with mass communications. Eco himself argued with Bompiani that his editor's suggested title actually had little to do with the rest of the collection of essays, which was being published solely as a submission for the university chair competition. Bompiani countered that the title was a perfect one. His insistence forced Eco to compose the introductory essay explaining the contrast between apocalyptic and integrated intellectuals now demanded by the title.

The intellectual debate that erupted after the publication of *Apocalyptic and Integrated Intellectuals* and *The Superman of the Masses* was no doubt eventually responsible for an important editorial decision in 1965 on the part of the publishers of *L'Espresso*, one of Italy's two major weekly news magazines, to employ Eco as a book reviewer and essayist on topics of general interest. This close collaboration became even more important after Eco achieved international fame as a novelist, for in 1985 Eco expanded his contributions to *L'Espresso* to include a weekly column entitled "La bustina di Minerva" ("Minerva's Matchbook"). One of the most successful editorial ventures in contemporary Italian journalism, his column is the source of many of the essays reprinted in various collections in Italy and translated into a number of foreign languages. Eco's work as a journalist is thus by no means separated from his theoretical writings, nor are these occasional writings merely a minor aspect of his total literary production. In fact, his journalistic writings have helped to create precisely the kind of ironic, self-reflexive, and well-informed readership that both his fiction and his theoretical

---

[7] For Eco's discussion of the genesis of the book see *Apocalypse Postponed*, p. 54; or the original in *Apocalittici e integrati*, pp. x–xii.

essays require. The column's title refers to a specific kind of wooden match sold in Italy primarily to smokers. Fanatic smokers, like Eco (whose addiction to nicotine is legendary), frequently write addresses, phone numbers, and notes for future reference on the reverse sides of the matchbook covers. Such a title for a weekly column emphasizes the occasional, ephemeral nature of the single-page, double-column essays that range over an enormous number of topics.

Eco's notion of what an essay represents retains the sense of a provisional trial or test found in the title of Montaigne's original masterpiece that helped to define this literary genre. There is little doubt that in the fast-moving, journalistic columns of weekly news magazines, Eco has perhaps found the perfect expression for his rapidly changing perspective on developments in popular culture. In the original 1964 edition of *Apocalittici e integrati*, Eco underscored the fact that his methodology was "conceived in the conditional tense" and that any attempt to define mass culture "cannot amount to more than a chain of hypothetical syllogisms with the premises in the subjunctive mood and the conclusion in the conditional"; without a sound methodology upon which to base any general theory of mass media, Eco believed any attempt to create a general theory would be comparable to the fruitless exercise of proposing a "theory of next Thursday."[8]

If *The Open Work* had embraced the aesthetic principles of the contemporary avant-garde, *Apocalyptic and Integrated Intellectuals* set out to define divergent attitudes on the part of intellectuals to popular or mass culture. The apocalyptic intellectual rejects mass culture as anti-culture, is obsessed with decadence, and generally refuses to see any positive benefits from such innovations as cinema, cartoon strips, pulp novels, science fiction, and the like. Expressions of popular culture actually demonstrate, for such individuals, the proof that "high" culture has been debased and corrupted, usually by a capitalist economic system. For Eco, the members of the influential Frankfurt

[8] *Apocalypse Postponed*, p. 33; *Apocalittici e integrati*, pp. 23–24.

school (Adorno, Horkheimer, Gunther Anders) represented the archetype of apocalyptic intellectuals. In a preface to a later edition of this work, Eco uses Herbert Marcuse (a figure perhaps better known to English-speaking readers) as the perfect apocalyptic intellectual. Eco's convincing critique of such figures rests upon his contention that apocalyptic intellectuals never actually study the concrete mechanisms of mass culture but usually remain content only to employ what Eco calls negative "fetish categories,"[9] such as "mass" or "mass man," while uttering pious, aristocratic objections to the vulgarization of "high" culture in the contemporary world:

> The apocalyptic intellectual must on the other hand be reproached for never really attempting a concrete study of products and how they are actually consumed. Not only does the apocalyptic reduce the consumer to that undifferentiated fetish that is mass man, but while accusing mass man of reducing even the worthiest artistic product to pure fetish, he himself reduces the mass-produced object to a fetish. Rather than analyse these products individually in order to render their structural characteristics visible, the apocalyptic negates them *en bloc*.[10]

Integrated intellectuals, on the other hand, focus less upon decadence and emphasize the positive side of popular or mass culture, often producing texts which actually form part of mass culture itself rather than offering diatribes against it. Eco cites Marshall McLuhan, the author of the best-selling *Understanding Media* (1964), as the perfect example of this type. The traditional European intellectual would certainly be closer to the apocalyptic type, while North American intellectuals, particularly those interested in popular culture, are most often in the opposite camp.

What is most interesting about this typology of intellectual approaches to mass or popular culture is Eco's rejection of both positions. In fact, Eco claims that apocalyptic texts on the demise of

---

[9] *Apocalypse Postponed*, p. 23; *Apocalittici e integrati*, p. 7.
[10] *Apocalypse Postponed*, p. 25; *Apocalittici e integrati*, p. 14.

civilization as we know it actually "constitute the most sophisticated product on offer for mass consumption" and believes that the two seemingly opposed attitudes are, in reality, quite complementary.[11] What Eco rejects in both camps is an intellectual passivity toward popular culture: while the negative, critical approach to popular culture ignores its mechanisms and its possible links to social conditions in the real world, the positive, embracing attitude toward mass culture is equally unanalytical but is also uncritical as well. Ever the medievalist, Eco maintains that this juxtaposition is no recent phenomenon but may be traced back as least as far as a debate between St. Bernard and the Abbot Suger over the use of medieval cathedrals to communicate religious messages to the unlettered masses. St. Bernard (the apocalyptic intellectual) preferred stark, unadorned churches, while Suger (the integrated intellectual) believed that the uneducated masses could be instructed in Christian doctrine by translating the official Christian culture into artistic images capable of immediate consumption by the masses. It is typical of Eco's clever turn of mind that a relatively obscure medieval argument could be used to illuminate a contemporary intellectual debate on popular culture.

A key concept in Eco's critique of apocalyptic intellectuals is that of the "consolatory" function of their diatribes, an idea that will be expanded in other essays on concrete expressions of popular culture, such as the characters of Superman or James Bond. Eco believes that the most dangerous aspect of an apocalyptic approach to mass culture is that this consolatory attitude allows the reader to assume an attitude that is extremely detrimental to retaining a free and critical judgment:

> the apocalyptic intellectual offers the reader *consolation*, for he allows
> him to glimpse, against a background of catastrophe, a community
> of "supermen" capable, if only by rejection, of rising above banal

[11] *Apocalypse Postponed*, p. 18; *Apocalittici e integrati*, p. 4.

mediocrity. At the very least, the elected few who write and read: "Us two, you and I – the only ones to understand, and be saved: the only ones not part of the mass." When I say "superman," I'm thinking of the Nietzschean (or pseudo-Nietzschean) origin of many of these attitudes. However, I use the term in the cunning sense suggested by Gramsci, for whom the model of the Nietzschean superman could be found in the heroes of nineteenth-century serial novels, such as the Count of Monte Cristo, Athos, Rodolphe de Gerolstein or (a generous concession) Vautrin.[12]

Eco's interest in the serial novel of the past century and contemporary "supermen" will be discussed in relation to several specific essays on such figures (James Bond, Superman, Steve Canyon), but before turning to Eco's specific studies in mass culture, the connections of the ideas in *Apocalyptic and Integrated Intellectuals* to *The Open Work* or even to the structuralist methodology Eco claimed to find in Scholastic philosophy should not be overlooked. In fact, Eco understood perfectly that in order to develop a theory of the avant-garde in aesthetics, any such theory would of necessity have to come to grips with popular culture. And since so much apocalyptic discourse focuses upon decadence and bad taste or kitsch in popular art, Eco's essay "The Structure of Bad Taste" represents a crucial document in this regard.

In this essay, Eco presents one of his earliest "pre-semiotic" definitions of a work of art. This definition not only presupposes the concept of an "open" work from his past writings, but it embodies insights Eco learned from Roman Jakobson's linguistic theory, hinting at his future espousal of semiotic theory as a master theoretical tool capable of dealing with both high and popular culture in the decade following the publication of *Apocalyptic and Integrated Intellectuals*:

> Any work of art can be viewed as a message to be decoded by an addressee. But unlike most messages, instead of aiming at transmitting a univocal meaning, the work of art succeeds precisely insofar as it appears ambiguous and open-ended. The notion of the open work

[12] *Apocalypse Postponed*, p. 18; *Apocalittici e integrati*, p. 5.

can be satisfactorily reformulated according to Jakobson's definition of the "poetic" function of language. Poetic language deliberately uses terms in a way that will radically alter their referential function (by establishing, among them, syntactic relationships that violate the usual laws of the code). It eliminates the possibility for a univocal decoding; it gives the addressee the feeling that the current code has been violated to such an extent that it can no longer help. The addressee thus finds himself in the situation of a cryptographer forced to decode a message whose code is unknown, and who therefore has to learn the code of the message from the message itself . . . ambiguity is not an accessory to the message: it is its fundamental nature.[13]

At this point in his intellectual development, Eco's views on popular culture are heavily indebted to the theories of an avowedly apocalyptic intellectual, Dwight MacDonald – especially MacDonald's definitions of "Masscult" and "Midcult" or kitsch. While Eco rejects MacDonald's radical apocalyptic attack upon all forms of popular culture, he nevertheless shares MacDonald's irritation with Midcult or kitsch corruptions of high art, such as the Revised Standard Version of the Bible, the Book-of-the-Month Club, and some of Hemingway's later prose, which, according to both MacDonald and Eco, represents a corruption of Hemingway's earlier prose style for commercial purposes. In reacting to MacDonald's views, Eco is more interested in identifying the *structure* of bad taste or kitsch than in denouncing its ill effects. In fact, the very title of his essay suggests Eco's fundamental indebtedness to structuralist theory, just as his citation of Jakobson's notion of poetic language points toward his growing interest in semiotics. Following general structuralist principles, Eco defines a work of art as a "system of relationships" containing stylistic elements Eco defines as *stylemes*. Thus, in structural terms, kitsch is

a styleme that has been abstracted from its original context and inserted into a context whose general structure does not possess the

[13] *The Open Work*, pp. 195, 196; *Apocalittici e integrati*, pp. 87, 92–93 (the English translation of the original has been edited and shortened).

same characters of homogeneity and necessity as the original's, while the result is proposed as a freshly created work capable of stimulating new experiences.[14]

Eco offers a number of fascinating illustrations of his view that bad taste represents a fundamental pastiche structure composed of stylemes taken out of their original high-cult framework. The nineteenth-century Italian portrait painter Giovanni Boldini, Eco believes, is a perfect example of kitsch, since his portraits are virtually alike and constitute "stylematic sirens, to be consumed from the waist up and looked at from the waist down": the faces and the clothes in his paintings are modified from picture to picture merely to please the demands of the client.[15] In an even more telling example, Eco demonstrates how a famous phrase at a crucial point in a great work of art, Alessandro Manzoni's *I promessi sposi* (*The Betrothed*, 1840–42) was employed, probably unconsciously, by Edmondo De Amicis's *Cuore* (*Heart: A School Boy's Journal*, 1886) in an entirely different and kitsch context. In Manzoni's novel, the tragic phrase "La sventurata rispose" ("The poor wretch answered") marks the beginning of the downfall of the tragic nun of Monza, Gertrude. Its kitsch repetition in a slightly different but recognizable form in De Amicis – "E quell'infame rise" ("And that rascal smiled") – occurs in De Amicis's novel at a completely undramatic moment and essentially represents a waste of the energy of Manzoni's masterpiece, as well as a corruption of the freshness and dramatic impact of the phrase, now taken from its original context.[16]

Unlike the apocalyptic intellectual, such as MacDonald, who condemns popular taste *per se*, Eco's view of the subject is far more nuanced. For him, the most important consideration resides in the use

[14] *The Open Work*, p. 201; *Apocalittici e integrati*, p. 110.
[15] *The Open Work*, p. 203; *Apocalittici e integrati*, p. 112.
[16] *The Open Work*, pp. 204–05; *Apocalittici e integrati*, pp. 113–14. As is so often typical of Eco's theoretical works, this particular passage has its origins in a very early occasional essay first collected in *Diario minimo* in 1962 but not included in *Misreadings*, the English translation of selected pieces from this anthology.

to which such artefacts of popular culture are put. If they are used by a manipulative power structure to obfuscate reality and to conceal the power relationships present within our contemporary world, or to mask an ideological message delivered through such popular culture phenomena as comic strips, then the intellectual's task must not be merely to denounce this aspect of popular culture. Such purposeless denunciations amount to a logical absurdity, something akin to denouncing the weather. Eco believes, instead, that a contemporary intellectual must deconstruct – to employ a term popular in current critical practice – the manner in which such a dangerous message is hidden beneath a highly consumable popular culture artefact.

Eco's suspicion of popular culture laden with ideological overtones returns us to the notion of the "consolatory" function of writing on popular culture or in popular culture itself. As David Robey's introduction to the English translation of *The Open Work* underlines, Eco rejects popular culture that reaffirms

> the public's sense of the essential rightness and permanence of the world in which they live. The great fault of the mass media, for Eco, is to convey a standardized, oversimplified, static, and complacent vision that masks the real complexity of things and implicitly denies the possibility of change. . . . The solution, therefore, is not to raise popular entertainment to the level of art – Eco is not saying that the public should be fed on a diet of modern open works – but to work for forms of entertainment that are "honest." This means, on the one hand, entertainment that does not have false artistic pretensions [kitsch] . . . On the other hand, what is more important, "honest" entertainment is that which is ideologically sound . . . because it acknowledges the complexity, the problematic character of the historical circumstances in which we live, because it allows for the possibility of change and serves as a stimulus to reflection and criticism, because it generates a sense of independence and choice instead of conformism and passivity.[17]

[17] David Robey, "Introduction," in Eco, *The Open Work*, pp. xvii–xviii. In an essay to

As far back as the mid-1950s, Eco had surmised that behind every great intellectual there was probably a detective novel in his or her closet, if not in his or her library. Now the future best-selling novelist hastens to admit that every reader, and not merely the reader familiar only with popular culture, feels a basic, psychological need to consume works that aim to provoke only an elemental sensation of pleasure:

> All these supercilious condemnations of mass taste, in the name of an ideal community of readers involved solely in discovering the secret beauties of the cryptic messages produced by high art, neglect the average consumer (present in just about all of us) who at the end of the day may resort to a book or a movie in the hope that it may evoke a few basic reactions (laughter, fear, pleasure, sorrow, anger) and, through these, reestablish some balance in his or her physical or intellectual life. A well-balanced cultural context does not require the eradication of this sort of message; it only needs to keep them under control, dose them, and see to it that they are not sold and consumed as art.[18]

The contemporary intellectual's task thus involves what Eco will soon begin to call a "semiological guerrilla warfare": messages in popular culture must be decoded to reveal their latent ideological content in order to prevent the mass media from becoming an instrument of passive control.[19]

Let us now turn to three articles in *Apocalyptic and Integrated Intellectuals* that deal specifically with popular culture artefacts (in this

---

"Umberto Eco: Theory and Practice in the Analysis of the Media," in Zygmunt G. Baranski and Robert Lumley, eds., *Culture and Conflict in Postwar Italy: Essays on Mass and Popular Culture* (New York: St. Martin's Press, 1990), pp. 160–77.

[18] *The Open Work*, p. 194; *Apocalittici e integrati*, p. 84.

[19] It is not by accident that this phrase "guerriglia semiologica" appears in a paper read in 1967 and in the conclusion of Eco's first work of semiotic theory, *La struttura assente*, published in that same year; it was reprinted as "Per una guerriglia semiologica" in the anthology on Italian ideologies entitled *Il costume di casa: evidenze e misteri dell'ideologia italiana*, pp. 290–98; it is translated as "Towards a Semiological Guerrilla Warfare" in *Travels in Hyperreality: Essays*, trans. William Weaver (New York: Harcourt Brace Jovanovich, 1986), pp. 135–44.

case, different American comic strips) – the chapters on *Steve Canyon*, *Superman*, and *Peanuts*, analyzed in the same order as they appear in the book. Eco's discussion of *Steve Canyon* departs from the very first strip drawn by artist Milton Caniff, who created the series on 11 January 1947 after years of success had earned him a weekly audience of some 30 million fans with *Terry and the Pirates*. The essay focuses upon eleven frames of the first installment which introduce the new character, his surroundings, his secretary at "Horizons, Unlimited," and a vamp named Copper Calhoun, who telephones Canyon's office through her male secretary. Canyon refuses the call because of the imperious attitude of the secretary. Yet, in the final frame, Copper Calhoun (blowing cigarette smoke and dressed in a black costume typical of the *femme fatale* of the cinema) exclaims: "I want that man!! . . . Get him!" Eco's essay includes a detailed analysis and commentary on each separate frame, all reproduced for the reader's convenience. Eco defines Canyon as "an iconographic element that can be studied iconologically, like the miniature of a saint with its canonical attributes and a fixed kind of beard or aureola"; this figure is a "prototype" from the 1940s, representing a "discreet mingling of Mediterranean and Oriental glamour, and this refers in turn to the two main theatres of war, from which the Americans subsequently imported their models for post-war eroticism"; Copper Calhoun is the prototype of the *femme fatale*, a "skillful blend of Snow White, the Veronica Lake of *I Married a Witch* and Hedy Lamarr."[20]

After his detailed comments on individual frames of the comic strip, Eco moves to the theoretical implications of his specific remarks. He posits the existence of a "semantics of comics" by searching for the specific devices through which a comic strip communicates to its mass public. There is, first of all, the device of the balloon, the fundamental idea of a comic strip, which functions as a linguistic sign. Balloons drawn with a sharp point and connected to a

---

[20] "A Reading of Steve Canyon," p. 22; *Apocalittici e integrati*, p. 140.

character's face indicate that the words within the bubble are spoken by that character. Balloons with zig-zag edges like the teeth of a saw signify various strong emotions (fear, anger, etc.). Sounds are rendered graphically – usually by onomatopoeia such as "Smack!," "Pow!," "Zip!," "Gulp!," and so forth, often printed in special type for emphasis. There is also a codified syntax of frame composition, and the relationship between one frame and the next often contains a montage similar to that employed by the cinema. The fundamental difference between comic strips and film remains, however. Film merges a series of still pictures into movement, while the comic strip breaks up the continuum of motion into separate and static elements. Nevertheless, a number of stylistic features normally identified with the cinema are also employed in the comic strip (jump cuts, classical montage juxtaposing diverse images à la Eisenstein, close-ups, medium close-ups, long shots, wide-angle shots, crane shots, pans and tracks), and Eco's discussion of *Steve Canyon* reflects a connoisseur's intimate knowledge of American popular culture in both film and cartoons.

In Eco's conclusion to his discussion of *Steve Canyon* he offers a definition of characters in popular culture that he will employ for other media as well. Steve Canyon, Copper Calhoun, and all such figures represent "stereotypes" or "topoi." They are not "types," if "type" is understood in the sense associated with the literary theory of Lukács to mean a literary character embodying an important aspect of a given period's historical reality. Such cartoon stereotypes as Steve Canyon or Superman nevertheless incarnate a number of important societal or cultural values, all marking a "substantial allegiance to the values of an American way of life tinged with the Hollywood Legend":

> Our "reading" of the *Steve Canyon* page has confronted us with the fact that the comic strip represents an autonomous literary sub-genre, possessing its own structural patterns, an original mode of communication with the reader and an interpretative code which

the reader already shares and which the author refers to constantly in order to organize his message. This message is conveyed in accordance with a whole range of tacitly accepted formative rules. It is directed consciously at the average intelligence, imagination and taste of the strip's adopted readers.[21]

The English translation of this chapter of *Apocalyptic and Integrated Intellectuals* ends with such a general conclusion. In the Italian original, however, Eco's discussion continues, offering a comparison between *Steve Canyon* and other American comic strips. Eco first rejects providing an analysis of Harold Gray's *Little Orphan Annie*. Such a straw-man target is much too simple, since "his ideological line is precise . . . profoundly reactionary."[22] Instead, Eco focuses upon Al Capp's *Li'l Abner*, a cartoon strip praised by liberals and progressives, such as John Steinbeck or Theodore White, for its relentless satire of every popular American institution. Eco concludes, however, that the progressive reputation of Capp's strip is only an illusion and that paradoxically, the ideological content of *Li'l Abner* matches that of *Steve Canyon*: a belief in the possibility of reform and progress combines with an absolute faith in the American political or social system itself. Capp's reformist satire of American values parallels the consolatory function of the diatribes apocalyptic intellectuals produce against popular culture, and like such elitist fulminations, Capp's sarcastic jabs at American institutions never move his audience to change them.

While Eco's reading of the eleven frames taken from the first images of *Steve Canyon* are thought-provoking interpretations of the comic strip series, they cannot reasonably be said to reflect a general theory of popular culture. Eco's skill as an intelligent reader, rather than any systematic theory applied to the cartoons, seems to explain the interpretations Eco provides for the ideological underpinning of various cartoon series. Thus, Eco concludes that *Little Orphan Annie*

---

[21] "A Reading of Steve Canyon," p. 25; *Apocalittici e integrati*, p. 151.

[22] Eco, *Apocalittici e integrati*, p. 175 (author's translation).

reflects what he will term in the chapter on *Peanuts* "the supporter of a nationalistic McCarthyism, a paleocapitalist classism, a petty bourgeois philistinism ready to celebrate the pomps of the John Birch Society."[23] Eco's discussion of Donald Duck and the comic strip's ideological foundation even admits that his conclusion embodies common knowledge:

> We all know that the figure of Donald Duck's Uncle Scrooge sums up all the defects of a generic capitalism founded on the ownership of money and the exploitation of one's fellow-man solely for profit: the Dickensian name of this character serves to direct this implied criticism towards a notion of nineteenth-century capitalism (akin to the use of child labour in coal mines and corporal punishment in the schools) which modern society obviously no longer fears and which anyone can feel free to criticize.[24]

We might compare Eco's analysis of *Steve Canyon* or other aspects of popular culture during this "pre-semiotic" phase of his career to another similar display of brilliance by a scholar from another generation, Leo Spitzer. Spitzer's famous explication of an American advertising jingle devoted to "Sunkist oranges"[25] goes far beyond the possibilities of normal *explications de texte*, even though Spitzer would have his reader believe that anyone understanding his critical method might be capable of duplicating his results. But both Spitzer's critical *tour de force*, and Eco's illuminating essays on popular culture, reflect an erudition and a literary intelligence few of their peers can match. The results Spitzer and Eco would have us attribute to the success of a critical theory are extremely difficult to duplicate by critics lacking their unique talents.

---

[23] "The World of Charlie Brown," in *Apocalypse Postponed*, p. 38; *Apocalittici e integrati*, p. 263.

[24] *Apocalypse Postponed*, p. 38; *Apocalittici e integrati*, p. 264.

[25] See Leo Spitzer, "American Advertising Explained as Popular Art," in *Essays on English and American Literature*, ed. Anna Hatcher (Princeton University Press, 1962), pp. 248–77; the essay originally appeared as part of Spitzer's *A Method of Interpreting Literature* (Northampton, Mass.: Smith College, 1949), pp. 102–49.

The famous essay on "The Myth of Superman," first published in 1962, considers the entire series of strips devoted to the Man of Steel, not merely a related series of frames. It is also more heuristic in its theoretical suggestiveness than the essay on *Steve Canyon*. Not surprisingly, Eco finds *Superman* replete with a status-quo ideology: in fact, he claims that *'the only visible form that evil assumes is an attempt on private property,"* while "good is represented only as charity."[26] But Eco now focuses upon what he calls the "iterative scheme" (*lo schema iterativo*) in the *Superman* mythology. The iterative scheme functions as a redundant message in *Superman*, and his emphasis upon such redundancy in popular culture points us not only backward to Eco's theories on the open work but also forward to his future studies of reader response. Thus, in his essay on *Superman*, Eco begins to concern himself not just with a work or message or even the code such a work or message embodies, but also its implied or actual audience (its receiver), as well as the audience's means of decoding the message it receives.

Popular narratives, either in fiction or in the comic strips that mimic popular fiction, embrace such redundant iterative schemes. This holds true not only for comic strips such as *Superman*, but also in the popular detective novels of Sherlock Holmes, Nero Wolfe, or Maigret:

> A series of events repeated according to a set scheme (iteratively, in such a way that each event takes up again from a sort of virtual beginning, ignoring where the preceding event left off) is nothing new in popular narrative. In fact, this scheme constitutes one of its more characteristic forms. . . . [In the detective novel] The attraction of the book, the sense of repose, of psychological extension which it is capable of conferring, lies in the fact that plopped in an easy chair or in the seat of a train compartment, the reader continuously recovers, point by point, what he already knows, what he wants to know again: that is why he has purchased the book. He derives

[26] "The Myth of Superman," in *The Role of the Reader*, pp. 123, 124; *Apocalittici e integrati*, pp. 258, 259 (the italics are Eco's in both the original and the English translation).

pleasure from the nonstory (if indeed a story is a development of events which should bring us from the point of departure to a point of arrival where we would never have dreamed of arriving); the distraction consists in the refutation of a development of events, in a withdrawal from the tension of past-present-future to the focus on an *instant*, which is loved because it is recurrent.[27]

Unlike the apocalyptic intellectual, who generally fulminates against the destructive effects of popular culture on contemporary society, Eco recognizes and appreciates why we all (Eco included) enjoy repetitious stories or comic strips celebrating a superhero who can never be changed, overcome, or threatened because he or she is invincible. Popular culture, in its many and varied forms, relies more than high culture upon such repetitive iterative schemes containing an extremely high redundancy in their messages: "the greater part of popular narrative is a narrative of redundance."[28] Any danger to the intellect and to society at large supposedly derived from popular culture comes not from the redundant messages themselves but, instead, from the implicit or explicit manipulation of popular culture for ideological reasons. Thus, so long as we are aware of the ideological positions of such comic strips as *Little Orphan Annie* or *Superman*, Eco seems to imply, they can do us little serious harm.

Eco's explanation for why a reader traditionally hungers for such high-redundancy messages in the iterative scheme links his interests in literary theory with his desire for the reform of society at large. For Eco, contemporary industrial society assails the individual with "a continuous load of information which proceeds by way of massive jolts, implying a continual reassessment of sensibilities, adaptation of psychological assumptions, and requalification of intelligence," and as a result, even the most cultured intellectuals turn to redundant

[27] "The Myth of Superman," in *The Role of the Reader*, pp. 117, 119–20; *Apocalittici e integrati*, pp. 245, 250.
[28] "The Myth of Superman," in *The Role of the Reader*, p. 120; *Apocalittici e integrati*, p. 251.

narrative as "an indulgent invitation to repose, the only occasion of true relaxation offered to the consumer," while high culture or superior art "only proposes schemes in evolution, grammars which mutually eliminate each other, and codes of continuous alternations."[29] From the psychological perspective of the harried reader, Eco thus now cautiously accepts at least part of the "consolatory" function of literature, a function he will criticize in other contexts. In his own fiction, of course, Eco will later exploit the generic conventions of the detective novel to the fullest, showing himself to be one of the genre's great contemporary connoisseurs.

If, in his examinations of comic strips with ideological overtones, Eco focuses upon unmasking their latent values, we must turn to "The World of Charlie Brown" and his praise for the cartoon world created by Charles M. Schulz in *Peanuts* for a picture of a comic strip that, in spite of its origins in popular culture, nevertheless offers an almost completely positive message unblemished by ideological manipulation. His opening assessment of the genre in this essay, however, is not encouraging:

> The comic strip is commissioned from above, it operates according to all the mechanisms of hidden persuasion, it presupposes in the consumer an attitude of escape that immediately stimulates the paternalistic aspirations of the producers. And, as a rule, authors conform: thus the comic strip, in most cases, reflects the implicit pedagogy of a system and acts as hidden reinforcement of the dominant myths and values.[30]

The only explanation Eco provides for some individual comic-strip writers who transcend this generally depressing scenario is that of individual genius. Some artists – Schulz, Jules Feiffer, George Harriman in *Krazy Kat* – went beyond the iron boundaries of this mass culture genre and

---

[29] "The Myth of Superman," in *The Role of the Reader*, p. 121; *Apocalittici e integrati*, p. 252.
[30] "The World of Charlie Brown," in *Apocalypse Postponed*, pp. 37–38; *Apocalittici e integrati*, p. 263.

these artists, working within the system, performed a critical and liberating function. As usual, it is a matter of individual genius: to be able to develop a language so incisive, clear and effective as to dominate all the conditions within which that language must operate.[31]

The fact that Eco falls back upon the extremely traditional argument of "original genius" to explain the differences between those comic strips which are consolatory and those which are not reflects the extent to which his thinking, at this point in his career, is as much dependent upon older critical methodologies as it is upon such new critical instruments as semiotics.

The Superman of the Masses offers a fascinating companion piece to the writings collected together in *Apocalyptic and Integrated Intellectuals*, even if it does not provide any fundamentally novel theoretical progress toward a strictly semiotic theory of popular culture in the mass media. The seven chapters of this book appeared in article form between 1965 and 1974 before being collected together in 1976 as *The Superman of the Masses*. Like so many of Eco's best writings, this book retains the air of an occasional work rather than a theoretical treatise. In Eco's preface to the 1974 edition of *Apocalyptic and Integrated Intellectuals*, he had declared that he first employed "semiotic tools" in his studies of Ian Fleming and Eugène Sue.[32] In the additional prefatory note to the 1977 edition of the same collection, Eco went on to claim that his *Apocalyptic and Integrated Intellectuals*

> definitely opened the way to semiotic studies for me. With *Open Work*, I studied the language of the avant-garde movements; with *Apocalittici*, I studied the language of their opposite (or, as some will say, of their fatal complement). But in the face of two apparently different phenomena, in which language was used in such different ways, I needed a unifying theoretical framework. And this framework

---

[31] "The World of Charlie Brown," in *Apocalypse Postponed*, p. 39; *Apocalittici e integrati*, p. 265.

[32] *Apocalypse Postponed*, p. 54; *Apocalittici e integrati*, p. xiii.

became clear to me precisely while I was writing the essay on kitsch, where I begin to make use of Jakobsonian linguistics.[33]

In his preface to *The Superman of the Masses*, however, Eco adds a disclaimer to any consideration of the work as a semiotic theory of popular culture and mass media, remarking, instead, that the anthology reflects a mixture of several kinds of criticism. There is a sociology of popular narrativity; a study of ideologies expressed in the form of a history of ideas; and finally "exploratory contributions to a textual semiotics not obsessed by the demands of formalization" wherein, with one exception (the essay on James Bond), the essays are never "pure examples of the semiotics of narrativity" but are, rather, works in which "semiotic tools are employed only when they are useful."[34]

By far the most important essays in the book are those devoted to the James Bond novels or to Eugène Sue's *Les Mystères de Paris*. Let us limit our discussion to the first work, which Eco himself declares to be the most indebted to semiotics in the collection. In this essay, Eco departs from a reading of Fleming's first Bond novel – *Casino Royale* (1953) – and outlines what he terms the "elements for the building of a machine that functions basically on a set of precise units governed by rigorous combinational rules."[35] He then proceeds to outline five levels of narrative structure in all of the Bond novels, structures based upon the opposition of characters and values. Eco isolates some fourteen such structures: four point to oppositions between four characters (Bond–M; Bond–Villain; Villain–Woman; Woman–Bond); the others constitute oppositions between values that find their personification in the four different characters (Free World–Soviet Union; Great Britain–Non-Anglo-Saxon Countries; Duty–Sacrifice;

---

[33] *Apocalypse Postponed*, p. 56; *Apocalittici e integrati*, p. xv.
[34] *Il superuomo di massa*, p. vii (author's translation; this section of the essay is not included in the English translation).
[35] "Narrative Structures in Fleming," in *The Role of the Reader*, p. 146; *Il superuomo di massa*, p. 147.

Cupidity–Ideals; Love–Death; Chance–Planning; Luxury–Discomfort; Excess–Moderation; Perversion–Innocence; Loyalty–Disloyalty). Having identified the basic variables in the Bond narratives, Eco then demonstrates that such opposed binary pairs constitute "the elements of an *ars combinatoria* with fairly elementary rules":

> Bond is sent to a given place to avert a "science-fiction" plan by a monstrous individual of uncertain origin and definitely not English who, making use of his organizational or productive activity, not only earns money, but helps the cause of the enemies of the West. In facing this monstrous being, Bond meets a woman who is dominated by him and frees her from her past, establishing with her an erotic relationship interrupted by capture by the Villain and by torture. But Bond defeats the Villain, who dies horribly, and rests from his great efforts in the arms of the woman, though he is destined to lose her.[36]

In fact, Fleming's plot structures can be outlined in eight different steps fixed according to the rules of the combination of oppositional pairs. They unfold by a prearranged scheme capable of many variations but always remain fundamentally the same: "the fundamental rule of the game is 'Bond moves and mates in eight moves'."[37] For Eco, a Fleming novel resembles a basketball game between the Harlem Globetrotters and their usual white patsies. The audience knows at the outset the Harlem team will win. Nevertheless, they derive pleasure "in watching the trained virtuosity with which they defer the final moment, with what ingenious deviations they reconfirm the foregone conclusion, with what trickeries they make rings around their opponents," just as a Fleming novel exploits "that element of foregone play which is typical of the escape machine geared for the entertainment of the masses."[38] In contrast to other

[36] "Narrative Structures in Fleming," in *The Role of the Reader*, p. 160; *Il superuomo di massa*, p. 166–67.
[37] "Narrative Structures in Fleming," in *The Role of the Reader*, p. 156; *Il superuomo di massa*, pp. 161–62.
[38] "Narrative Structures in Fleming," in *The Role of the Reader*, pp. 160–61; *Il superuomo di massa*, p. 168.

leftist critics of the era, who saw in Ian Fleming's literary creation only the reflection of a reactionary, even a McCarthyite ideology with Manichaean overtones, Eco's reading of James Bond emphasizes Fleming's skill at constructing a narrative apparatus that is remarkably close in tone and structure to the classic fairy tales of Western culture.

In spite of Eco's *post-facto* declaration that his theories about popular culture were marked by a growing interest in semiotics during this period, David Robey seems correct when he remarks that "to judge from the Bond and Sue essays, therefore, the impact of Eco's semiotics on his analyses of the media was not all that substantial."[39] Even though Eco labeled the essay on James Bond a "pure" example of semiotic analysis in retrospect in 1977, a cursory examination of the textual criticism Eco performs in that article places its methodology directly in the tradition of narrative theories current during the 1960s before semiotics became fashionable. The binary pairs of characters or values owed an obvious debt to the theories of Claude Lévi-Strauss, who was, ironically, one of the harshest critics of *The Open Work*. Eco's critical perspective in the essays on Sue and Bond embraces eclectic responses to narrative theories typical of French structuralists, as well as ideas associated today with the Russian formalists, with Roland Barthes's early essays on popular culture, and with the works by French or Italian followers of Vladimir Propp's studies of fairy tales, especially those of Tzvetan Todorov. The most influential writings associated with these and other critics Eco could have known appeared in Italy as much as a decade earlier then when they were published in England or America in translation. Bompiani, the publishing house for which Eco worked in Milan, was involved in circulating translations of such works, but every major Italian publishing firm of the period (Einaudi, Feltrinelli, Laterza, Il Mulino, Rizzoli) was also involved in disseminating foreign theories throughout Italian culture. The interchange of ideas could often

---

[39] David Robey, "Umberto Eco: Theory and Practice in the Analysis of the Media," in Baranski and Lumley, eds., *Culture and Conflict in Postwar Italy*, p. 171.

become quite confusing. Eco himself originally planned to translate Roland Barthes's *Elements of Semiology* (1964) for the little magazine, *Marcatré*, but after the death of Elio Vittorini, he learned from friends at Einaudi that Vittorini had wanted to bring this work out himself, and so he abandoned his original plan, leaving the field free for Einaudi. Barthes himself, who had published the essay in a journal of limited circulation (*Communications*), initially believed the essay could not justify publication in book form. But after the success of the Italian translation, the essay received a French edition as well, and was subsequently translated into dozens of foreign languages, making Barthes known all over the world as one of the first and most persuasive exponents of semiotics.[40]

One seldom-mentioned influence upon Eco's thinking during this period should be noted, the poetics of the French literary movement Oulipo (Ouvroir de Littérature Potentielle or "Workshop of Potential Literature"), founded in 1960 by Raymond Queneau and other writers and to which such figures as Italo Calvino (Eco's friend) and Georges Perec belonged. While Calvino actively joined the group only in 1973, the movement's aesthetic theories were widely disseminated a decade earlier by Italian translations published at Einaudi, the publisher for whom Calvino worked at the time. Oulipo's theories defined literature in general and narrative in particular as a combinative process – exactly the perspective embraced by Eco in his essays on James Bond and Eugène Sue.[41] Oulipo's ideas thus paralleled structuralist, formalist, and semiotic theory during the period, but they were put forward

[40] I am indebted to a letter from Umberto Eco dated 30 January 1996 for this detailed information on the role he and others played in popularizing foreign methodologies. Italy's role as a catalyst in spreading such new theories has unfortunately been frequently ignored. Russian formalist theory, for instance, was first translated into Italian long before significant quantities of these critical works were available in English translations.

[41] For an analysis of Oulipo and translations of the major texts of the movement, including writings by Queneau, Calvino, and even American members of the group, see Warren F. Motte Jr., *Oulipo: A Primer of Potential Literature* (Lincoln: University of Nebraska Press, 1987).

not by literary theorists but by practicing writers of great talent and ingenuity. Such notions surely had an impact upon Eco's own practice as a novelist years later, and it was not by accident that in 1983, Eco himself translated and Einaudi published Queneau's most significant and complex work, *Exercises de style* (*Esercizi di stile*), only two years after the international success of *The Name of the Rose*.[42]

After publishing anthologies of occasional essays on popular culture, Eco's studies of mass media convinced him that he required a more general set of theoretical principles which would allow either a literary theorist or a social critic to examine both high and popular culture, not only "classic" works of art (the object of traditional aesthetics) but contemporary mass media as well. Moreover, such a comprehensive perspective would have to emphasize the intricate relationships between such "texts" (now defined as *any* product of human culture) and the ideology or the culture of the society that produced them. Emerging from an intellectual milieu indebted to a number of different philosophical points of view on contemporary society, Eco was to move beyond structuralism toward a vision of semiotics as a master discipline that would respond to such a Herculean theoretical task.

[42] Raymond Queneau, *Esercizi di stile*, trans. Umberto Eco (Turin: Einaudi, 1983).

four

§

From semiotics to narrative
theory in a decade of radical
social change

The tumultuous political and cultural changes in Europe associated
with the year 1968 began in France, even if ultimately inspired by
events in the United States. Italy's conservative political and cultural
establishment was profoundly changed by events that spilled over
into the peninsula from France. Radical and unforeseen transform-
ations in Italian political institutions, schools, universities, and facto-
ries resulted.[1] While the disastrous impact of political terrorism
from both the right and the left threatened to unravel the delicate
social fabric underpinning Italy's democratic government, the
screaming headlines announcing the latest exploit of the Red Brig-
ades were ultimately not so important as a series of profound and
permanent changes within Italian society during this period that all
called established tradition and authority into question in a variety
of ways and within a variety of cultural contexts. The year 1968 also
marks Umberto Eco's move beyond an essentially structuralist
analysis of popular culture in his pre-semiotic period to his active
support of a theoretical perspective he considered more fruitful, that
of semiotics.

Eco's first venture into semiotic theory resulted in the publication of

---

[1] Robert Lumley (the editor of the recent English edition of Eco's *Apocalypse
Postponed*) provides a good study of social change during this decade in *States of
Emergency: Cultures of Revolt in Italy from 1969 to 1978* (London: Verso, 1990).

La struttura assente (The Absent Structure).[2] Subtitled "Introduction to Semiological Research," *The Absent Structure* has never been translated completely into English, although one chapter of the work, "Series and Structure," appears in the English version of *The Open Work.*[3] *The Absent Structure* itself was an amplified and greatly modified version of another work, *Appunti per una semiologia delle comunicazioni visive (Notes for a Semiology of Visual Communications,* 1967) that Eco had first written for the use of students in his university lectures.[4]

During the year following the appearance of *The Absent Structure,* the International Association for Semiotic Studies decided to employ the term "semiotics," a conscious shift to the language used by the American philosopher Charles S. Peirce (1839–1914), rather than the term "semiology" employed by French theorists, such as Ferdinand de Saussure in his seminal *Course in General Linguistics* (1916) or Roland Barthes in *Elements of Semiology.* Eco was elected Secretary-General of the association in 1969 and would later organize its first international congress in Milan in 1974. His own work during this decade to disseminate semiotics as an academic discipline was remarkably successful. Not only was Eco awarded the first Italian university Chair of Semiotics at the University of Bologna in 1971, but he also founded, in that same year, the first international semiotics journal published in Italy (*VS: Versus – Quaderni di studi semiotici*). This journal is still in existence and publishes essays in Italian, English, and French. It has done much to popularize semiotic research among academics and often includes major essays by Eco himself that are later revised and republished elsewhere. In addition, his frequent trips abroad as visiting professor (particularly in the United States and France) won

---

[2] *La struttura assente: introduzione alla ricerca semiologica* (Milan: Bompiani, 1968); reprinted as *La struttura assente: la ricerca semiotica e il metodo strutturale* (Milan: Bompiani, 1994), the edition to which subsequent page citations refer.

[3] *The Open Work,* pp. 217–35.

[4] Milan: Bompiani, 1967. Like *The Absent Structure,* this work remains untranslated, essentially because its arguments were eventually subsumed by later and more comprehensive books.

him a significant following among foreign intellectuals and academics, and he became something of an intellectual jet-setter or superstar, identified everywhere with the study of popular culture through the methodology of semiotics even before his fame was exponentially increased by his first novel.

Eco's publications during this decade are only partially available in English translation. *The Absent Structure* was followed in 1971 by *Le forme del contenuto* (*The Forms of Content*). Two sections of this work are translated in *The Role of the Reader*: "The Semantics of Metaphor" and "On the Possibility of Generating Aesthetic Messages in an Edenic Language."[5] *The Forms of Content* was followed by another book, *Trattato di semiotica* (*A Theory of Semiotics*, 1975), Eco's most comprehensive and systematic contribution to formal semiotic theory. Not only is this book available in English, but it was also written originally in English (with the assistance of David Osmond-Smith) after Eco decided to abandon an earlier translation of *The Absent Structure*. Eco subsequently translated the English version into Italian, and an Italian edition appeared in 1975, followed by the English-language original in 1976. Finally, in 1979 Eco published a series of essays composed after the appearance of *A Theory of Semiotics*: *Lector in fabula: la cooperazione interpretativa nei testi narrativi* (literally, The Reader in the Story: Interpretative Cooperation in Narrative Texts).[6] *The Reader in the Story* was joined by an English volume in that same year – *The Role of the Reader: Explorations in the Semiotics of Texts*[7] – that is not quite identical with the contents of *The Reader in the Story*.

---

[5] *The Role of the Reader*, pp. 67–89 and 90–104. Both essays are revised versions of pp. 93–144 from *Le forme del contenuto* (Milan: Bompiani, 1971). On p. 7 of this work, Eco notes that *The Forms of Content*, in conformity with the decision of the International Association for Semiotics Studies, employs the term "semiotics" rather than "semiology."

[6] *Lector in fabula: la cooperazione interpretativa nei testi narrativi* (Milan: Bompiani, 1979).

[7] As noted elsewhere, *The Role of the Reader* contains selections from many of Eco's previous works, including *The Open Work, Apocalyptic and Integrated Intellectuals, The Superman of the Masses, The Absent Structure*, and *The Forms of Content*. But it also reprints

In addition to the theoretical books listed above intended for the specialist in semiotic, literary, or cultural theory, Eco also published two extremely important collections of his occasional essays, most of which had appeared either in his weekly column in *L'Espresso* or in *Il Corriere della sera*, Milan's major newspaper: *Il costume di casa: evidenze e misteri dell'ideologia italiana* (*Home Customs: Evidence and Mysteries of Italian Ideology*, 1973); and *Dalla periferia dell'impero: cronache da un nuovo medioevo* (*From the Periphery of the Empire: Chronicles from a New Middle Ages*).[8] The titles of these two collections, as much as their contents, underline Eco's interest in establishing a dialogue with the general reading public during a period which witnessed rapid social and cultural change throughout Italy. As the titles also suggest, the first collection focuses upon Italian topics, while the second anthology broadens the author's horizons to concentrate upon the United States.

Several questions immediately arise from an examination of the trajectory of Eco's career during this period. First, why did Eco abandon the structuralist approach to popular culture that in his widely acclaimed essays on mass media had provided such a workable

radically rearranged and revised versions of the key sections of *Lector in fabula*, including the following sections: "Il lettore modello," pp. 50–66; "Livelli di cooperazione testuale," pp. 67–85; "Le strutture discorsive," pp. 86–101; "Le strutture narrative," pp. 102–10; "Peirce: I fondamenti semiotici della cooperazione testuale," pp. 175–99; "Applicazioni: *Il mercante di denti*," pp. 186–93; and "Applicazioni: *Un drame bien parisien*," pp. 194–230.

[8] Some of the essays in *Il costume di casa: evidenze e misteri dell'ideologia italiana* and *Dalla periferia dell'impero: cronache da un nuovo medioevo* have appeared in English. Eco's first English anthology of such occasional essays, *Travels in Hyperreality*, contains the following pieces from *Home Customs* – "Towards a Semiological Guerrilla Warfare" (pp. 135–44); "Sports Chatter" (pp. 159–65); "Two Families of Objects" (pp. 183–85); "Lady Barbara" (pp. 187–89) – as well as a number of works in *From the Periphery of the Empire* – "Travels in Hyperreality" (pp. 1–58); "Living in the New Middle Ages" (pp. 73–85); "Casablanca: Cult Movies and Intertextual Collage" (pp. 197–211); "Cogito Interruptus" (pp. 221–38); "In Praise of St. Thomas" (pp. 257–68); and "De Interpretatione" (pp. 281–88). The rest of the essays in this anthology derive from a subsequent Italian collection, *Sette anni di desiderio* (Milan: Bompiani, 1983). A more recent English anthology, *Apocalypse Postponed*, contains a single essay from *Home Customs*–'The Italian Genius Industry" (pp. 211–24) – and another in *From the Periphery of the Empire* – "Does the Audience have Bad Effects on Television?" (pp. 87–102).

methodology? Second, what specific contributions did Eco make to the development of semiotic theory in the writings of this period? Third and most important, did Eco's turn to narrative theory in *The Reader in the Text* (written at the same period as he composed his first novel, *The Name of the Rose*) reflect a theoretical step back from the imperialistic claims he formerly made for semiotics as a theory encompassing all of human culture and a turn to more modest aims in elaborating a theory of textual interpretation? In short, did Eco the storyteller replace Eco the theorist? Eco's move from structuralism to semiotics and his specific contributions to semiotic theory will be the focus of this chapter. The remaining chapters of this study will examine the complex relationship between Eco the theorist and Eco the storyteller.

Eco's interest in semiotic theory must also be put into the context of the times. As Teresa de Lauretis has noted,[9] structuralist theory initially received a warm welcome among Italian intellectuals of the 1960s. Structuralism seemed to offer a methodology preferable either to the discredited philosophical idealism of Croce or to the dogmatically deterministic Marxist theory that was advanced to replace Croce. Italian academics lacked a convincing methodology upon which to base textual interpretation, such as America's New Criticism or Russian formalism, and for a brief time structuralism seemed to provide that. Moreover, structuralism's impulse toward interdisciplinarity and its links to the social sciences, particularly linguistics, seemed like a breath of fresh air to Italians who were exploring a variety of what would eventually be called "strumenti critici" (critical tools)[10] in

---

[9] See Teresa de Lauretis, "Semiotics, Theory and Social Practice: A Critical History of Italian Semiotics," *Cine-Tracts* 2, no. 1 (1978), 1–14; reproduced in a revised form in her *Umberto Eco* (Florence: La Nuova Italia, 1981), pp. 31ff.

[10] In fact, an important journal founded by Cesare Segre, Maria Corti, and others was entitled precisely *Strumenti critici* and soon became identified with semiotic analyses of literature. Not surprisingly, the periodical was first published by Turin's Einaudi from its foundation in 1966 until 1982 and was subsequently picked up by Il Mulino of Bologna. Like Einaudi and Bompiani, Il Mulino represents one of a small number of Italian publishers that disseminate new critical ideas through translations. Il Mulino may also be said to function as the University of Bologna's "university" press, even

an attempt to overcome what they perceived to be Italian intellectual provincialism.

Critics of structuralist theory believed it concealed an unacceptable idealist premise in assuming the existence of structures immanent in a text. Its methodology was therefore vitiated by an essentially tautological attempt to verify the existence of formal structures already presumed to be contained within its object of study. Perhaps an even more damning critique of structuralism, from Eco's point of view, was the growing suspicion that structuralist theory masked an essentially conservative approach to social change, since structuralist methodology consciously avoided social, political, or ideological values, ultimately representing an essentially non-historical or ahistorical methodology. Such objections sound remarkably similar to those advanced earlier by Eco in his study of the aesthetics of St. Thomas Aquinas. It will be recalled that Eco saw in Scholasticism a methodological precursor to structuralism. Such disinterest in context and historical development typical of both Scholasticism and structuralism flies directly in the face of the kind of social concern Eco believed intellectuals had an obligation to develop in their work, a concern clearly reflected in Eco's examinations of the ramifications of popular culture in his "presemiotic" writings. Thus, as Teresa de Lauretis remarks:

> in the changing historical situation that culminated in the political events of 1968, structuralism came to denote a reactionary and narrow view of the critical activity, while its early innovative charge and conceptual tools were assumed, developed, and sharpened by semiotics . . . in Italy structuralism was transformed into semiotics by a conscious political shift.[11]

Eco treats the relationship of structuralism to semiotics in a number of different works from this period. Besides being discussed in *The Absent Structure*, Eco provided a prefatory essay to an Italian anthology of

---

though the very concept of a "university press," so important a force in the Anglo-Saxon academic world, has no real Italian equivalent.
[11] De Lauretis, "Semiotics, Theory and Social Practice," p. 5.

Russian essays on the structuralist origins of semiotics that appeared in 1968.[12] In a widely read anthology devoted to new critical tools or methodologies for the analysis of literature that appeared two years later, Eco introduced the chapter on what he was still calling "semiology" and discussed its kinship to structuralism at length.[13] Eco believed that the codes underlying the very discipline of semiotics could be described as systems held together by structural laws or, to use another term, "structures." In offering a summary definition of semiology, Eco called it a "totalitarian point of view" that encompassed "all of the phenomena of culture at all levels"; semiology thus transcended any mere textual criticism and represented a broader theoretical approach to a larger "world of signs." Eco concluded that the notion of "semiological criticism" would best be considered in a much broader context as a "criticism of culture."

Semiotic theory appealed to Eco precisely because it pointed toward cultural theory and was not a purely literary theory developed for the analysis of only high culture classics. Since Eco's most important earlier books, *The Open Work* or *Apocalyptic and Integrated Intellectuals,* included brilliant studies of comic strips, popular songs and mystery novels as well as analyses of literary classics or art works associated with the avant-garde, it is not surprising that Eco would prefer a theoretical perspective, such as semiotics, that paid appropriate attention to popular culture as well as to high culture, mass media as well as the artistic avant-garde. The European intellectual most frequently identified with semiotics during the 1960s was certainly Roland Barthes, whose *Mythologies* (1957) or the previously cited

[12] See Eco's essay, "Lezione e contraddizioni della semiotica sovietica," in Remo Faccani and Umberto Eco, eds., *I sistemi di segni e lo strutturalismo sovietico* (Milan: Bompiani, 1969), pp. 13–31, which contains copious references to the Italian translations of Russian formalists, structuralists, and semioticians that appeared in the 1960s.

[13] See "La critica semiologica," in Maria Corti and Cesare Segre, eds., *I metodi attuali della critica in Italia* (Turin: Edizioni RAI Radiotelevisione italiana, 1970), pp. 369–87. The bibliography contained in Eco's essay also provides an excellent reflection of how important the editorial work of houses such as Einaudi was in changing the way literature was analyzed in Italy during the 1960s and 1970s.

Elements of Semiology departed from de Saussure's linguistic model to study French popular culture (wrestling, soap, toys, tourism, etc.). *Mythologies* has been described by a historian of cultural theory as "quite simply one of the founding texts of cultural studies,"[14] and Eco could not help but be influenced by Barthes's example.

Many Italian intellectuals, both from the traditional Marxist old left and from the new left taking shape during this decade, dismissed mass culture out of hand as part of the capitalist consumer society they professed to despise and had vowed to destroy. Eco, on the other hand, had already criticized such apocalyptic approaches to the mass media. While Eco certainly objected to any ideological manipulation of mass media as much as the ideologues of the period, he would never have accepted the radical position totally rejecting mass culture typical of poet, novelist, and film director Pier Paolo Pasolini, even though Pasolini himself wrote a number of essays applying semiotic theory to the cinema.[15] Eco's attraction to semiotics was more than an intellectual interest in developing an overlapping theory that might encompass both great works of literature and products of the mass media. He also preferred a methodological grounding that provided him with as much intellectual freedom as possible, not only freedom to criticize society's institutions and to work for their reform but also the latitude to take issue with fashionable leftist ideologies sweeping over West European institutions.

The Absent Structure reflects the intellectual situation described above, particularly the rejection of structuralist theory. A major portion of the work, including the only selection from it in English significantly entitled "Series and Structure," is devoted to a critique of

---

[14] John Storey, *Cultural Theory and Popular Culture* (Athens: University of Georgia Press, 1993), p. 77.

[15] For Pasolini, see Zygmunt Baranski, "Pier Paolo Pasolini: Culture, Croce, Gramsci," in *Culture and Conflict in Postwar Italy*, pp. 139–59; Pasolini's semiotic writings, largely devoted to the cinema, are published in English translation as *Heretical Empiricism*, eds. and trans. Louise K. Barnett and Ben Lawton (Bloomington: Indiana University Press, 1988).

structuralist theory, including the views of cultural anthropologist Claude Lévi-Strauss, who earlier had attacked Eco's *The Open Work*. Eco goes directly to the philosophical differences between structuralism and what he calls "the poetics of serial thought" (which, for Eco, was primarily linked to the music of Stockhausen, Berio, and Boulez). Eco connects serial thought to the theory of the open work as well, thus forging a link between his past ideas and his present interest in the methodology of semiotics, and he identifies serial thought with "the production of a structure that is at once open and polyvalent."[16] He then asks if it is possible to conceive of a series in structural terms, notes the difficulties associated with various French terms for structure (*structurel, structural*), and concludes that while "serial thought produces open-structured (*structurelles*) realities (even when these realities appear unstructured) . . . structuralist thought deals with structural (*structurales*) laws."[17] What is most distinctive about structuralism, in Eco's opinion, is that it embodies models of thought proposed by linguistics or communications theory, as well as the general notion that human culture can be interpreted as a series of coded messages moving between addresser and addressee. The notion that human culture can be viewed as a complex combination of messages and codes is, of course, at the heart of semiotics. But unlike semiotic theory, structuralist thought implicitly hypothesizes that every code is based upon a more elementary code, a primary code – "formally and logically speaking, an *Ur*-code" which would constitute by itself the

real Structure of all communication, all language, all cultural manifestation, all acts of signification, from articulate speech to the most complex syntagmatic chains such as myths, from verbal language to the "language" of cuisine or fashion.[18]

[16] "Series and Structure," in *The Open Work*, p. 218; *La struttura assente*, p. 304.
[17] "Series and Structure," in *The Open Work*, pp. 218–19; *La struttura assente*, p. 305.
[18] "Series and Structure," in *The Open Work*, p. 220; *La struttura assente*, p. 306.

For Eco, serial thought accepted the fact that each message calls its code into question and is a discourse on the language generating it. But most importantly, serial thought avoided the search for any ultimate structure and emphasized, instead,

> the *identification of historical codes in order to question them, thereby generating new forms of communication.* The main goal of serial thought is to allow codes to evolve historically and to discover new ones, rather than to trace them back to the original generative Code (the Structure). Thus, serial thought aims at the production of history and not at the rediscovery, beneath history, of the atemporal abscissae of all possible communication.[19]

While Eco is ultimately making a case for semiotic as opposed to structuralist methodology, he is also remaining faithful here to his most original insights in *The Open Work*. In the comprehensive semiotic theory that will emerge in *A Theory of Semiotics*, Eco will embrace the Peircean concept of "unlimited semiosis" precisely because he will identify this idea with another, more philosophically sound way of arguing for the openness of texts. This link of *The Absent Structure* to *The Open Work* is evident not only in Eco's critique of Lévi-Strauss and structuralism but also emerges in Eco's analysis of contemporary advertising in this first book informed by "semiological" reasoning.[20] The analysis of advertising is not the only practical form of criticism Eco offers as an example of his methodology in this book (he also discusses architecture and film). His readings of advertisements for Camay soap, a swimming suit, the Volkswagen Beetle, a piece of anti-Vietnam War propaganda, and Knorr cream of asparagus soup – while displaying his usual wit and intellectual pyrotechnics – reach conclusions we might expect after an examination of *The Open Work*, *Apocalyptic and Integrated Intellectuals*, and *The*

---

[19] "Series and Structure," in *The Open Work*, pp. 220–21 (the italics are Eco's); *La struttura assente*, p. 307.

[20] *La struttura assente*, pp. 165–88 (no English translation exists).

Superman of the Masses. Eco finds that advertising messages are so conventional "every message only repeats what the listener already expected and already knew," and that the ideology reflected by advertising is that of consumption. The ultimate message of every advertisement, no matter how complex, can be boiled down to the following redundant message: "We invite you to consume product X because it is normal that you consume something and we propose to you our production instead of another, employing precisely the kind of persuasion of which, by now, you already know all the mechanisms."[21] While Eco's readings of advertising are amusing, they have not yet transcended the methodology of earlier books that relied primarily upon information theory and the concept of redundancy versus openness.[22]

Even though Eco affirms that we actually never learn anything from advertising and that no new message is ever communicated to the public, he nevertheless believes that revealing this fact to advertising's mass audience will have a positive effect upon the public's civic consciousness. That Eco envisioned a socially useful role for semiotic theory and not merely that semiotics serve a narrow, theoretical, or academic purpose can be seen from an important *caso* or scandal – that of Aldo Braibanti, arrested under the charge of *plagio*. *Plagio* does not mean "plagiarism" in this case, even though that is the first reference any hurried consultation of an Italian dictionary will suggest. It is, instead, an unusual crime recognized as far back as ancient Roman law and retained by the Rocco Code, the fascist legal code much of which was still in place during the 1960s in Italy. *Plagio* involves holding another person within one's psychological power and bending him or her to one's will. In the case of Braibanti, a man

---

[21] *La struttura assente*, pp. 187–88 (author's translation).

[22] I agree with David Robey, who believes that "there is little that is distinctively semiotic about the analysis" and that Eco's position in *La struttura assente* is still that of *Apocalyptic and Integrated Intellectuals* (see Robey, "Umberto Eco: Theory and Pratice in the Analysis of the Media," in Baranski and Lumley, eds., *Culture and Conflict in Postwar Italy*, p. 173).

who not only held leftist political views but also was a homosexual, the crime of *plagio* ultimately involved luring "helpless" young men into liaisons with shady political *and* moral overtones and then dominating their wills, presumably forcing them to commit perverse sexual acts and to espouse leftist political views. The case ultimately evolved into a heated debate over patterns of authority in Italy. A number of important Italian intellectuals – Eco, Alberto Moravia, Adolfo Gatti, Cesare Musatti, and others – published a volume that examined the charges against Braibanti and the subsequent trial from a moral, political, legal, psychoanalytic, social, and (in Eco's case) semiotic perspective.[23] What is significant about Eco's contribution to the volume is that for the first time, semiotics was associated with a progressive political cause and disassociated from an abstract academic setting. Arguments based upon semiotics or associated with a semiotic methodology, even of the rudimentary sort Eco employed in his scathing analysis of the glaring stupidities in documents connected with Braibanti's arrest and trial, came to symbolize reform and progressive change for an entire generation of university students, intellectuals, and well-informed middle-class readers. Eco's essay is particularly interesting, since the charge of *plagio* rests entirely upon verbal "acts" and verbal evidence rather than actual facts or actions, as it was Braibanti's alleged mental domination over other individuals, and not what he had actually done, that constituted his crime of *plagio*. Such verbal "acts," of course, are precisely the kinds of *signs* that are the focus of any semiotic analysis of human behavior. Eco's goal was to demonstrate through his minute analysis of trial testimony, the prosecution's accusations, and sensationalistic journalistic accounts of the affair that

> in a society in which words are used especially for their emotive
> value [rather than for their referential value], men are not free . . .

---

[23] See *Sotto il nome di plagio* (Milan: Bompiani, 1969); Eco's contribution, "Sotto il nome di plagio," was subsequently reprinted in *Il costume di casa* in 1973 but has yet to receive an English translation.

> When a society is held prisoner by these linguistic tabus, anyone
> who seeks to act critically is subject to tremendous experiences and
> remains a prisoner of the fabric of words with which he is suffocated,
> like a character from Kafka who, in the end, never succeeds in
> understanding what is the nature of the power that overwhelms
> him.[24]

Eco's analysis of Braibanti's case, like his treatment of advertising in
The Absent Structure, does not reflect a totally semiotic methodology,
and there is much in his impassioned plea for justice in the Braibanti
affair that could just as easily have been written by an author
uninterested in semiotics. But the effect of Eco's intervention into the
debate resulted in the identification of semiotics with the forces of
social change in Italy, a perspective that helped to popularize
semiotics in Italy among even a non-academic readership.

While Eco's *impegno politico*, his desire to utilize cultural theory in
the service of civic causes, may be demonstrated by his intervention
in the Braibanti affair, it would be his theoretical critique of structuralism, and not his practical readings of advertising, that would lead
Eco toward more original contributions to semiotics in several
important essays from *The Forms of Content* that have appeared in
English translation in *The Role of the Reader*. "The Semantics of
Metaphor" returns to familiar territory from *The Open Work*, depart-
ing from a passage in *Finnegans Wake* by James Joyce to examine the
theoretical status of metaphoric language itself. Borrowing a concept
from the work of Charles S. Peirce that would become one of the key
features of Eco's semiotic theory, Eco first defines *Finnegans Wake* as
"itself a metaphor for the process of unlimited semiosis,"[25] and then
proceeds to examine a sentence in Joyce which had caused one of
Joyce's most accomplished explicators, James Atherton, to throw up
his hands when confronted with the obligation to explain Minucius

---

[24] "Sotto il nome di plagio," in *Il costume di casa*, pp. 94–95 (author's translation).
[25] "The Semantics of Metaphor," in *The Role of the Reader*, p. 70; *Le forme del contenuto*
p. 98.

Mandrake:[26] "Now, fix on the little fellow in my eye, Minucius Mandrake, and follow my little psychosinology, poor armer in slingslang."[27] For Eco, the meaning of this mysterious reference not only sheds light on Joyce, but, even more significantly, serves as a perfect demonstration of how metaphor embodies a semiotic process inherent in the very nature of aesthetic language. While Atherton had identified "Minucius" with Minucius Felix, an early church father, he could make no sense of "Mandrake." True to his reputation as a connoisseur of popular culture, Eco offers the suggestion that Mandrake actually refers to Mandrake the Magician, the main character in the comic strip by Lee Falk and Phil Davis – not an outrageous supposition, since Joyce knew such comic strips as *Mutt and Jeff*. Then Eco turns to the early version of *Finnegans Wake* and discovers that in the 1924 version of this passage, Mandrake does not appear. He explains this by the obvious fact that the cartoon strip with the magician figure appeared for the first time in 1934, a chronological fact that is consistent with what we know about Joyce's revision of his text between 1936 and 1939. The puzzle about why Minucius and Mandrake are linked together in *Finnegans Wake* still remains. Eco suggests that the comic-strip origin of the reference to Mandrake itself supplies the solution to the puzzle. The historical character Minucius was surnamed Felix. Felix, of course, is also the name of an extremely famous cartoon figure, a cat created in 1923 by Pat Sullivan. Eco's description of how Joyce arrived at the metaphor of "Minucius Mandrake" also shows us the manner in which metaphor functions in general:

> Minucius refers by contiguity to Felix, Felix refers by contiguity (belonging to the same universe of comic strips) to Mandrake. Once the middle term has fallen, there remains a coupling that does not seem justified by any contiguity and thus appears to be metaphoric . . . each metaphor produced in *FW* is, in the last analysis, compre-

[26] See James Atherton, *The Books at the Wake* (New York: Viking, 1960).
[27] Joyce, *Finnegans Wake*, p. 486.

hensible because the entire book, read in different directions, actually furnishes the metonymic chains that justify it.[28]

The key idea here is that metaphors can be invented not because words refer to things but, instead, because "language, in a process of unlimited semiosis, constitutes a multidimensional network of metonymies, each of which is explained by a *cultural convention* rather than by an original resemblance."[29] In other words, every definition of metaphor that depends upon a resemblance between one element of language and another errs, since this operation requires no outside referent. It is precisely the aesthetic function of language to "create connections which as of yet do not exist," thereby expanding the possibilities of any linguistic code to which the language refers.[30] Eco thus emphasizes not only the arbitrariness of metaphor but also its completely historical nature. Another example, that of "white-collar worker," illustrates the same point. At one time all or most office employees wore white collars on their shirts. The contiguity of "employee" and "white collars" was thus codified during a precise historical moment. Today, when office employees are normally allowed to wear any kind of shirt they wish, the contiguity is "no longer factual, but semiotic," since associated with the lexeme "employee" there exists the connotation "wears white collars," and as a result, the contiguity that was once a factual or an empirical contiguity has been transformed by the passage of time into a continuous code, where the kinship between "employee" and "white collar" is no longer natural but has become "cultural."[31] Eco believes that an analysis of how metaphor functions, as well as the general

---

[28] "The Semantics of Metaphor," in *The Role of the Reader*, p. 72; *Le forme del contenuto*, p. 101.

[29] "The Semantics of Metaphor," in *The Role of the Reader*, p. 78 (my italics); *Le forme del contenuto*, p. 108.

[30] "The Semantics of Metaphor," in *The Role of the Reader*, p. 79; , *Le forme del contenuto*, p. 110.

[31] "The Semantics of Metaphor," in *The Role of the Reader*, p. 80; *Le forme del contenuto*, p. 111.

workings of aesthetic language in general, demonstrate the fundamental correctness of the semiotic principle of unlimited semiosis.
The explanations we seek when studying human behavior are not
derived from some *Ur*-code that is at the foundation of all communication, as structuralists maintained. Such explanations can only be
found within human culture itself, are completely historical in
character, and semiotics provides the key to unlocking their secrets.

Eco draws a similar conclusion in a much more entertaining essay
entitled "On the Possibility of Generating Aesthetic Messages in an
Edenic Language." A humorous narration of the creation of language
in the Garden of Eden, Eco's account demonstrates that even the
simplest language can create aesthetic messages by altering the forms
of the messages. Beginning with the Peircean concept of unlimited
semiosis, Eco employs a mythical fable typical of the philosophical
ruminations of the best writings of Giacomo Leopardi to show that
the aesthetic use of a language generates self-contradictions within
that language, and that any such contradictions at the level of its form
of expression involve contradictions in the form of its content.

Eco also examines the Peircean concept of unlimited semiosis in
some detail in an essay, "Peirce and the Semiotic Foundations of
Openness," written in 1976 and included in both *The Reader in the Story*
and in translation in *The Role of the Reader*. By this time, Eco had
clearly chosen to associate his semiotic writings with the philosophical tradition associated with Peirce's "semiotic," a term Peirce found
first employed in the closing paragraphs of John Locke's *Essay
Concerning Human Understanding* (1690),[32] rather than the tradition of
"semiology" associated with Ferdinand de Saussure's linguistic model
and his French followers. In Eco's words,

> the process of unlimited semiosis shows us how signification, by
> means of continual shiftings which refer a sign back to another sign

[32] For a history of the term, see John Deely, *Basics of Semiotics* (Bloomington: Indiana University Press, 1990).

or string of signs, circumscribes *cultural units* in an asymptotic fashion, without even allowing one to touch them directly, though making them accessible through other units. Thus one is never obliged to replace a cultural unit by means of something which is not a semiotic entity, and no cultural unit has to be explained by some platonic, psychic, or objectal entity. Semiosis explains itself by itself: this continual circularity is the normal condition of signification and even allows communicational processes to use signs in order to mention things and states of the world.[33]

The circularity of unlimited semiosis, where signs refer back to other signs which refer, yet again, still again to other signs – and not to objective referents in reality, subjective mental states, or Platonic universals – guarantees that social and historical reality will never be ignored by a semiotic perspective, since signs and their codes are directly conditioned, as Eco had already demonstrated in numerous previous essays on mass media, by the societies in which or the historical periods during which they are created. It is worth noting that Eco's use of Peirce's concept of unlimited semiosis guarantees the validity of his own theories of textual openness (a not insignificant achievement, since no writer likes to discard his most interesting ideas). Indeed, Eco's theory of the open work depends, in theoretical terms, precisely upon Peirce's notion of unlimited semiosis, something Eco did not realize when he first published *The Open Work*.

Eco's reliance upon Charles Peirce brings us to Eco's most systematic work of semiotic theory, *A Theory of Semiotics*.[34] Since a great deal that is most original about this work was already contained in *The Absent Structure* but was rewritten within a more methodical framework in *A Theory of Semiotics*, it will be unnecessary here to provide an elaborate and minute description of the book's contents.

---

[33] "Peirce and the Semiotic Foundations of Openness," in *The Role of the Reader*, p. 198; the Italian version of this essay (revised for English translation) may be found in *Lector in fabula*, pp. 27–49.

[34] *A Theory of Semiotics* (Bloomington: Indiana University Press, 1976); for the Italian edition, see *Trattato di semiotica generale* (Milan: Bompiani, 1975).

Eco's basic approach is to provide discussions of two major topics: a theory of codes and a theory of sign production. Following Peirce, Eco defines a sign as *"everything* that, on the grounds of a previously established social convention, can be taken as *something standing for something else."*[35] His claims for semiotics as a discipline are broad:

> In culture every entity can become a semiotic phenomenon. The laws of signification are the laws of culture. For this reason culture allows a continuous process of communicative exchanges, insofar as it subsists as a system of systems of signification. *Culture can be studied completely under a semiotic profile.*[36]

The section of *A Theory of Semiotics* devoted to the theory of codes repeats, but in a much more orderly and rational fashion, the argument of *The Absent Structure* that signs refer only to other signs and not to "real" objects or referents. The belief that a sign corresponds to anything objective Eco labels the "referential fallacy." It is partly in response to this persistent belief that Eco prefers the term "sign-function" to sign: the sign-function consists of two functives (expression and content) that are mutually correlated but which may become another functive, thus giving rise to another and different sign-function. Peirce's concept of unlimited semiosis again becomes fundamental to Eco's argument:

> a cultural unit never obliges one to replace it by means of something which is not a semiotic entity, and never asks to be explained by some Platonic, psychic or objectal entity. *Semiosis explains itself by itself*; this continual circularity is the normal condition of signification and even allows communication to use signs in order to mention things. To call this condition a "desperate" one is to refuse the human way of signifying, a way that has proved itself fruitful insofar as only through it has cultural history developed.[37]

Of special interest for literary theory (as well as Eco's first novel) are his

[35] *A Theory of Semiotics*, p. 16; *Trattato*, p. 27.
[36] *A Theory of Semiotics*, p. 28; *Trattato*, p. 43.
[37] *A Theory of Semiotics*, p. 71; *Trattato*, p. 104.

remarks on the concept of "interpretation," which he prefers not to call "decoding" but rather "understanding, on the basis of some previous decoding, the general sense of a vast portion of discourse" and which is akin to the specific kind of philosophical inference Peirce usually calls "abduction" or sometimes defines as "making an hypothesis."[38] Logical deduction moves from a general Rule (all the beans from this bag are white), and given a Case (these beans are from this bag), it infers a Result (these beans are or must be white). Induction, on the other hand, from a plurality of Results (all the beans I picked up were white) and a plurality of Cases (they all came from this bag), infers a probable Rule (all the beans in this bag are white). Abduction is interesting because it invents or hypothesizes a general Rule from a single Result: these beans are white; now, if I suppose that there is a Rule according to which all the beans in this bag are white, then the Result could be a Case of that Rule.[39] Abduction, as the key element of semiotic logic, will later become William of Baskerville's preferred form of thought in *The Name of the Rose*, making this character the first consciously semiotic detective in literature (although many of his literary ancestors practiced abduction without recognizing its Peircean dimensions). In concluding his discussion of the theory of codes, Eco seems to return to his first major theoretical book, *The Open Work*, when he affirms that "the message (or the text) appears as an *empty form to which can be attributed various possible senses*."[40]

The second section of Eco's work treats the theory of sign production and interpretation, and perhaps the most intriguing aspect of it is the discussion of "the aesthetic text as invention," in which Eco reclassifies the categories of classic rhetoric under semiotic rubrics and asserts that reading a literary text requires all three types of logic mentioned above: induction (inferring general rules from individual

---

[38] *A Theory of Semiotics*, p. 131; *Trattato*, p. 185.
[39] Eco provided this extremely clear outline of deduction, induction, and abduction in correspondence sent to me on 30 January 1996.
[40] *A Theory of Semiotics*, p. 139; *Trattato*, p. 196.

cases), abduction (testing both old and new codes with a hypothesis), and deduction (checking whether what has been understood on one level can determine artistic events on another). His definition of aesthetic abduction leads him to a topic that will occupy his next book, the role of the reader in receiving the author's message. Aesthetic abduction requires proposing certain tentative codes in order to make the author's message understandable, since the addressee does not initially know what the sender's rule was. While the reader may simply try to understand what the author meant, he may also try out other interpretive possibilities on the text, but "in so doing, he never wants to completely betray the author's intentions":

> In this dialectic between fidelity and initiative two kinds of knowl-
> edge are generated: (a) a combinational knowledge about the entire
> range of possibilities available within the given codes; (b) a historical
> knowledge about the circumstances and the codes (indeed all the
> norms) of a given artistic period . . . A responsible collaboration is
> demanded of the addressee. He must intervene to fill up semantic
> gaps, to reduce or to further complicate the multiple readings
> proposed, to choose his own preferred paths of interpretation . . .
> Thus the aesthetic text becomes a multiple source of *unpredictable*
> *"speech acts"* whose real author remains undetermined, sometimes
> being the sender of the message, at others the addressee who
> collaborates in its development.[41]

Eco refuses to accept the kind of radical deconstructionism that completely denies any authorial intentionality. He will later defend and expand this critique of deconstructionist thought in *The Limits of Interpretation* (1990) after dramatizing its pernicious effects in his second novel, *Foucault's Pendulum* (1988).

Critics who discuss the development of Eco's semiotic theory from the appearance of *The Absent Structure* in 1968 through not only *A Theory of Semiotics* in 1976 but also *Semiotics and the Philosophy of Language*, which appeared in 1984,[42] generally agree that Eco's basic

---

[41] *A Theory of Semiotics*, p. 276; *Trattato*, p. 343.

[42] *Semiotics and the Philosophy of Language* (Bloomington: Indiana University Press, 1984)

viewpoint has remained fundamentally the same. One perceptive critic of *A Theory of Semiotics* has described it as having "a distinctly ecumenical character," and as aiming at the recuperation of "a quasi-totality by absorbing concepts purveyed by various semiological theories."[43] This general, even abstract character is also noted by David Robey, who believes that for Eco, "semiotics . . . is really a high-level metalanguage" and that Eco's interest in such abstract theory may be inspired primarily by "the needs of the moment, by a systematic effort on Eco's part to establish semiotics internationally as a new academic institution."[44] Teresa de Lauretis perhaps captures the most original features of Eco's semiotic theory best by stressing the role Peirce's concept of unlimited semiosis plays in *A Theory of Semiotics*. While Eco's semiotic theory disregards "real" referents as not being directly accessible to semiotics, it deals with this same "real" world indirectly – through cultural units that are, unlike "real" referents, accessible to semiotic analysis.[45] It is Eco's emphasis upon the importance of culture that moves him to a materialist conclusion, arguing that codes (upon which meaning and communication depend and which result in the production of signs) are created and transformed only within a historical setting:

> semiotics recognizes as the only testable subject matter of its discourse the social existence of the universe of signification, as it is revealed by the physical testability of interpretants – which are, to reinforce this point for the last time, *material expressions*.[46]

or the original, *Semiotica e filosofia del linguaggio* (Milan: Bompiani, 1984). The bulk of this collection of essays assembles five articles on signs, symbol, metaphor, and code that originally appeared in the *Enciclopedia Einaudi* between 1976 and 1980. Two other articles on "Dictionary vs. Encyclopedia" and "Mirrors" in the anthology will be discussed in an analysis of *The Name of the Rose* in chapter 5.

[43] Jean-Jacques Nattiez, *Music and Discourse: Toward a Semiology of Music*, trans. Carolyn Abbate (Princeton: Princeton University Press, 1990), p. 20.

[44] Robey, "Umberto Eco: Theory and Practice in the Analysis of the Media," in Baranski and Lumley, eds., *Culture and Conflict in Postwar Italy*, p. 175.

[45] See de Lauretis, *Umberto Eco*, pp. 43–65.

[46] *A Theory of Semiotics*, p. 317; *Trattato*, p. 379.

Once Eco finally rejected any possibility for a theory of semiotics to "know" the reality of its referents and accepted Peirce's circular process of unlimited semiosis that refers sign-functions to other sign-functions but never to concrete referents, it was inevitable that Eco should turn toward further theoretical consideration of the "receiver" or the "reader." He does so in *The Reader in the Story*, which appeared only a few years after *A Theory of Semiotics*. *The Reader in the Story* was written while Eco composed his first novel, *The Name of the Rose*, an important fact that must be remembered when reading that literary work. More than abstract theoretical considerations linked to the creation of a general theory of semiotics, however, was responsible for Eco's turn toward the reader in his work. His own progressive political and cultural stance as a man dedicated to such principles as pluralism, freedom of information, democracy, and intellectual tolerance were also important considerations in this regard. For it is precisely within the social or cultural world Eco posits as the domain of semiotics – which is also the world of ideology and mass communications – that messages or readers may be manipulated for ideological or political ends. Eco's desire that semiotics play a civic role in a modern technological society, assisting readers to uncover the ideology inherent in potentially manipulative messages, can be seen in an essay read at a scholarly convention in 1967 and included in the collection *Home Customs* in 1973. The piece – appearing in English translation in *Travels in Hyperreality* as "Towards a Semiological Guerrilla Warfare" – argues that mass communication is a powerful instrument but is impossible to control, even by totalitarian powers. Unlike the means of production, which can be controlled by either individuals or the community as a whole, the means of communication cannot be controlled by either. Politicians, censors, and even educators falsely believe, says Eco, that they can control the means of communication by controlling the Source and the Channel. But they fail to realize that the addressees, the receivers of such messages, receive only an empty form that each addressee fills up with his or her own cultural models. Today, as events in Communist China have demonstrated, even the most severe totalitarian dictatorship can be perforated by faxes, electronic mail, and the ubiquitous CNN television network. As Eco puts it, "the battle for the survival of man as a responsible being in the Communications Era is not to be won where the communication originates, but where it arrives."[47] Eco's theoretical shift of attention toward the destination of the message or text and away from the process of how the message or text is sent thus has both philosophical and political implications for his thought.

In his introductions to both *The Reader in the Story* and *The Role of the Reader* that collects the most important sections of the Italian originals, Eco emphasizes that his focus upon the reader was implicit in his first important theoretical work, *The Open Work*, since "an open text is a paramount instance of a syntactic-semantico-pragmatic device whose foreseen interpretation is a part of its generative process."[48] Once again, he refers back to the critique of his first book he received from the distinguished structuralist, Claude Lévi-Strauss, and admits that in a critical atmosphere dominated by structuralism, "the idea of taking into account the role of the addressee looked like a disturbing intrusion, disquietingly jeopardizing the notion of a semiotic texture to be analyzed in itself and for the sake of itself."[49] The Italian preface (not translated entirely for the English anthology) also underlines Eco's belief that the problem of interpretation had characterized all of his work and that between 1963 and 1975 – that is, between the publication of *The Open Work* and the publication of the Italian edition of *A Theory of Semiotics* – almost all of his efforts had been directed toward uncovering the "semiotic foundations of this

[47] "Towards a Semiological Guerrilla Warfare," in *Travels in Hyperreality*, p. 142; *Il costume di casa*, p. 297.
[48] *The Role of the Reader*, p. 3. The reader should be advised that Eco's English "Introduction: The Role of the Reader," composed for the English edition of *The Role of the Reader*, summarizes ideas in *Lector in fabula* but is not a direct translation of the Italian edition.
[49] *The Role of the Reader*, p. 3.

experience of openness which I had described, but for which I had not provided the rules, in *The Open Work.*"[50] The Italian preface also underlines the fact that unlike all his previous books, which examined a wide variety of cultural phenomena, *The Reader in the Story* has narrowed its focus strictly to narrative literature.[51] This sharp turn toward narrative theory points toward Eco's own experiments with the writing of fiction that were in progress while *The Reader in the Story* was being completed.

The basis for Eco's discussion of the reader's presence in the story is his definition of the model reader. Viewed from the perspective of semiotic communication, "the author must foresee a model of the possible reader (hereafter Model Reader) supposedly able to deal interpretively with the expressions in the same way as the author deals generatively with them."[52] Conversely, Eco defines the "author" as "nothing else but a textual strategy establishing semantic correlations and activating the Model Reader."[53] In practice, however, Eco admits that it is almost impossible to predict what will occur when the actual reader is different from the average reader postulated by the author. Texts such as *Superman* comic strips or Fleming's Bond novels, for example, are aimed at eliciting a very precise response, but paradoxically even such "closed" texts may be read at a number of very different levels – the naive level or that demonstrated by Eco's own earlier analyses of the ideological foundations of the comic strip or the spy novels. In contrast to the implied model reader of such mass cult works, major works of literature such as Joyce's *Ulysses* or *Finnegans Wake* literally demand the kind of model reader presumed by the author when Joyce created these complex novels.

Eco gives a number of interesting examples to substantiate his claims. For example, one can read Kafka's *Trial* as a "trivial criminal novel, but at this point the text collapses."[54] Nor can the ideal reader

[50] *Lector in fabula*, p. 8 (author's translation).
[51] Ibid., p. 10.   [52] Ibid., p. 7.   [53] *The Role of the Reader*, p. 11.
[54] Ibid., pp. 9–10.

of *Finnegans Wake* be either a Greek from the classic age of Pericles or an illiterate man of Aran. Overriding everything else, however, is his concern that certain limits of interpretation be recognized. Concentrating upon *fabula* or story as opposed to plot (following the definitions provided by the Russian formalist theorists), Eco notes that the reader experiences the *fabula* of a narrative step by step, the result of a "continuous series of abductions made during the course of the reading."[55] As the reader proceeds, in order to make the kinds of forecasts he must make to understand the text, from time to time he must move outside the text to make what Eco defines as "inferential walks" to gather intertextual support for understanding what he is reading. A significant portion of the entire book (as well as the English translation) Eco devotes to a minute, exhaustive, analysis of Alphonse Allais's *Un drame bien parisien* (1890). It is a metaliterary text that must be read twice, since it calls for both a naive and a sophisticated critical reading wherein the latter represents an interpretation of the former.[56]

Clearly, Eco prefers open to closed texts, James Joyce to Ian Fleming, Alphonse Allais to *Superman*. Such texts, which may often not only be literary but also metaliterary, provide the kind of textual "pleasure" popularized by Roland Barthes because "they have been planned to invite their model readers to reproduce their own processes of deconstruction by a plurality of free interpretive choices."[57] Eco admits that intentional or unintentional misinterpretations of texts can and do occur. Ideologically blinded readers consistently produce aberrant readings of texts. Such false acts of textual cooperation can also be highly amusing on a theoretical level. Eco cites the most famous suggestions offered by Borges of such aberrant readings: a reader may purposely apply improper codes to a given text, as the Argentine novelist suggests, reading the *Odyssey* as if it

---

[55] *Ibid.*, p. 31.
[56] "Lector in Fabula: Pragmatic Strategy in a Metanarrative Text," in *ibid.*, pp. 200–60; *Lector in fabula*, pp. 194–225. [57] *The Role of the Reader*, p. 40.

were written *after* the *Aeneid* or reading the *Imitation of Christ* as if it were written by Céline! But that is not the purpose of reading. While not offering a lengthy defense of his belief, at the close of his introduction to *The Role of the Reader*, Eco asserts his faith in the possibility of drawing limits to aberrant interpretations while, at the same time, allowing the reader the liberties of choice implied by the narrative strategy of an author concerned with his model reader's freedom:

> I think, however, that it is possible to distinguish between the free interpretative choices elicited by a purposeful strategy of openness and the freedom taken by a reader with a text assumed as a mere stimulus.[58]

Eco will later address the question of the limits of interpretation in a more systematic manner in subsequent collections of essays. But before Eco returned to the problem of the limits of interpretation in his theoretical writings, he would publish *The Name of the Rose* shortly after *The Reader in the Text* appeared in print in Italy. Eco therefore turned his hand to a practical demonstration of his theories of semiotics and his notion of the model reader, using the subject-matter of so many of his theoretical works – narrative fiction – to test his hypotheses about literature in a concrete manner.

[58] *Ibid.*, p. 40.

five

&

"To make truth laugh":
postmodern theory and practice
in *The Name of the Rose*

When Eco published his first work of prose fiction in September 1980, a novel with a medieval setting, no one (least of all the author himself) could have imagined its unparalleled international success. Within Italy, of course, Eco was extremely well known to the educated public because of the fame of his earlier theoretical works on popular culture, narrative theory, and semiotics. In addition, he continued a long collaboration with the major Italian news magazine, *L'Espresso*, that had begun in 1965 and would eventually include providing the magazine with a high-profile weekly column ("La bustina di Minerva") every week. Eco had also guaranteed himself a substantial following in Italian universities by publishing a popular guide to the preparation of humanistic theses required for graduation from these institutions of higher learning in Italy, a publication equal in popularity to the *MLA Handbook* or the *Chicago Manual of Style* in the United States: *Come si fa una tesi di laurea: Le materie umanistiche* (*How to Write a Doctoral Thesis: The Humanistic Subjects*, 1977).[1] Critical approval of Eco's novel inside the peninsula with the award of the prestigious Premio Strega in 1981 was therefore not so surprising. But the absolutely unprecedented popular reception of this book both inside Italy and abroad with sales of tens of millions of copies all over the

---

[1] Milan: Bompiani, 1977 (no English translation exists).

world and translations in some thirty different languages was impossible to imagine. For Eco's severest critics, the "apocalyptical" intellectuals who were suspicious of any other intellectual they suspected of gaining fame through an interest in popular culture, Eco's international success only confirmed their suspicion of the direction of his intellectual development. In 1986, French director Jacques Annaud turned *The Name of the Rose* into a film starring Sean Connery (an actor type-cast as the very James Bond character Eco had analyzed in a classic essay earlier in his career), Christian Slater, and F. Murray Abraham (fresh from an Oscar-winning performance in 1984 with *Amadeus*). In only a brief time after the appearance of the novel, Umberto Eco's reputation transcended the relatively small circle of scholars and intellectuals familiar with his theoretical work, and he gained international fame.

The Name of the Rose constitutes the single most successful Italian book in terms of its sales in the twentieth century, and its very success as both a bestseller and a long-seller around the world sparked a critical debate about its meaning and significance that continues to inspire extremely sophisticated commentary. The critical literature on this novel has itself become something of a cottage industry, ranging from practical guides providing translations of the many foreign language passages to assist the popular reader, to more learned tomes addressing theoretical issues the author implicitly raises with his text.[2]

---

[2] For treatments of Eco's first novel, the most important books (listed in chronological order) are the following: Renato Giovannoli, ed., *Saggi su "Il nome della rosa"* (Milan: Bompiani, 1985); Adel J. Haft, Jane G. White, and Robert J. White, eds., *The Key to "The Name of the Rose"* (Huntington Park, NJ: Ampersand Publications, 1987); Theresa Coletti, *Naming the Rose: Eco, Medieval Signs, and Modern Theory* (Ithaca, NY: Cornell University Press, 1988); M. Thomas Inge, ed., *Naming the Rose: Essays on Eco's "The Name of the Rose"* (Jackson, Miss.: University of Mississippi Press, 1988); Brian McHale, *Constructing Postmodernism* (London: Routledge, 1992); Bruno Pischedda, *Come leggere "Il nome della rosa"* (Milan: Mursia, 1994); and Roberto Cotroneo, *La diffidenza come sistema: Saggio sulla narrativa di Umberto Eco* (Milan: Anabasi, 1995). A complete listing of the numerous popular and scholarly articles devoted to *The Name of the Rose* would be impossible here. An English-language bibliography of articles and reviews on Eco's first novel can be found in Jackson R. Bryer and Ruth M. Alvarez, "Appendix: A Preliminary Checklist of English-Language Criticism," in Inge, ed., *Naming the Rose*, pp. 173–98.

The unusually different audiences attracted to *The Name of the Rose*, ranging from the great mass of readers of bestsellers to the most serious of intellectuals and scholars, were anticipated by the author himself on the dust-jacket of the first Italian edition. This material – unfortunately not printed on the cover of the English-language edition which was aimed almost exclusively at the popular market – was provided by Eco himself and defines three different kinds of readers he anticipated for *The Name of the Rose*:

> Difficult to define (Gothic novel, medieval chronicle, detective story, ideological narrative à clé, allegory) this novel (whose story entwines itself with History, since the author asserts, perhaps mendaciously, that not one word is his own) may perhaps be read in three ways. The first category of readers will be taken by the plot and by the *coups de scène*, and will accept even the long bookish discussions and the philosophical dialogues, because it will sense that the signs, the traces, and the revelatory symptoms are nesting precisely in those inattentive pages. The second category will be impassioned by the debate of ideas, and will attempt to establish connections (which the author refuses to authorize) with the present. The third will realize that this text is a textile of other texts, a "whodunit" of quotations, a book built of books. In any case, the author refuses to reveal to any category of readers what the book means. If he had wanted to advance a thesis, he would have written an essay (like so many others that he has written). If he has written a novel, it is because he has discovered, upon reaching maturity, that those things about which we cannot theorize, we must narrate.[3]

The concluding sentence of the above passage, an important allusion to the ideas of the philosopher Ludwig Wittgenstein (1859–1951), warns us that *The Name of the Rose* proposes to unite theory and practice, the theory of narrative and narrative itself. It also implicitly

Giovannoli's anthology contains Italian translations of the most important critical appraisals of the book in the major European languages.

[3] I cite this translation from Walter E. Stephens, "Ec[h]o in Fabula," *Diacritics* 13 (1983), 51, one of the very best reviews to have been published on the novel. Pischedda, *Come leggere "Il nome della rosa"*, p. 32, notes that Eco himself was the author of the material on the dust-jacket.

underscores the fact that Eco the storyteller has begun to overtake, but not eliminate, Eco the theorist. Purist academics searching for a super-theory of human culture may well view Eco's marriage of semiotic theory and narrative practice as a step backward, as a move away from "hard" theory. On the contrary, my own belief is that only Eco's immersion in theory during the years preceding his daring and successful transition to becoming a novelist made such an abrupt turn in his career possible.

Moreover, on the dust-jacket Eco defines his model reader in such a manner that he or she embodies a series of non-mutually exclusive traits. In the first place, Eco's model reader may be identified, in some respects, with the avid consumer of bestsellers concentrating upon plot and story-line – the same model philistine castigated by modern-ist writers of a previous generation. To underline the novel's links with popular, even pulp literature associated with popular culture, Eco's intriguing tale of the strange happenings taking place in an Italian monastery in late November 1327 – including the death of seven different monks (two by suicide and five by murder) and the concluding destruction of the entire abbey by fire – is set within the traditional and familiar genre of the detective story. Early on in Eco's career, as we have already noted, he stated that the detective story was a "perpetual temptation" for the man of culture, and with his first entrance into the practice of fiction, as opposed to a theoretical appraisal of fiction in literary or cultural theory, he succumbs to such a temptation completely and with amazingly successful results.

A second group of readers implicitly envisioned by the author represents those readers who see any historical treatment of the past as a thinly veiled allegory for events in the present. Eco's account of the genesis of the novel in his *Postille a "Il nome della rosa"* (1983, appearing in English in 1984 as *Postscript to "The Name of the Rose"*) lends weight to this approach, for in this brief but important assessment of his own novel, Eco notes that he began writing in March of 1978.[4] March 1978

[4] Umberto Eco, *The Name of the Rose Including Postscript to "The Name of the Rose"*, trans.

will always represent an unforgettable historical moment for every Italian, for on the 16th of that month, Aldo Moro (1916–78), then President of the Christian Democratic Party and Prime Minister of Italy on three different previous occasions, was kidnaped by Red Brigade terrorists and murdered a few months later. Moro was responsible for the so-called "opening to the left" within the Christian Democratic Party and more specifically for the "historic compromise" between the Christian Democrats and the Communist Party led by Enrico Berlinguer (1922–84) that was an important step in the evolution of Italy's Communist Party toward a brand of Eurocommunism and social democracy. Eco and many other Italian intellectuals were profoundly shocked by Moro's assassination.

Readers without any knowledge of this specifically Italian background to Eco's novel will nevertheless not find it difficult to see the warring forces of the papacy and the empire Eco's novel depicts as reflecting a similar conflict between the two opposing groups of nations engaged in the ideological struggle of the Cold War. And even if the model reader envisioned by Eco's text excludes a consideration of such a general allegory, it is nevertheless true that twentieth-century popular culture evinces a particular fascination with the Middle Ages, as can be seen from the many films or musicals set in that era, the popular histories of the period by such best-selling writers as Barbara Tuchman, or the countless works of science-fiction or romance with a medieval or pseudo-medieval setting. In an essay written in 1973 for the collection *From the Periphery of the Empire: Chronicles from a New Middle Ages* and now translated and reprinted as "Living in the New Middle Ages" in *Travels in Hyperreality*, Eco himself drew a parallel between a Middle Ages witnessing the collapse of a "great peace" and the end of what he calls the "crisis of the Pax

William Weaver (San Diego: Harcourt Brace, 1994), p. 509; or in Umberto Eco, *Il nome della rosa. In appendice Postille a "Il nome della rosa"* (Milan: Bompiani, 1989), p. 510. Here and subsequently, I cite from these two paperback editions rather than other hardcover editions, since the separately published copies of *Postscript* or *Postille* are extremely difficult to locate.

Americana."[5] While this was written at the height of the Vietnam War and certainly does not foreshadow the demise of the other empire much dearer to the hearts of European intellectuals, the Soviet Union, Eco returned to this theme in 1983 after the publication of his novel in an essay entitled "Dreaming of the Middle Ages," which was collected in the original Italian in *On Mirrors* and subsequently translated into English and included in *Travels in Hyperreality*. Once again, Eco defines the Middle Ages as the infancy of the modern world and outlines ten different contemporary approaches to the period, including the Middle Ages as a pretext or a mythological stage upon which to set contemporary characters; as ironic visitation (Eco's example is the ironic way Sergio Leone reconstructs American Western films); as an age of elementary and dangerous feelings (Wagner's operas); as a romantic setting (stormy castles, ghosts); as a perennial setting for neo-Thomism (the application of the philosophy of St. Thomas Aquinas to contemporary problems); as a moment of national identity (particularly in the nineteenth century); as a decadent environment (the Pre-Raphaelites or D'Annunzio); as a period inspiring philological reconstruction by scholars; and as the home of anti-scientific and occult philosophies (such as the cults of the Templars or the Rosicrucians, or the Nazis' reputed quest for the Holy Grail); and finally as a model for millennial thought.[6] The attentive reader may find elements of all these different Middle Ages in Eco's novel, although they are not necessarily viewed in a positive light by the author who includes them.

The third group of readers implied by Eco's model reader is, of course, the most sophisticated category and would include the "educated reader" as well as the scholar-specialist or critic such as the author himself. But the most important characteristic of Eco's model reader is that he or she must encompass the entire range of

---

[5] *Travels in Hyperreality*, pp. 74–76; *Dalla periferia del impero*, p. 194.
[6] *Travels in Hyperreality*, pp. 68–72; Eco, *Sugli specchi e altri saggi: Il segno, la rappresentazione, l'illusione, l'immagine* (Milan: Bompiani, 1990), pp. 78–89.

possibilities – from the consumer of best-sellers to the erudite
academic in search of sources and literary allusions (the same kind of
imaginary reader a modernist such as James Joyce had in mind). What
differentiates Eco from Joyce, however, is his postmodernist (as
opposed to Joyce's modernist) sensibility, for Eco has quite consciously set out with *The Name of the Rose* to write a novel that may serve as a
postmodernist manifesto and a practical demonstration of the possibility of appealing to a wide variety of audiences at the same time. It is
also important to note that Eco is not interested in appealing only to
this third and smaller group, which would certainly have to include
the avant-garde. In fact, he specifically rejects the older, modernist
identification of "popularity" and "lack of value" that he and the
other members of Gruppo 63 had tenaciously argued in their attacks
upon Italian novelists they considered too popular in the 1960s, such
as Giuseppe Tomasi di Lampedusa (1896–1957), Giorgio Bassani
(1916–), and Carlo Cassola (1917–87).

Eco asserts that "it is possible to find elements of revolution and
contestation in works that apparently lend themselves to facile
consumption" – that is, in works of popular culture – while at the
same time maintaining that "certain works, which seem provocative
and still enrage the public, do not really contest anything" – an
aesthetic and philosophical position that can only be termed postmodern.[7] And there is little doubt that Eco wanted his first novel to be
construed not only as a work of fiction but also as a statement of
postmodernist aesthetics. His German translator, Burkhart Kroeber,
has quite rightly pointed to an important interview Eco gave to the
Italian daily, *La Repubblica* (15 October 1980) in which the author
declared: "It is my ambition that nothing in my book be by me but
only texts already written," so that the book might be compared to a
reliquary "produced with a medieval artisan's technology: disparate
pieces, assembled together around the bones of a saint who is more

---

[7] *The Name of the Rose*, p. 526; *Il nome della rosa*, pp. 527–28.

than one thousand years old."[8] This cannot but remind Eco's readers
of yet another provocative essay which deals with the repetition of
commonplaces in a work of popular culture, the film *Casablanca*:
"Two clichés make us laugh but a hundred clichés move us because
we sense dimly that the clichés are talking among themselves,
celebrating a reunion."[9] Eco goes on in the essay to discuss more
current "postmodern" films, and it is clear that intertextuality –
conceiving of a literary text as "a textile of other texts, a "whodunit"
of quotations, a book built of books," as Eco put it on the cover of the
novel – constitutes one of the key elements in the fashioning of a
postmodern narrative.

Looking back on Eco's career before the appearance of *The Name of
The Rose*, it seems clear that much of his intellectual development –
especially his interest in the so-called "open" work, as well as his
fascination with the reader's role in literary response – reaches a
culmination in the publication of his first novel. Eco himself coyly
refuses to "interpret" his work but nevertheless discusses the book in
great detail in his *Postscript to "The Name of the Rose."* As this essay is
now appended to every Italian paperback edition of the novel, as well
as to the most recent English paperback edition, it now represents a
true postscript. Matei Calinescu calls attention to the fact that even
Eco's "postscript" to his novel represents a rewriting or "revisiting"
(to employ Eco's favorite term) of "The Philosophy of Composition"
by Edgar Allan Poe, a step-by-step explanation of his poem, "The
Raven."[10] Eco himself refers to Poe's explanation of his famous poem
in the *Postscript* and ironically does so in the context of refusing to
"interpret" his own novel. The precedent of Poe is doubly important

[8] Cited by Burkhart Kroeber, "Il misterioso dialogo di due libri: Eco e Calvino," in
Giovannoli, ed., *Saggi su "Il nome della rosa'*, p. 73 (author's translation).
[9] *Travels in Hyperreality*, p. 209; the original essay first appeared in *L'Espresso* in 17 August
1975 and was then collected with the essays of *Dalla periferia del impero* (p. 142).
[10] Matei Calinescu, *Five Faces of Modernity*, p. 276. Eco provides a lengthy discussion of
Poe's "Philosophy of Composition" in his Norton Lectures at Harvard University in
1992–93, now published as *Six Walks in the Fictional Woods* (see chapter 7 for a detailed
discussion of this work).

here, not only because Poe provides a literary precedent for Eco's *Postscript* but also because Poe is universally regarded as the inventor of the modern detective story, the popular genre to which Eco's novel is indebted and the conventions of which Eco plays with in a particularly postmodern fashion.

Nevertheless, in spite of Eco's ironic declaration that his *Postscript* is not intended as an interpretation, there are few better discussions of the essence of postmodernism than Eco's tongue-in-check *Postscript*. In researching medieval chronicles for background for his novel, Eco declares:

> I rediscovered what writers have always known (and have told us again and again): books always speak of books, and every story tells a story that has already been told. Homer knew this, and Ariosto knew this, not to mention Rabelais and Cervantes. My story, then, could only begin with the discovered manuscript, and even this would be (naturally) a quotation.[11]

In what is perhaps not only the most amusing but the most useful definition of postmodernism in print, Eco compares the postmodern attitude to that of a lover:

> The postmodern reply to the modern consists of recognizing that the past, since it cannot really be destroyed, because its destruction leads to silence, must be revisited: but with irony, not innocently. I think of the postmodern attitude as that of a man who loves a very cultivated woman and knows he cannot say to her, "I love you madly," because he knows that she knows (and that she knows that he knows) that these words have already been written by Barbara Cartland. Still, there is a solution. He can say, "As Barbara Cartland would put it, I love you madly." At this point, having avoided false innocence, having said clearly that it is no longer possible to speak innocently, he will nevertheless have said what he wanted to say to the woman . . . Irony, metalinguistic play, enunciation squared.[12]

[11] *The Name of the Rose*, pp. 511–12; *Il nome della rosa*, p. 513.
[12] *The Name of the Rose*, pp. 530–31; *Il nome della rosa*, p. 529.

There are many other statements in the *Postscript* that certainly show Eco's first novel to have been the product of a very careful reflection upon both literary history and literary theory. Besides the creation of a model reader that is based upon a recognition of a wide range of potential literary audiences and a conscious desire to appeal to them all at very different levels – the kind of "double coding" that such postmodern theorists as Charles Jencks, Linda Hutcheon, or Matei Calinescu discuss[13] – Eco also depends upon a healthy dose of literary tradition in order to fashion his postmodern narrative. In the first place, as he notes in the *Preface*, he chooses what he terms "the most metaphysical and philosophical" literary form – the detective novel.[14] Moreover, taken as a whole, the *Postscript* presents a relatively accurate list of the kinds of writers who will be used, abused, and parodied in Eco's novel: James Joyce, Sir Arthur Conan Doyle, Jorge Luis Borges, Alessandro Manzoni, Rabelais, and a host of medieval writers, from Saint Thomas Aquinas (whose undignified demise will be repeated with the death of the head of Eco's monastery, constituting a moment of comic relief in the narrative) to Bernard of Cluny, whose twelfth-century Latin poem provides the novel's title and the famous untranslated last line of the book in Latin: "Stat rosa pristina nomine, nomina nuda tenemus" ("yesterday's rose endures in its name, we hold empty names" [*De contemptu mundi*, I, 952]).[15]

A brief outline of the plot of *The Name of the Rose* may be useful here. The most significant aspect of Eco's narrative craft is the consummate skill with which he shifts constantly between various levels in his novel in order to appeal to all three of his audiences. The setting is late November of 1327 in an Italian Benedictine monastery in the north of Italy to which a Franciscan, William of Baskerville, and his Benedictine novice, Adso of Melk, journey. William comes as

---

[13] See Calinescu, *Five Faces of Modernity*, p. 285.

[14] *The Name of the Rose*, p. 524; *Il nome della rosa*, p. 524.

[15] See Haft, White, and White, eds., *The Key to "The Name of the Rose"*, p. 175. This handy little book from which the translation of the Latin line is taken is an invaluable reference when reading the novel.

the envoy of Louis IV of Bavaria (*d.* 1347) to initiate negotiations between Pope John XXII (*d.* 1334) and a group of Franciscans critical of the pope and the Catholic Church because of the church's tolerant attitude toward accumulated wealth and its neglect of the poverty Christ originally preached. When William arrives, he is greeted with an emergency situation: a monk has been found dead and soon others are discovered dead, perhaps murdered. He is asked to solve the mysteries before the pope's party arrives, since the group to arrive contains an inquisitor, Bernard Gui, who will take advantage of the crimes at the monastery to scuttle the negotiations. William thus begins to explore the mysteries of the Aedificium (the main structure of the monastery) and the monastery's gigantic library built in the form of a Piranesi-like labyrinth with the requisite supply of secret passages, booby traps, and dark, deep secrets. In the course of William's investigation, the reader learns a great deal about the church history of the period, particularly the various heretical movements opposed to the property accumulated by the church in its role as a temporal power, as well as a wealth of detail about the various kinds of manuscripts that might well have been in a real monastery's library of the period. The novel ends with the accidental finding that an old, blind monk from Spain, Jorge of Burgos, is the evil mind behind most of the terrifying events at the monastery. This revelation, as well as the discovery that Jorge's crimes and machinations were designed to conceal the lost book of Aristotle on comedy, comes to William too late, and he and Adso narrowly escape death in a conflagration that engulfs the entire monastery and its priceless library (including the manuscript of Aristotle that represented what Alfred Hitchcock would have called the "McGuffin" of the story – the necessary mechanism around which the entire plot had revolved).

William is a particularly anachronistic kind of medieval monk, and his anachronisms reflect Eco's postmodern sense of humor. He is singularly adept at applying the teachings of Roger Bacon (*c.* 1214–*c.* 92),

William of Occam (*c.* 1285–1349), and Marsilius of Padua (*c.* 1275–1342), which in a medieval scholar is to be expected. But he also has a more than passing acquaintance with contemporary semiotic theory by Peirce and Umberto Eco as well! Apparently William has smoked a medieval form of marijuana, he has a pair of eyeglasses, and he is equipped with a magnet which eventually serves him well when lost in the labyrinth of the library. William of Baskerville is thus a combination of Sherlock Holmes, a philosophical skeptic, a semiotician, and a monk. This combination of seemingly disparate traits follows the best traditions of the most famous protagonists of detective fiction from Poe through Conan Doyle down to the present day.[16]

As Eco aptly put it, postmodern literature is "irony, metalinguistic play, enunciation squared," and more than anything else, he applies this aesthetic principle to the concept of literary tradition in *The Name of the Rose*. His work represents a pastiche and a parody of a number of other traditions – some obvious, others less so – that enable the novel to appeal to all his intended audiences simultaneously. Let us examine some of the most obvious and most revealing examples of this playfulness with literary history, beginning with the most important – that of the detective novel. Clearly, the protagonist William of Baskerville points the average reader to Sherlock Holmes, Sir Arthur Conan Doyle, and specifically to the famous tale, "The Hound of the Baskervilles." Like the indefatigable Watson, who narrates the stories of the world's foremost investigative detective and lives with him in a

---

[16] There are a number of important discussions of the detective story tradition to which my treatment of Eco is indebted. Still unsurpassed as a historical treatment of the genre are two books by Howard Haycroft: *Murder for Pleasure: The Life and Times of the Detective Story* (New York: D. Appleton-Croft, 1941); and his anthology, *The Art of the Mystery Story: A Collection of Critical Essays* (New York: Biblo and Tannen, 1967, rpt. of 1946 original edition). One of the best essays on the contemporary use of detective fiction is an article by Michael Holquist, "Whodunit and Other Questions: Metaphysical Detective Stories in Postwar Fiction," *New Literary History* 3 (1971), 135–56. Also very useful are Dennis Porter, *The Pursuit of Crime: Art and Ideology in Detective Fiction* (New Haven: Yale University Press, 1981); and, for the Italian context, Stefano Tani, *The Doomed Detective: The Contribution of the Detective Novel to Postmodern American and Italian Fiction* (Carbondale, Ill: Southern Illinois University Press, 1984).

modest apartment in London's Baker Street, William of Baskerville
has his own Watson – his novice Adso, who recounts the story of the
terrible happenings at the monastery when he is an old man. Jorge of
Burgos, the villain of Eco's novel, certainly suggests the evil Moriarty,
the "Napoleon of crime," as Sherlock Holmes calls his nemesis in
"The Final Problem."[17] And Jorge of Burgos is more than a match for
Eco's medieval detective, for he thwarts William of Baskerville
completely at the conclusion of Eco's tale.

Of course, for the postmodern model reader (as opposed to the
empirical reader more typical of the general consumer of bestsellers
and detective fiction), an antagonist named Jorge of Burgos must also
call to mind Jorge Luis Borges (1889–1986), the blind librarian-writer
of metafiction from Argentina. Several of Borges's short stories
resonate through Eco's novel – in particular "The Library of Babel"
and "Death and the Compass," not to mention a number of the
Argentine's brief essays or reviews on the history of detective
fiction.[18] Eco specifically refers to Borges in the *Postscript*: "I wanted a
blind man who guarded a library (it seemed a good narrative idea to
me), and library plus blind man can only equal Borges, also because
debts must be paid."[19] What Eco does not say here but what he
implies is that the equation "can only equal" derives from a theory of
postmodern fiction, not from logical necessity. Only when literature
is defined as "irony, metalinguistic play, enunciation squared" does
the equation blind man plus library *inevitably* equal Borges. Eco's
Postscript maintains much the same view of the literary function of the
detective story as Borges did years earlier (in 1942) in a review entitled
"On the Origins of the Detective Story." Borges was a conservative
thinker where literary tradition was concerned, and in this early

[17] See William S. Baring-Gould, ed., *The Annotated Sherlock Holmes* (New York: Clarkson
N. Potter, Inc., 1973), 2nd rev. ed., II: 303.
[18] For Eco and Borges, see especially the previously cited Stephens, "Ec[h]o in fabula";
and Deborah Parker, "The Literature of Appropriation: Eco's Use of Borges in *Il nome
della rosa*," *Modern Literature Review* 85 (1990), 842–49.
[19] *The Name of the Rose*, p. 515; *Il nome della rosa*, p. 515.

review he argues that "the literature of our time is exhausted by interjections and opinions, incoherences and confidences: the detective story represents order and the obligation to invent."[20] Borges means by this remark that a detective story resembles a sonnet or a sestina – it has a relatively fixed narrative form with certain rules that must be followed.[21] The bravura of a writer is underlined not by breaking all of the rules but by creating something original while following them, much as Ezra Pound tried his hand at sestinas because the acknowledged masters of metrics in the Middle Ages (Arnaut Daniel, Dante, Petrarch) had done so, and to be a great poet, in Pound's opinion, meant excellence within a tradition as opposed to a complete and radical break from literary history.

The intricate literary games (enunciation squared) played by Eco in *The Name of the Rose* are fascinating, for they aim at every instance at a postmodern bridging of the gap between the erudite, academic, philosophical reader and the avid consumer of best-selling pulp fiction and detective stories. In the process, Eco not only manipulates literary tradition in entertaining ways, but he also incorporates academic scholarship into his fiction as well. Let us examine a classic case of this – William of Baskerville's first Holmes-like proof of his prowess at detection. The skill with which William's model Sherlock could meet an individual for the first time in his life and immediately pronounce intimate details about this person has become so well known that it has produced a phrase recognized by every English-speaking schoolboy – "Elementary, my dear Watson!" Eco cannot resist the temptation to show that William is equal to Sherlock in this regard, and in the first chapter ("Prime") of the first day of his narrative, as William and Adso work their way up to the monastery, they meet Remigio of Varagine, the monastery's cellarer (later arrested by Bernard Gui for

[20] Jorge Luis Borges, *Borges: A Reader* (New York: E. P. Dutton, 1981), p. 148.
[21] In fact Haycroft's *The Art of the Mystery Story* contains a number of articles outlining the "code" that has been or should be followed by detective fiction: "Twenty Rules for Writing Detective Stories" by S. S. Van Dine; "Detective Story Decalogue" by Ronald A. Knox; and "The Detective Club Oath."

heresy). Without being asked by Remigio whether or not William had seen a stray horse (Abbot Abo's favorite horse Brunellus), William announces to his astounded interlocutor:

> "The horse came this way and took the path to the right. He will not get far, because he will have to stop when he reaches the dungheap. He is too intelligent to plunge down that precipitous slope . . . We haven't seen him at all, have we, Adso?" William said, turning toward me with an amused look. "But if you are hunting for Brunellus, the horse can only be where I have said."[22]

When Remigio is surprised by William's remarks (they happen to be an accurate description of the facts) and asks how William knew the horse was named Brunellus, William's reply further increases our admiration for his Holmes-like powers:

> "Come, come," William said, "it is obvious you are hunting for Brunellus, the abbot's favorite horse, fifteen hands, the fastest in your stables, with a dark coat, a full tail, small round hoofs, but a very steady gait, small head, sharp ears, big eyes. He went to the right, as I said, but you should hurry, in any case."[23]

When asked subsequently by Adso how he came upon this information, William's answer begins with the kind of information we would expect from Holmes – hoofprints on the fresh snow, the size of the horse inferred from the proportions of the hooves, the direction indicated by a broken blackberry bush on the right fork of the road on which some long black horsehair had been caught, and so forth. But this empirical evidence typical of any basic detective work gives place to other literary or philosophical considerations. Adso notes that the small head, the sharp ears, and the big eyes (not to mention the name Brunellus itself) could not possibly be inferred from the empirical information, and it is precisely here that William parts company, in some respects, from his modern British counterpart:

[22] *The Name of the Rose*, p. 23; *Il nome della rosa*, pp. 30–31.
[23] *The Name of the Rose*, p. 23; *Il nome della rosa*, p. 31.

"I am not sure he has those features, but no doubt the monks firmly believe he does. As Isidore of Seville said, the beauty of a horse requires 'that the head be small, siccum prope pelle ossibus adhaerente, short and pointed ears, big eyes, flaming nostrils, erect neck, thick mane and tail, round and solid hoofs.' If the horse whose passing I inferred had not really been the finest of the stables, stableboys would have been out chasing him, but instead, the cellarer in person had undertaken the search. And a monk who considers a horse excellent, whatever his natural forms, can only see him as the auctoritates have described him, especially if" – and here he smiled slyly in my direction – "the describer is a learned Benedictine."

"All right," I said, "but why Brunellus?"

"May the Holy Ghost sharpen your mind, son!" my master exclaimed. "What other name could he possibly have? Why, even the great Buridan, who is about to become rector in Paris, when he wants to use a horse in one of his logical examples, always calls it Brunellus."[24]

William has clearly gone beyond the boundaries of any empirical investigation – he has begun to make broad hypothetical inferences rather than to deduce from logical premises. And while the initial impact of his virtuoso performance will strike every common reader as a masterful literary parody of Sherlock Holmes's investigative style – all we lack is for William to exclaim in triumph, "Elementary, my dear Adso!" – in the midst of his explanation, Eco has transformed William (at least for the more erudite reader) into a very different kind of thinker. William has become a semiotician employing a method that is far closer to the abduction discussed by Peirce or Eco himself than to the logical deductions we associate with real-world detectives or a host of fictional investigators.

Eco's anachronistic transformation of William into a contemporary semiotician becomes clear from an examination of the essays

---

[24] *The Name of the Rose*, p. 24; *Il nome della rosa*, p. 32.

included in an anthology co-authored by Eco and Thomas A. Sebeok entitled *Il segno dei tre* (*The Sign of Three: Dupin, Holmes, Peirce*, 1983).[25] This collection is an important contribution to the history of semiotic theory which underlines the interesting parallels between the methods of the two most famous detectives of nineteenth-century fiction – Poe's Dupin and Conan Doyle's Holmes – and the semiotic theory of Charles S. Peirce, the American thinker so fundamental to Eco's own theory of semiotics. Eco's particular contribution to the volume, an essay entitled "Horns, Hooves, Insteps: Some Hypotheses on Three Types of Abduction," is itself indebted to an essay by Carlo Ginzburg (one of Eco's colleagues at the University of Bologna) which is also reprinted in the anthology but which originally appeared in a different form as early as 1978.[26] Ginzburg's essay, plus Eco's own interest in linking the reasoning processes associated with Sherlock Holmes and Charles S. Peirce, ultimately provide the literary "sources" for the Brunellus episode in *The Name of the Rose*.

Ginzburg's "Clues: Morelli, Freud, and Sherlock Holmes" outlines the rise in the nineteenth century of what he calls "the conjectural model" for the construction of knowledge in the social sciences which utilized obscure or seemingly insignificant clues in a speculative fashion to construct an epistemological model that would be different from the mathematical-scientific model proposed by Galileo or Newton. Ginzburg demonstrates this kind of logic in three very different fields: in the art connoisseurship of Giovanni Morelli, which aimed at identifying the authorship of a Renaissance painting by

---

[25] Bloomington: Indiana University Press, 1983; Italian edition, *Il segno dei tre* (Milan: Bompiani, 1983).

[26] As Pischedda, *Come leggere "Il nome della rosa"* notes (pp. 40–41), Ginzburg's essay – reprinted in *Il segno dei tre* (pp. 95–136) – originally appeared as "Spie: radici di un paradigma indiziario" in *Rivista di storia contemporanea*, 7 (1978) and was subsequently reprinted in A. Gargani, *Crisi della ragione: nuovi modelli nel rapporto tra sapere e attività umane* (Turin: Einaudi, 1979), a work that Eco himself reviewed in *Alfabeta* (no. 9, January 1980) and reprinted in *Sette anni di desiderio*, pp. 34–39. In the Eco and Sebeok anthology, Ginzburg's essay is entitled "Clues: Morelli, Freud, and Sherlock Holmes" (pp. 81–118).

studious attention to rather insignificant details (the shape of an ear, the curve of a hand); in the psychoanalytic essays of Sigmund Freud, who mentions Morelli's method in his essay on the Moses of Michelangelo and whose own method (such as his fascination with seemingly unimportant slips of the tongue or only apparently banal cases of forgetfulness) was not dissimilar to Morelli's; and in the detection of Sherlock Holmes, whose character Conan Doyle based upon the diagnostic techniques of medical doctors he knew personally. Ginzburg believes the reasoning process common to Morelli, Freud, and Holmes and many other important disciplines that arose in the last century is ultimately indebted to symptomatology, a medieval model of medical semiotics. Ginzburg defines this older model as "the discipline which permits diagnosis, though the disease cannot be directly observed, on the basis of superficial symptoms or signs, often irrelevant to the eye of the layman."[27] Freud himself once told his patient, the "Wolf-Man," how interesting he found the Holmes mysteries, and he also admired Morelli's methodology.

What makes Ginzburg's essay pertinent to Eco's first novel (and what must have attracted Eco's attention when he first read Ginzburg) is the next step in the essay, which demonstrates how the kind of reasoning typical of Morelli, Freud, and Holmes has antecedents in prehistory when mankind lived by hunting and hunters had to learn to reconstruct the appearance and movement of their prey through their tracks (Eco would call these tracks "signs"). Ginzburg declares that lurking behind the symptomatic model is "the gesture which is the oldest, perhaps, of the intellectual history of the human race: the hunter crouched in the mud, examining a quarry's tracks."[28] Folklore from the distant Middle Eastern past tells of three brothers who meet a man who has lost a camel; without seeing the animal themselves,

---

[27] Carlo Ginzburg, "Clues: Morelli, Freud, and Sherlock Holmes," in Eco and Sebeok, eds. *The Sign of Three*, p. 87; Eco and Sebeok, eds., *Il segno dei tre*, p. 105.

[28] Ginzburg, "Clues: Morelli, Freud, and Sherlock Holmes," in Eco and Sebeok, eds., *The Sign of Three*, p. 91; Eco and Sebeok, eds., *Il segno dei tre*, p. 109.

they nevertheless describe it to the man. Believing that only the thieves could provide such an accurate description, the camel's owner has the three brothers arrested and brought before a judge. Only their convincing reconstruction of how they managed to infer what the camel looked like without seeing it saves them from execution. This ancient folktale, like so many other folk motifs in European literature, made its debut in Western literature through an Italian collection of short stories – the *Novelle* of Giovanni Sercambi (1348–1424) – that was subsequently included in a very popular compendium of oriental tales published in Venice in the sixteenth century as *Peregrinaggio di tre giovani figliuoli del re di Serendippo* (*The Travels of the Three Sons of the King of Serendippo*). This book, in turn, went into numerous editions and European translations, given the fashion of oriental subject-matter in the eighteenth century, and the story of these three brothers (now transformed into the three sons of the king of Serendippo) was so popular that Horace Walpole coined the word "serendipity" in 1745 to mean a happy and unexpected discovery. A few years before, Voltaire had read the French version of the book and incorporated the tale in the third chapter of *Zadig*: following this literary tradition, Zadig describes some missing animals he has never seen, and when he is accused (like the three brothers and the three sons before him) of stealing the animals he has described in great detail, he wins his freedom by outlining the reasoning process that allowed him to provide such a precise description. In concluding this intriguing bit of literary detection and after providing a fascinating tour of literary history, Ginzburg notes that in Voltaire's elaboration of this old folktale "lies the embryo of the detective story. It inspired Poe and Gaboriau directly, and perhaps indirectly Conan Doyle."[29]

The fact that folklore, literary tradition, reasoning in a variety of disciplines in the nineteenth-century social sciences, and the logic behind the detective story could all be related by Ginzburg to a new

[29] Ginzburg, "Clues: Morelli, Freud, and Sherlock Holmes," in Eco and Sebeok, eds., *The Sign of Three*, p. 102; Eco and Sebeok, eds., *Il segno dei tre*, p. 125.

epistemological model must have intrigued Eco, who immediately borrowed and even parodied this tradition in *The Name of the Rose* in the Brunellus episode. More than a linkage to the methods of Sherlock Holmes, therefore, Eco's aim was to underline the semiotic bases of human understanding and more specifically the theories of Charles S. Peirce that were so important to his own book, *A Theory of Semiotics*.

As Marcello Truzzi points out in a contribution to *The Sign of Three*, an analysis of Conan Doyle's mystery tales reveals "at least 217 clearly described and discernible cases of inference (unobtrusive measurement) made by Holmes" and reaches the surprising conclusion that "although Holmes often speaks of his *deductions*, these are actually quite rarely displayed in the canon. Nor are Holmes' most common inferences technically *inductions*. More exactly, Holmes consistently displays what C. S. Peirce has called *abductions*."[30] The important difference between a deduction and an abduction is that while a deduction follows logical rules and need have no reference to external reality, abductions require external validation, since they are, in Peirce's terms, presumptive inferences or hypotheses.

Eco's essay in *The Sign of Three* linking the detective novel to Peirce's abductions was certainly conceived in 1978, the year when Ginzburg published the first draft of his essay and the same year Eco began writing *The Name of the Rose*. A reading of Eco's essay makes perfectly clear that Eco's invention of the protagonist William of Baskerville must have been indebted not only to the literary traditions of the detective novel familiar to generations of pulp-fiction readers but also to the most sophisticated contemporary epistemological scholarship on the history of philosophy and scientific methodology, as in Ginzburg's work, not to mention Eco's own semiotic theory treating signs, abductions, and Peirce's theory of unlimited semiosis. By placing William of Baskerville at the end of a long tradition of discourse on inferential thinking based ultimately upon semiotic

---

[30] Marcello Truzzi, "Sherlock Holmes: Applied Social Psychologist," in Eco and Sebeok, eds., *The Sign of Three*, p. 69; or in Eco and Sebeok, eds., *Il segno dei tre*, p. 84.

theory as well as reflecting a direct debt to the detective novel, Eco has created a symbolic figure whose investigation now embodies an extremely serious argument, the outcome of which will underscore Eco's own views not only on literary tradition but on metaphysics as well.

The success or failure of William's attempts to resolve the mysteries at the monastery is thus fraught with more meaning than can be bounded by the genre of the detective novel. And it is Eco's goal to combine themes that are derived from the pulp-fiction–detective novel tradition, on the one hand, and more serious, theoretical problems from the disciplines of semiotics and literary or cultural theory. An excellent way of demonstrating this two-pronged approach to his subject-matter is Eco's treatment of the pattern of the Apocalypse in *The Name of the Rose*. Looking for a pattern in the deaths inside the monastery, William begins to discern one derived from the prophecy of the seven angels with the seven trumpets in the Book of Revelation (8:6–10:10). The manuscript illustrator Adelmo (the first body found in the abbey) has fallen from the high window of the Aedificium, creating a bloody path on the snow below, a death that seems to reflect the angel who announces "hail and fire, mixed with blood" (8:7).[31] Actually, we later discover that Adelmo was not murdered but committed suicide, thus making any pattern based on seven murders meaningless from the outset. When Venantius is found drowned in a tub of blood, it recalls the prophecy of the second angel, where "a third of the sea became blood" (8:9). Berengar is found poisoned in the balneary, causing William to note that in the third prophecy, the angel poisons one third of the waters with wormwood (8:10). When Severinus has his head crushed by a planetary sphere representing the sun, the moon, and the other stars, it practically forces William to conclude that the murderer is now following a pattern based upon the Book of Revelation, since the

[31] In all citations from the Holy Bible, I cite from the New Revised Standard Version (Grand Rapids, Mich.: Zondervan Publishing House, 1989).

fourth angel speaks of striking a third of the sun, moon, and stars, darkening the skies (8:12). When Malachi dies of a mysterious poison that seems to have possessed the power of a thousand scorpions, William is finally convinced that the pattern is a valid one, even though he himself realizes that the reference to scorpions in the description of the fifth angel and the fifth trumpet is somewhat problematic, since the text in the Book of Revelation speaks of *locusts* with a sting like that of scorpions. (9:10).

By the time Malachi's body is discovered, William has deduced that only the people who know Greek are dying (a true conclusion from the facts he has unearthed) and that the pattern of the deaths in the monastery follows that in the Book of Revelation (a false conclusion but one which is warranted by the facts at William's disposal). Jorge of Burgos comes from Spain, and since William knows (correctly) that most of the important medieval commentaries on the Book of Revelation also came from Spain – including a beautiful one written in the eighth century by Beatus, the abbot of Liébana that Eco himself has analyzed – William naturally assumes that Jorge is the Moriarty-like mastermind behind the deaths.[32] This Spanish connection to the Apocalypse, plus the fact that Jorge himself delivers a dramatic sermon based upon apocalyptic references (the pattern of the seven angels and their trumpets) in the chapter entitled "Compline," finally convinces William that the murders in the abbey follow a pattern from the Book of Revelation (a false inference) and that Jorge is the most obvious suspect (a true inference but for the wrong reasons). When the sixth victim, the abbot himself, suffocates in the narrow passageways after being lured into the labyrinth by Jorge, this seems to fulfill the prophecy which speaks of many things, among them a horseman who kills with fire and smoke and sulphur coming from the

---

[32] See Umberto Eco, *Il beato di Liébana* (Milan: Ricci, 1973), for a beautiful reproduction of the major illuminations in the commentary and Eco's introduction in Italian; for a translation of the introduction, see Eco's "Waiting for the Millennium," *FMR* 2 (July 1984), 63–92. This text becomes one of the major sources for Eco's novel.

horses' mouths (9:18). Finally, after William–Sherlock confronts Jorge–Moriarty in the labyrinth of the library, he finally catches a glimpse of the only surviving manuscript copy of Aristotle's treatise on comedy bound in a volume that includes works in Arabic, Syriac, Latin, and (of course) Greek. Jorge prevents William from rescuing this priceless work by eating the pages of the manuscript which he has poisoned to prevent readers from surviving the experience of reading it. In the ensuing struggle, Jorge dies and the entire monastery with its magnificent library burns to the ground, including the Aristotle manuscript. Ironically, just as William realizes that he has been mistaken all along in following a pattern of crimes based upon an assumed master criminal following a pattern from the Book of Revelation, Jorge's death confirms the pattern: the last angel of the Book of Revelation (11:9–10) speaks of John, the assumed author of the work, eating a scroll given to him by an angel which "was sweet as honey in my mouth, but when I had eaten it, my stomach was made bitter."

While the pattern William presumes to have discovered seems to reveal an ordered mind or a rational plot behind seemingly irrational events, the belief in the existence of such a mind or plot arises from William's errors in making abductions or inferences as a detective-semiotician. Adelmo's death, the beginning of the pattern, results from suicide, caused by remorse for the monk's homosexuality, not murder. Malachi, and not Jorge, kills Severinus. Jorge never based any of his actions initially upon a literary pattern from the Book of Revelation, but after the fifth death, he became convinced, like William, that such a pattern was in operation as part of a divine plan to punish his enemies and those who would have disseminated Aristotle's theories of comedy and undermined authority and established, traditional, religious values. Actually, the pattern from the Book of Revelation can be discerned only by an almost intentional disregard for most of the *details* of the descriptions of the seven angels and their seven trumpets. One must fixate upon only those details that fit *an already preexisting pattern* in the mind of the investigator (in this case, William), in order to see the crimes as reflecting the last book of the Bible. In effect, William constructed an inferential hypothesis – an abduction – which utterly failed when tested against reality. The fact that William ultimately solved the crime was a purely chance affair, and given the disastrous results of his investigation – the destruction of the entire abbey, including the priceless manuscript – there is little about which he should be congratulated.

True to his philosophical bent, William admits his error:

> "There was no plot," William said, "and I discovered it by mistake."
> ... "I have never doubted the truth of signs, Adso; they are the only things man has with which to orient himself in the world. What I did not understand was the relation among signs. I arrived at Jorge through an apocalyptic pattern that seemed to underlie all the crimes, and yet it was accidental. I arrived at Jorge seeking one criminal for all the crimes and we discovered that each crime was committed by a different person, or by no one. I arrived at Jorge pursuing the plan of a perverse and rational mind, and there was no plan ... I should have known well that there is no order in the universe."[33]

William continues his sad confession of failure, citing an anachronistic reference to a German thinker – supposedly one of Adso's countrymen. In reality, it is a famous citation from the *Tractatus Logico-Philosophicus* of Ludwig Wittgenstein:

> The order that our mind imagines is like a net, or like a ladder, built to attain something. But afterward you must throw the ladder away, because you discover that, even if it was useful, it was meaningless. Er muoz gelîchesame die leiter abewerfen, sôer an ir ufgestigen ... Is that how you say it?'
> "That is how it is said in my language. Who told you that?"
> "A mystic from your land. He wrote it somewhere, I forget where. And it is not necessary for somebody one day to find that

---

[33] *The Name of the Rose*, pp. 491–92; *Il nome della rosa*, pp. 494–95.

manuscript again. The only truths that are useful are instruments to be thrown away."[34]

William's abductions assume the existence of order and purpose in his world and in the universe. The common reader of *The Name of the Rose*, as one perceptive critic has noted, is also drawn into accepting William's mistaken hypotheses or inferences as part of the brilliant perceptions of a master sleuth for several reasons: because readers, in general, are accustomed to seek out patterns and order in narrative; and most particularly, because readers of the classic detective or mystery novels enjoy a specially intriguing tradition of intricate criminal plots involving complex patterns. For example, Agatha Christie's *The ABC Murders* has a series of murders following an alphabetical pattern; the crimes in Ellery Queen's *Ten Days Wonder* follow the Ten Commandments; those in S. S. Van Dine's *The Benson Murder Case* are based upon nursery rhymes; and so forth.[35] Life, unfortunately, rarely follows either the rules of detective fiction or those of semiotic theory, and by showing William to be a spectacular failure both as a detective and as an inventor of semiotic abductions, Eco wants to underline how dangerous our assumptions of order in the universe really can be. I also believe that Eco cites this reference to Wittgenstein to inform us that he no longer believes semiotics represents an all-encompassing master discipline. Like the ladder that is discarded when the philosopher reaches his or her goal, semiotics represents a useful tool in the search for a contingent and limited truth, but a tool that should never be confused with Truth itself.

As we have seen, the early Brunellus episode in the novel sets the stage for Eco's double purpose in *The Name of the Rose*: it both suggests to the general reader that he or she has opened a consumable whodunit; and it promises for the erudite scholar and "the happy

---

[34] *The Name of the Rose*, p. 492; *Il nome della rosa*, p. 495.
[35] I am indebted to David H. Richter's "Eco's Echoes: Semiotic Theory and Detective Practice in *The Name of the Rose*," *Studies in Twentieth-Century Literature* 10, no. 2 (1986), 213–36 for a discussion of this relationship.

few" a learned discourse on metaphysics and linguistics. During the course of his investigation, William discovers a message written in a cipher which derives from a zodiacal alphabet.[36] It is clearly the key to the *finis Africae*, the section of the library's labyrinth where Jorge conceals the only copy of Aristotle's theory of comedy that has been the root cause of the deaths in the monastery. In the stable of the monastery, near the same Brunellus of William's first and seemingly brilliant abduction, Adso recalls the comically incorrect Latin spoken by the unfortunate wretch Salvatore, who has been consigned to Bernard Gui's inquisition. Salvatore speaks a confusing jumble of every known European and classical language but none of them accurately or coherently. Once he had said "tertius equi" to Adso, meaning to say "the third horse." In reality, due to his miserable Latin grammar, he had in fact said "the third of a horse." As Adso explains:

> "I was remembering poor Salvatore. He wanted to perform God knows what magic with that horse, and with his Latin he called him 'tertius equi.' Which would be the *u*."
>
> "The *u*?" asked William, who had heard my prattle without paying much attention to it.
>
> "Yes, because 'tertius equi' does not mean the third horse, but the third of the horse, and the third letter of the word 'equus' is *u*. But this is all nonsense . . ."
>
> William looked at me, and in the darkness I seemed to see his face transformed. "God bless you, Adso!" he said to me. "Why, of course, suppositio materialis, the discourse is presumed de dicto and not de re . . . What a fool I am!"[37]

It is doubtful that the general reader has followed this chain of reasoning completely. But William's reference in Latin to *suppositio materialis* is a learned reference to one of the theories of William of Occam, and the sentence may be rendered as follows: "Why, of

---

[36] See Eco, *The Name of the Rose*, p. 165, or *Il nome della rosa*, p. 170, for the diagram of the message.

[37] *The Name of the Rose*, p. 457; *Il nome della rosa*, p. 460.

course, the material supposition, the discourse is presumed about the word itself and not about the thing for which it stands."[38] Put in philosophical, and not narrative terms, William's mistakes and his failure to understand the events in the monastery are based upon a misconception about language. Language does not necessarily refer to something in the *outside* world, something concrete that stands in a one-to-one relationship to the word which is a sign; language may also be *metareferential* and refer to *itself*, just as Eco's *The Name of the Rose* is both a novel and a book that refers to and is made up of many other novels. The learned reader will thus not be surprised to discover that the Latin phrase uttered by William in his moment of epiphany derives from William of Occam's *Summa totius logicae* (I, 63, 67), where the philosopher, who Eco originally wanted as his novel's protagonist, argued that material supposition occurs when a term stands for the vocal or written word rather than for that which it signifies.[39] The fact that "tertius equi" can refer to the third letter in the noun *equus* suddenly makes William understand that his cipher providing the way into the *finis Africae* refers not to other things but to other letters of the alphabet in the words that refer to things. Thus the mysterious phrase "primum et septimum de quatuor" ("the first and the seventh of the four") refers not to anything specific but the first and seventh letters of the number four in the phrase written over the mirror, "super thronos viginti quatuor!" ("on their thrones sat the twenty-four elders!"). When William and Adso push the first and seventh letters in the Latin word *quatuor*, the mysterious passage opens and they enter the forbidden chamber with ease. This discovery leads to the ultimate destruction of the monastery and the loss of the only copy of Aristotle's manuscript. William and Adso have the dubious satisfaction of concluding that Jorge was the evil genius behind some but not

---

[38] Haft, White and White, eds., *The Key to "The Name of the Rose"*, pp. 169–70. I owe this observation to an article by Robert Caserio, "The Name of the Horse, *Hard Times*, Semiotics, and the Supernatural," *Novel* 20 (1986), p. 8.

[39] Haft, White, and White, eds., *ibid.*, p. 170 provides the source for this citation.

all of the events taking place during the novel's narration. Their unsuccessful investigation constitutes a rejection of the literary tradition of the ingenious and infallible detective. And Eco employs the failure of his two medieval sleuths to cast a postmodern veil of doubt not only upon semiotics as a master discipline capable of understanding all facets of human culture but also over the very power of reason itself.

The extraordinary quality of *The Name of the Rose* is that a book such as this one, filled with obscure Latin quotations, medieval lore, and complex philosophical questions, might also have become such a phenomenal bestseller and long-seller. Eco's narrative strategy, as an explicit postmodernist statement, aimed at a marriage of popular audiences and themes with themes for an audience closer to a university faculty meeting. Much of Eco's popular success must be accredited to his clever choice of a narrative voice in Adso, the novice of William of Baskerville, who is a careful but naive observer of all that goes on in the novel's narrative. At the age of eighty, Adso looks back on the events of his youth (he was then 18). In Eco's words, he wanted to tell the story

> through the voice of someone who experiences the events, records them all with the photographic fidelity of an adolescent, but does not understand them (and will not understand them fully even as an old man, since he then chooses a flight into the divine nothingness, which was not what his master had taught him) – to make everything understood through the words of one who understands nothing.[40]

Eco also notes, and with obvious satisfaction, that the cultivated readers liked his narrator least, while the general audience of relatively unsophisticated readers identified with Adso's ignorance, innocence, and relative lack of understanding. Adso allowed Eco's common readers to *enjoy* the story, in other words, without feeling

---

[40] *The Name of the Rose*, p. 518; *Il nome della rosa*, p. 518.

guilty or running to the encyclopedia to check dates and sources.[41] It is precisely Adso's lack of intellectual sophistication, like that of Watson before him in Conan Doyle's Holmes mysteries, that appeals to the average reader.

A number of cleverly constructed narrative frames separate the contemporary reader from the events recounted in the novel. Adso first recounts his story in manuscript form during the next to the last decade of the fourteenth century, recalling the events in his old age. His manuscript is edited by Dom J. Mabillon in the eighteenth century. Mabillon's edition is translated by the Abbé Vallet in 1842. And Vallet's translation is supposedly the work that is transcribed in 1968 by our narrator – let us call him Umberto Eco for convenience, although contemporary narrative theory forbids us from identifying him with the actual person Umberto Eco. As the preface to the work reads, "Naturally, a manuscript."[42] Eco reminds us immediately of the long and glorious tradition of narrative fiction based upon imaginary manuscripts – Ariosto, Cervantes, Manzoni – that he is imitating.

Adso also provides the only romantic elements in the novel through a fleeting encounter with an unnamed peasant girl who makes love to him, an experience which he relates through reference to a series of learned texts Eco took from a number of sources – particularly from the Song of Solomon, its medieval commentaries, and Saint Hildegard's mystic description of ecstatic rapture. Even Adso's account of how he awakens after his first and only experience of physical love refers us to a book – this time a metaliterary reference, since the passage in question is Dante's *Inferno* v, which itself speaks of how Paolo and Francesca fell in love because of a book they read: "I let out a cry and fell as a dead body falls," Adso remembers decades later in his narrative in the future.[43] But Eco's description of this remembrance in Italian – "lanciai un urlo e caddi

---

[41] *The Name of the Rose*, p. 518; *Il nome della rosa*, p. 518.
[42] *The Name of the Rose*, p. v; *Il nome della rosa*, p. 10.
[43] *The Name of the Rose*, p. 250; *Il nome della rosa*, p. 253.

come cade un corpo morto" – also echoes perhaps the most famous line in Dante's poem, the point where Dante the pilgrim and the poet-narrator of the *Divine Comedy* faints after hearing what he construes (falsely) as the tragedy of Paolo and Francesca, when he should be condemning these two lovers with the righteous indignation of a prophet, a point of view that Dante the pilgrim eventually assumes during his long journey through the afterlife.[44] At this point in the pilgrim's adventure through the afterlife, Dante the pilgrim has not yet understood the nature of evil and is almost as naive as Adso will always remain. In contrast to Dante the pilgrim, who learns through his experiences, Adso never really grasps the meaning of William of Baskerville's teachings or example.[45]

Adso also never learns the name of his beloved, the woman with whom he had the only sexual experience of his entire lifetime: "This was the only earthly love of my life, and I could not, then or ever after, call that love by name."[46] This important detail about Adso, the relatively minor role women play in the novel in general (not really a surprising trait in a book treating of medieval monasteries), and the fact that the novel opens with the narrator's account about how a traveling companion (presumably a woman) steals the only copy of the nineteenth-century translation of Adso's manuscript immediately following their flight from Prague during the 1968 Russian invasion – all these facts have led some feminist critics to attack Eco for his supposedly sexist approach to gender.[47] This is

---

[44] A recent poetic translation renders this famous Italian verse – "E caddi come corpo morto cade" – as "Swooning as in death, I fell like a dying body" (see Robert Pinsky, *The Inferno of Dante* [New York: Farrar, Giraux & Strauss, 1994], pp. 52–53). Mark Musa's translation of the same line in iambic pentameter blank verse reads: "and fell to Hell's floor as a body, dead, falls" (Dante, *The Divine Comedy: Vol. I : Inferno* [New York: Penguin, 1984], p. 113).

[45] For an excellent discussion of this point, see chapter 2 of Theresa Coletti's *Naming the Rose.*

[46] *The Name of the Rose*, p. 407; *Il nome della rosa*, p. 409.

[47] Thus Diane Elam in *Romancing the Postmodern* (London: Routledge, 1992), can claim that "Eco's ironic postmodernization of issues of genre and history is vitiated by being mortgaged to a classical portrayal of gender" (p. 33), implying that every postmodernist

certainly an exaggeration and an ideological distortion of Eco's perspective.

Adso's object of desire is unattainable (only the first of many unattainable objects of desire in Eco's three novels, as we shall subsequently see), and that unattainable quality is underlined by the fact that Adso fails to learn the girl's name and will never find out what it is after she is arrested for witchcraft. We are reminded of Adso's nameless object of desire at the finale of the novel, when, decades later, the world-weary Adso as an old, disillusioned, and certainly no wiser man, delivers the previously cited final lines of the book from which its problematic title is derived: "Stat rosa pristina nomine, nomina nuda tenemus" ("yesterday's rose endures in its name, we hold empty names"). Eco's *Preface* once again sheds light on the reason behind this puzzling title:

> The idea of calling my book *The Name of the Rose* came to me virtually by chance, and I liked it because the rose is a symbolic figure so rich in meanings that by now it hardly has any meaning left: Dante's mystic rose, and go lovely rose, the Wars of the Roses, rose thou art sick, too many rings around Rosie, a rose by any other name, a rose is a rose is a rose is a rose, the Rosicrucians. The title rightly disoriented the reader, who was unable to choose just one interpretation; and even if he were to catch the possible nominalist readings of the concluding verse, he would come to them only at the end, having previously made God only knows what other choices. A title must muddle the reader's ideas, not regiment them.[48]

novelist must, of necessity, be fascinated by the interests of American academic feminists. She also argues unconvincingly that Eco's definition of postmodernism and its reference to Barbara Cartland in *Preface to "The Name of the Rose'* provide proof of Eco's sexism. Other discussions of this issue include: Teresa de Lauretis, "Gaudy Rose: Eco and Narcissism," *Sub-Stance* 14 (1985), 13–29; and Thomas S. Frentz, "Resurrecting the Feminine in *The Name of the Rose*," *Pre/Text* 9, no. 3–4 (1988), 124–45. *The Name of the Rose* is simply not concerned with issues of gender in the strict constructionist sense applied by some feminist critics to literary texts.

[48] *The Name of the Rose*, p.506; *Il nome della rosa*, p. 508. For a treatment of the rose theme in literature, see Robert F. Fleissner, *A Rose by Another Name: A Survey of Literary Flora from Shakespeare to Eco* (West Cornwall, Conn.: Locust Hill Press, 1989).

Adso, both as a young novice and later as an older monk, never learns the fundamental lesson taught by William – that language and life itself are so rich in meanings that they must be treated as Eco's image of the rose, as an empty shell into which multiple meanings can be poured. William, according to Adso, "was not at all interested in the truth" but "he amused himself by imagining how many possibilities were possible," while Adso always remained "on the side of that thirst for truth that inspired Bernard Gui"[49] – and, we might add, Jorge of Burgos.

Yet it is precisely the fanatic thirst for truth and its corollary – the over-zealous search for heretics who deny the truth once it is known – that *The Name of the Rose* is directed against. By the author's own admission, his favorite line is an exchange between Adso and William: "'What terrifies you most in purity?' I asked. 'Haste,' William answered."[50] Haste, intolerance, the conviction that there is only one Truth and that only one interlocutor understands that single Truth – all these assumptions stand behind much of the world Eco pictures in *The Name of the Rose*. It is a world that Eco knows perhaps better than most other scholars, a culture that has provided him with models from everything from philosophy to semiotics and literary theory, but Eco realizes that it is not a world which would be very friendly to eclectic thinkers such as he who are convinced, on the contrary, that there are no certain truths; that no one person, church, government, or philosophy stands as the guardian of any authentic orthodoxy; and that the disciplines of linguistics and semiotics, properly applied, actually provide a theoretical underpinning for tolerance and the suspension of final judgments.

Because *The Name of the Rose* is ultimately about freedom, about tolerance, and about respect for difference, it is appropriate that the lost book William seeks and Jorge conceals is Aristotle's treatise on comedy. Comedy, as Jorge of Burgos quite rightly understands, is

---

[49] *The Name of the Rose*, p. 306; *Il nome della rosa*, p. 309.
[50] *The Name of the Rose*, p. 385; *Il nome della rosa*, p. 388.

always – in the hands of artists of genius, such as Aristophanes, Rabelais, Ariosto, Shakespeare, Molière, Mozart, or Fellini – a subversive force undermining established authority and customs. It is mankind's best and sometimes only protection against fanaticism of all sorts. Eco provides William with an eloquent statement of this position at the end of the novel:

> Fear prophets, Adso, and those prepared to die for the truth, for as a rule they make many others die with them, often before them, at times instead of them. Jorge did a diabolical thing because he loved his truth so lewdly that he hated anything in order to destroy falsehood. Jorge feared the second book of Aristotle because it perhaps really did teach how to distort the face of every truth, so that we would not become slaves of our ghosts. Perhaps the mission of those who love mankind is to make people laugh at the truth, *to make truth laugh*, because the only truth lies in learning to free ourselves from insane passion for the truth.[51]

Thus, the closing line in Latin that puzzled so many readers otherwise fascinated by Eco's novel actually provides a concrete example of how a word or a sign, such as "rose," can contain within itself an incredible range of meanings, historical associations, symbolisms, and yet remain only a sign, not a fixed truth. Others might see the passage as a pessimistic admission that humanity is forever doomed to remain separated from a single unequivocal Truth. Eco, however, had come to realize that the semiotic principle of unlimited semiosis can also imply an expansion of human liberty. That this realization came through the process of creating one of the postwar period's most popular novels confirms the conclusion on the original Italian book-jacket of the work. There, Eco came to the realization, happily for his readers: "upon reaching maturity, that those things about which we cannot theorize, we must narrate."

[51] *The Name of the Rose*, p. 491; *Il nome della rosa*, p. 494.

§

six

Interpretation, overinterpretation, paranoid interpretation, and *Foucault's Pendulum*

After the incredible success of *The Name of the Rose*, Eco turned his attention for roughly a decade to the question of textual interpretation – always a favorite theme in his critical essays – now incorporating this interest within the complex plot of a difficult novel, *Il pendolo di Foucault* (*Foucault's Pendulum*, 1988).[1] Like Eco's first novel, the context and meaning of which are clearly enriched by at least a passing knowledge of Eco's other theoretical works on narrative theory, semiotics, and popular culture, reading *Foucault's Pendulum* will probably constitute a more satisfying experience if the reader is familiar with the social or critical problems that interested Eco during the decade following the composition of his first fictional work. In short, a successful reading of the novel requires Eco's brand of model reader.

The least frequently cited of the specific works providing a theoretical background to Eco's second novel constitutes the most important clue to the writer's thinking at this point in his career. It is a theoretical introduction to a collection of Italian essays on esoteric interpretations of Dante from the nineteenth century – *L'idea deforme: interpretazioni esoteriche di Dante* (*The Distorted Idea: Esoteric Interpreta-*

---

[1] Milan: Bompiani, 1988; English translation by William Weaver, New York: Harcourt Brace Jovanovich, 1989. Subsequent citations will be taken from these two editions.

tions of Dante, 1989) – research carried out by Eco's students in a seminar at the University of Bologna on "hermetic semiosis" that took place in 1986.[2] The essay contains a relatively complete and well-developed outline of Eco's historical contextualization of contemporary theories on interpretation and overinterpretation, views that constitute the core of two books widely distributed both in Italian and in English – *I limiti dell'interpretazione* (*The Limits of Interpretation*, 1989) and the collection of Tanner Lectures Eco presented at Cambridge University in 1990. *The Limits of Interpretation*[3] is, in many ways, far less focused than Eco's earlier compilation, *The Role of the Reader*, and its arguments on narrative theory may seem at first glance less original. It includes a number of essays ranging from a discussion of Luigi Pirandello (dating from 1968 and already included in the collection *Sugli specchi*) to treatments of James Joyce, fakes in art, animals and semiotics, Pliny the Younger, and a host of other topics. The sections relevant to *Foucault's Pendulum* – Eco's introduction and the first three chapters of the book – were delivered as lectures or first published after the appearance of *The Name of the Rose*. Like Eco's preface to *The Distorted Idea*, they deal with problems of contemporary textual interpretation by providing a historical context for such theories, linking them to past practice in Renaissance hermeticism. These essays include Eco's introduction to the book; an essay entitled "Two Models of Interpretation" (originally published in two different places in 1985 and 1987); another essay entitled "Unlimited Semiosis and Drift: Pragmaticism vs. 'Pragmatism'" (originally delivered as a lecture in 1983 at Indiana University and later revised for a second lecture at Harvard University in 1989); and a third chapter called "Intentio Lectoris: The State of the Art," which was first given as a lecture in Germany and the United States in 1986 and 1987 and was

---

[2] "La semiosi ermetica e il 'paradigma del velame'," introduction to *L'idea deforme: interpretazioni esoteriche di Dante*, ed. Maria Pia Pozzato (Milan: Bompiani, 1989), pp. 9–37.

[3] Milan: Bompiani; English translation by various hands, Bloomington: Indiana University Press, 1989.

later anthologized in 1988 in another collection of essays dedicated to new Italian philosophy.[4]

In 1990, Eco delivered the Tanner Lectures at Cambridge University, and two years later these lectures, along with responses and critiques by Richard Rorty, Jonathan Culler, and Christine Brooke-Rose, were published by Cambridge University Press as *Interpretation and Overinterpretation* and subsequently translated into Italian in 1995.[5] The core of Eco's argument in this work – a historical discussion of theories of interpretation and overinterpretation – incorporates the arguments of both *The Distorted Idea* and *The Limits of Interpretation* and, in passing, offers interesting examples of interpretative problems taken from both of Eco's novels. While it provides the most readable and accessible outline of the views on textual interpretation that occupied Eco during the gestation of *Foucault's Pendulum* and in the years immediately following its publication, it nevertheless depends heavily upon views first expressed in *The Distorted Idea* and *The Limits of Interpretation*. Because of the close interconnection between Eco's theoretical and critical writings that serve as an intellectual background to Eco's second novel, I believe it is justified to discuss them *en masse* for the purposes of simplicity and economy. We shall subsequently discuss how they enlighten our understanding of *Foucault's Pendulum*.

After spending much of his intellectual life arguing for the "open" work and textual interpretation in which the reader's response plays an active, even a dominant, role, Eco now claims that "in the course of the last decades, the rights of the interpreters have been overstressed" and

---

[4] See Giovanna Borradori, ed., *Recoding Metaphysics: The New Italian Philosophy* (Evanston, Ill: Northwestern University Press, 1988), pp. 27–43 (same title). Eco's essay joins others by Massimo Cacciari (presently the Mayor of Venice), Gianni Vattimo, and a number of the most significant thinkers of contemporary Italy.

[5] Umberto Eco, *Interpretation and Overinterpretation* with Richard Rorty, Jonathan Culler and Christine Brooke-Rose, ed. Stefan Collini (Cambridge University Press, 1992); Italian translation *Interpretazione e sovrainterpretazione: Un dibattito con Richard Rorty, Jonathan Culler e Christine Brooke-Rose*, ed. Stefan Collini (Milan: Bompiani, 1995). The Italian edition contains a "Postfazione" by Sandra Cavicchioli (pp. 183–208) that analyzes the Cambridge debate following Eco's Tanner lectures.

rejects an idea humorously suggested by Tzvetan Todorov that "a text is only a picnic where the author brings the words and the readers bring the sense."[6] His argument involves three different concepts: the intention of the author (*intentio auctoris*); the intention of the reader (*intentio lectoris*); and what he calls the intention of the text (*intentio operis*). In common-sense terms almost entirely free of the kind of scholarly jargon typical of much contemporary literary theory, Eco argues that while the intention of the work cannot be reduced to a pre-textual intention of the empirical author (thereby agreeing with both New Critics and deconstructionists), an understanding of this empirical author's intention nevertheless may serve to assist the model reader (that reader posited by the intention of the text, the *intentio operis*) in excluding or discarding certain unlikely, improbable, or even impossible interpretations of a text. The empirical author is never, in Eco's view, a privileged interpreter of his or her text but becomes a potential model reader offering possible explanations for his or her creation. Unlikely, improbable, or impossible readings constitute overinterpretation and in certain extreme instances – best reflected by the crackpot theories held by many of the "Diabolicals" in *Foucault's Pendulum* – such readings may become paranoid overinterpretations.

Beginning with Dante's own statements that his poetry contained a non-literal sense under the "veil" of difficult verse, interpreters of *The Divine Comedy* such as Gabriele Rossetti (1783–1854), Eugène Aroux (1773–1859), and Luigi Valli (1878–1931) read Dante's admittedly complex poetic work for hints of secret messages, secret societies, and elaborate conspiracies. Eco calls these critics "Followers of the Veil" (the "Adepti del Velame"). They were by no means insane or simply eccentric cranks, and in some ways they resembled the many writers on Sherlock Holmes whose work assumes that the imaginary protagonist of Conan Doyle's mystery stories actually existed and lived on Baker Street with his faithful friend Watson. Many of the "Followers

---

[6] *Interpretation and Overinterpretation*, pp. 23, 24; *Interpretazione e sovrainterpretazione*, pp. 33, 34.

of the Veil" spent their lives in dedicated scholarship, writing numerous learned tomes to prove their theories. Rossetti and Aroux, in particular, found in Dante a host of symbols and images that according to them reflected Masonic and Rosicrucian traditions and even evidence of Dante's link to the Knights Templar (all groups that play a prominent role in *Foucault's Pendulum*). Such theories run directly counter to overwhelming historical evidence, unchallenged by no responsible scholars except those who are the "Followers of the Veil." This body of scholarship demonstrates beyond a shadow of a doubt that Rosicrucian philosophy originated at the beginning of the seventeenth century and that Freemasonry derives from the first part of the eighteenth century. From a historical perspective, Dante could not have known anything about either group. However, either group could have seen in Dante a precursor and may actually have incorporated elements of Dantesque imagery into their rituals.[7]

Eco believes that many aspects of contemporary literary theory – in particular deconstructionist theory identified with Jacques Derrida and practiced by numerous American literary theorists – have licensed arbitrary interpretations of literary texts in their desire to establish the theory that an author's intentions have no privileged position in criticism of his or her works. Eco's position is relatively simple and is neatly summarized in his rebuttal to objections raised by his Tanner Lectures: "I accept the statement that a text can have many senses. I refuse the statement that a text can have every sense."[8] His critique of postmodern theories of interpretation actually pays little attention to specific works, although Derrida or Foucault are obviously in his mind and are noted briefly. Instead, Eco's primary objective is to demonstrate that "most so-called 'post-modern' thought will look very pre-antique."[9]

---

[7] For detailed discussions of these interpretations of Dante, see the various essays in *L'idea deforme*; or the far more schematic discussion in Eco's *Interpretation and Overinterpretation*, pp. 53–60, *Interpretazione e sovrainterpretazione*, pp. 66–73.

[8] *Interpretation and Overinterpretation*, p. 141; *Interpretazione e sovrainterpretazione*, p. 169.

[9] *Interpretation and Overinterpretation*, p. 25; *Interpretazione e sovrainterpretazione*, p. 36.

Eco provides an historical context for understanding the attitudes present in some contemporary thinking about textual interpretation, going back in time to the ancient world and to Renaissance humanism. He offers a summary of the classical contribution to Western thought, underlining how several key principles inherited from ancient Greece and Rome still shape intelligent reading and should serve as criteria to separate rational ideas from irrational ones. From Greece, we derive our methods of understanding causes, which presuppose several logical rules: the principle of identity (A = A); the principle of non-contradiction (it is impossible for something to be both A and not A at the same time); and the principle of the excluded middle (either A is true or A is false and *tertium non datur*). These logical principles from Greek philosophy produce the "typical pattern of thinking of Western rationalism, the *modus ponens*: 'if p, then q; but p: therefore q'."[10] The Romans transformed Greek philosophical rationalism into an ethical and legal rationalism with more obvious social dimensions, in particular identifying irrationality with lack of moderation, while rationality was identified as standing within the *modus*, within limits or within measure. This notion became an ethical principle best expressed by Horace in his *Satires* (1. 1. 106–07): "There is a *mean* in things, fixed limits on either side of which right living cannot get a foothold."[11] The Greek world produced other less rationalistic philosophical traditions, particularly in the first several centuries of the Christian era, where Eco sees the triumph of hermetic philosophy. Hermetic ideas constitute a complex set of syncretic ideas symbolized by the myth of Hermes, a myth that basically denies all the logical principles discussed earlier (identity, non-contradiction, the excluded middle), as well as the causal chains such logical principles imply.

[10] *Interpretation and Overinterpretation*, pp. 26–27; *Interpretazione e sovrainterpretazione*, pp. 38–39. Similar arguments may also be found in both *L'idea deforme* and *The Limits of Interpretation*.

[11] Eco cites the original Latin in *Interpretation and Overinterpretation*, p. 26; *Interpretazione e sovrainterpretazione*, p. 37. I cite from Horace, *The Complete Works of Horace*, trans. and ed. by Casper J. Kraemer (New York: Random House, 1936), p. 6.

Needless to say, such a syncretic philosophy also violates the Latin notion of moderation, of a mean, and stresses the most immoderate kinds of philosophical positions.

Second-century hermeticism, in particular, rejects the law of the excluded middle and asserts that many things may be true at the same time even if they stand in contradiction to one another. To hold this position, books must be transformed into complex allegories – they say one thing but mean something quite different, often something secret and "hermetically" sealed from the non-initiated. Thus truth becomes identified with what is implied (but not explicitly stated) or what is concealed under the surface, much as the esoteric readings of Dante ignored literal readings of Dante's poem and looked, instead, for a reading more conducive to conspiracy theories. But as Eco asserts:

> where the coincidence of opposites triumphs, the principle of identity collapses. *Tout se tient*. As a consequence, interpretation is indefinite . . . Hermetic thought transforms the whole world theatre into a linguistic phenomenon and at the same time denies language any power of communication.[12]

Tout se tient – everything is connected: this French phrase becomes the key to the plot of *Foucault's Pendulum*[13] and represents for Eco a view of reality that he rejects. In *The Limits of Interpretation*, Eco provides an excellent example of this kind of thinking by analogy, what he calls "hermetic drift" or the "uncontrolled ability to shift from meaning to meaning, from similarity to similarity, from a connection to an-other."[14] It is a word game where one moves in six steps from one term (his example is *peg*) to another (Eco selects *Plato* as his target). Any connection will do – metaphorical, metonymical, phonetic. Thus we connect *peg* to *pig* by sound; *pig* to *bristle*, because pigs have

---

[12] *Interpretation and Overinterpretation*, p. 32; *Interpretazione e sovrainterpretazione*, pp. 43, 44.

[13] *Foucault's Pendulum*, pp. 179, 289, 618; *Il pendolo di Foucault*, pp. 145, 230, 490.

[14] *The Limits of Interpretation* (Bloomington: Indiana University Press, 1990), pp. 26–27; see also *I limiti dell'interpretazione* (Milan: Bompiani, 1990), which does not cite this specific illustration but which makes the same general argument.

bristles; *bristle* to *brush,* because Italian masters used pig bristles to make paint brushes; *bristle* to *Mannerism,* because bristles used for paint brushes suggest an artistic movement made famous by great Italian painters; *Mannerism* to *Idea,* because Mannerism employed a notion of *concetti* or abstract concepts and ideas in its artistic theory; and finally *Idea* to *Plato,* since Plato is an idealist philosopher. As Eco says, with this kind of reasoning, "one can always win."

It is thus perfectly consistent with Eco's theoretical thinking that the main character in his novel is named Casaubon. Isaac Casaubon (1559–1614) was a Swiss philologist at the beginning of the seventeenth century who established that the Corpus Hermeticum celebrated by Renaissance humanists as a mystical text composed by Hermes Trismegistus living in Egypt before the time of Moses must have been composed, on the contrary, after the Christian era and therefore had absolutely nothing to do with ancient Egypt. The kind of ahistorical thinking that would identify a text written after the Christian era with ancient Egypt is exactly the kind of textual interpretation Eco would call, at the very least, overinterpretation, and would more likely term paranoid interpretation. In discussing the origin of the name (Casaubon) for the narrator of his second novel, Eco specifically underscores in the Tanner Lectures the fact that as an empirical author he was in fact less clever than one of his readers (David Robey) who, in a review of the novel, suggested another explanation for Casaubon – a reference to a character in George Eliot's *Middlemarch* who is (very appropriately) composing a book entitled *A Key to All Mythologies.* Robey's suggestion would seem to be as heuristic as Eco's explanation, but Eco contends not only that he did not intend a reference to George Eliot but that he specifically rejected it in the novel itself to make sure that the link to Isaac Casaubon was perceived by the careful reader. In spite of the fact that Eco himself discusses Michel Foucault's ideas about the paradigm of similarity as parallel to the conspiracy theories of his novel's characters, Eco also specifically rejects any intentional reference to Michel Foucault, insisting that Léon Foucault (1819–68), the inventor of the famous pendulum proving experimentally the rotation of the earth, is the only Foucault he meant to signify.[15]

Eco does not reject a clever reader's right to see an allusion in a text the empirical author did not intend. He merely believes that some sort of reality check needs to be imposed upon textual interpretations, and he suggests the "consensus of the community" as a possible answer.[16] In effect, Eco argues that an interpretative community (a group of Italianists reading Eco, for example) functions as a check upon outlandish or paranoid interpretations. Suggestive interpretations will engender other equally heuristic readings of a text, while overinterpretations or paranoid interpretations will eventually be refused by the community. Comparing non-useful interpretations to the sterility of a mule, Eco suggests that such non-heuristic textual interpretations will be

> unable to produce new interpretations or cannot be confronted with the traditions of the previous interpretations. The force of the Copernican revolution is not only due to the fact that it explains some astronomical phenomena better than the Ptolemaic tradition, but also to the fact that it – instead of representing Ptolemy as a crazy liar – explains why and on which grounds he was justified in outlining his own interpretation.[17]

In his discussion of the esoteric Dante scholars who read the epic

[15] *Interpretation and Overinterpretation*, pp. 81–83; *Interpretazione e sovrainterpretazione*, pp. 97–99. The strongest argument for a connection between Michel Foucault and Eco's title is made by Thomas Stauder in "*Il pendolo di Foucault*: l'autobiografia segreta di Umberto Eco," *Il lettore di provincia*, 23 (1991), 3–22. Stauder (p. 5) argues that Foucault died in Paris 25 June 1984; Belbo, one of Eco's protagonists, dies between 23 and 24 June of the same year, while Casaubon passes his final night in the novel between 26 and 27 June of 1984. Stauder refuses to believe that these dates are accidentally related and also points to the fact that Michel Foucault's *Les mots et les choses* (first published in 1966; translated into English as *The Order of Things*) was required reading for a seminar Eco once offered in Bologna.

[16] *Interpretation and Overinterpretation*, p. 144; *Interpretazione e sovrainterpretazione*, pp. 172–73.

[17] *Interpretation and Overinterpretation*, pp. 150–51; *Interpretazione e sovrainterpretazione*, p. 180.

poem as a compendium of secret knowledge, Eco closes his remarks with an interesting discussion of the relative merits of these scholars providing paranoid interpretations, on the one hand, and those more traditional scholars (Gilson, Eliot, Pound, the New Critics) who read Dante's text through the prisms of the *Patrologia Latina* or medieval poetics, on the other. Why, Eco asks rhetorically, were these "Followers of the Veil" abandoned to the dustheap of academic footnotes? Perhaps, Eco suggests, because the latter group of textual readers, forming a community of consensus and employing what he calls the "healthy sense of [textual] economy, went to seek out the secret of Dante where it had lain clearly in view for some time, like the purloined letter."[18] Textual interpretation and learning in general have some characteristics in common with the detective novel, the *whodunit* invented by Edgar Allan Poe, whose tale "The Purloined Letter" is Eco's obvious point of reference. The common-sense argument Eco makes in all his discussions of overinterpretation is that in many instances the most sensible interpretation of a text, like the purloined letter, may be found directly under our noses.

Foucault's Pendulum requires more of its reader than did *The Name of the Rose*, in part because Eco's encyclopedic knowledge in the first novel was more sharply focused upon a single historical period (the Middle Ages). In addition, the various theoretical problems that shaped the narrative, most already outlined in Eco's other theoretical works, had already paved the way for a positive reception of the novel among the intelligentsia. For the general reader, the fact that such a complex work of literature could be packaged within the popular genre of the detective story, the *whodunit*, ensured a large audience for the work by appealing to several kinds of model reader – both highbrow and lowbrow. With *Foucault's Pendulum*, Eco adopts a far more complex narrative strategy, employing a narrator (Casaubon) and other central characters (Diotallevi, Belbo) that have important autobiographical links to the author's experience as a young man

---

[18] *L'idea deforme*, p. 37 (author's translation).

during the war and later as an associate of major publishing houses during most of his career.[19] Moreover, the narrative grants an important role to a computer named Abulafia (or Abu for short). Belbo's computer is named after Samuel ben Samuel Abraham Abulafia (1240–*circa* 1292), a thirteenth-century Jewish mystic who studied the infinite combinations of the Torah and developed a system of number and letter symbolism that was influential in the development of cabbalistic thinking. We have previously discussed Eco's interest in writing as a combinative process, a thesis associated with the Paris Oulipo group which included such major writers as Italo Calvino, Georges Perec, and Raymond Queneau, one of whose works Eco translated into Italian.[20] Now, Eco incorporates the essentially "postmodernist thematics of mechanical reproduction," as one recent critic has called it,[21] directly into the novel by using large narrative blocks (twelve in all[22]) written by Casaubon's friend Belbo and hidden within the locked computer files of Abulafia.

Belbo's computer files allow Eco to provide points of view that may be compared or contrasted to the first-person narrative of Casaubon, and it also permits him to change the time sequences of the story with relative ease. In fact, Eco's novel opens on the night of June 23–24, 1984 inside the Conservatoire des Arts et Métiers in Paris, waiting for the denouement of events that have begun some fourteen years earlier. Employing a technique not unlike that in film flashbacks, the story shifts abruptly to two days before, when Casaubon

---

[19] Roberto Controneo, *La diffidenza come sistema*, provides a discussion of Eco's use of autobiographical data in his second novel, a problem that will be discussed further along in this chapter.

[20] For Oulipo, see Warren F. Motte Jr., *Oulipo: A Primer of Potential Literature*.

[21] Brian McHale, *Constructing Postmodernism*, p. 182. McHale's book devotes an entire chapter to *Foucault's Pendulum*.

[22] Manlio Talamo, *I segreti del pendolo: percorsi e giochi intorno a "Il pendolo di Foucault" di Umberto Eco* (Naples: Simone, 1989), pp. 81–99, provides a useful outline of the structure of the novel, including the breakdown of the narrative blocks from Belbo's computer files. Also worth consulting is Luigi Bauco and Francesco Millocca, *Dizionario del pendolo di Foucault*, ed. Luciano Turrini (Ferrara: Gabriele Corbo, 1989).

broke the code lock to Belbo's computer and discovered his files. Casaubon's life during the last fourteen years thus intertwines with the various computer files left behind by a Belbo who will eventually be killed on the night of June 23–24, 1984 (the night that opens the narrative). The conclusion of the novel takes place shortly after Belbo's death as Casaubon goes to Belbo's native village in Piedmont, attempts to understand not only Belbo's past during the Resistance but also his death, and awaits the arrival of the Diabolicals who have caused Belbo's death and who will surely bring about his own demise.

The dangerous situation that results first in Belbo's death and in Casaubon's imminent death derives from a long, interconnected chain of overinterpretations that transcends the category of creative overinterpretation (the kind of creative misreading critics such as Harold Bloom or others have recommended) and lands squarely inside the boundaries of paranoid interpretation. While Casaubon is completing his university thesis on the history of the Knights Templar, at Pilade's Bar, a local watering-hole Casaubon compares to Rick's American Café from the film *Casablanca*, he meets Belbo, employed at the nearby Garamond Press. Belbo is obsessed with his computer Abulafia, and the two men become friends, with Belbo introducing Casaubon to his colleague at the press, Diotallevi. Diotallevi is an albino who aspires to be Jewish, even though his friends point out to him that his name is a traditional Christian name given to orphans in the Middle Ages and afterwards. Diotallevi is also obsessed with the combinative potential of the cabbala, the mass of esoteric and mystical writings that the Jewish religion has produced through the centuries.

Originating as far back as the third century of the Christian era, cabbala became an important intellectual phenomenon in medieval France and spread into Spain and Italy. Within the literature of this movement, the Sefirot or the ten complex images of God become crucial. These ten concepts are also employed by Eco as ten major divisions in his novel: Keter ("the supreme crown"); Hokhmah ("wisdom"); Binah ("intelligence"); Hesed ("love"); Gevurah ("power"); Tiferet ("beauty"); Nezah ("victory" or "lasting endurance"); Hod ("majesty"); Yesod ("foundation"); and Malkhut ("kingdom").[23] I cite Harold Bloom's translations of these terms from his work of critical theory, *Kabbalah and Criticism*, because it is quite likely that Eco himself was influenced by this book and by Bloom's lectures at the University of Bologna which took place before the composition of *Foucault's Pendulum*. Bloom himself discusses textual interpretation in this work in the light of Peirce's semiotic theory (something that would have attracted Eco to the book in the first place), and his theory of strong readings of literary works that of necessity constitute "misreadings" must certainly have occurred to Eco when he began to fashion the overtly paranoid textual interpretations that fill the pages of his second novel.[24]

Eco's use of the ten parts of the cabbalistic Sefirot to structure his novel continues a practice begun with *The Name of the Rose* – the citation of passages in a variety of languages (including ancient Hebrew) that are practically incomprehensible to any but the most erudite of readers. It is possible to detect some general meaning or design in the ten-part structure based on the Sefirot, and Eco plays with his reader, tantalizing him or her into attempting such a textual interpretation. Some critics, but not many, have even attempted to

[23] Harold Bloom, *Kabbalah and Criticism* (New York: The Seabury Press, 1975), p. 27.
[24] For example, Bloom declares that "a reading, to be strong, must be a misreading for no strong reading can fail to insist upon itself" (*ibid.*, p. 125); or again when Bloom lists four illusions about poetry – that poetry possesses or creates (1) a real presence; (2) a kind of unity; (3) a definite form; and (4) meaning (*ibid.*, p. 122). In *Kabbalah and Criticism*, many of Bloom's ideas about textual interpretation, taken to their logical conclusions, would result in the kind of deconstructionist destruction of meaning that Eco attacks in the followers of Derrida. One of the earliest manifestos of deconstruction in the United States was a collection of essays containing works by Harold Bloom, Paul De Man, Jacques Derrida, Geoffrey H. Hartman, and J. Hillis Miller: *Deconstruction and Criticism* (New York: Continuum, 1979). Bloom made an important contribution to this collection, an essay entitled "The Breaking of Form" (pp. 1–38), even though in the introduction to the collection Geoffrey H. Hartman describes Derrida, Miller, and De Man as true deconstructionists, while he claims that Bloom and he are "barely deconstructionists" and "may even write against it on occasion" (p. ix).

see some order in the selection of these ten concepts.[25] The temptation is enormous to begin to fashion an overarching interpretation of the entire novel based upon these ten cabbalistic concepts. However, I believe Eco employs them to tempt the unwitting reader, especially the model reader accustomed to intellectual games, into drawing the same kinds of false conclusions Eco's protagonists form during the course of the novel. We should remember that the moment of truth for William of Baskerville came when the monk-detective understood that the secret entrance to the labyrinth was found in the *suppositio materialis*, one of the theories of William of Occam. William had construed the phrase *tertius equi* to refer to a real horse in the real world when, in fact, the phrase merely referred to the third letter of the word for horse, not to a real horse. The Sefirot functions in much the same fashion in Eco's second work of fiction. While attacking paranoid interpretations, Eco wants his reader to experience how easily they may be created, and there is no better or simpler method of doing this than to use these concepts to divide his book, just as the canonical hours (certainly a logical thing to find in a medieval monastery) divided the chapter headings of the first novel without necessarily offering something crucial to the book's meaning. My suspicion that Eco is putting his reader on, in the vernacular sense, finds some textual backing in the preface that Eco ironically places at the beginning of the novel:

[25] For example, Bauco and Millocca's *Dizionario del pendolo di Foucault* (pp. 12–13) argues that the plot structure "non è casuale: l'ordine corrisponde a quello previsto dell'Alberto delle sifiroth (e dall'Adam Qadmon) ed esprime un graduale passaggio, una discesa nei vari gradi del divino, dall'Eterno verso il Mondo (Malkut)." In the cabbalistic theories of Isaac Luria (1534–72), the ten parts of the Sefirot form, in the particular order followed by Eco, the divine figure of Adam Qadmon or the Celestial Adam: the first three sefirot comprise the head, the fourth and the fifth the body; the sixth the trunk; the seventh and the eighth the legs, the ninth the sexual organs; and the tenth the totality of the image (*ibid.*, p. 19). There is no doubt that Eco knew of this doctrine and followed its order in his novel. That it means anything other than a general invitation to delve deeply into cabbalistic readings of the work, thereby producing in the model reader the same kinds of paranoid readings experienced by Eco's characters, would be difficult to prove.

Only for you, children of doctrine and learning, have we written this
work. Examine this book, ponder the meaning we have dispersed in
various places and gathered again; what we have concealed in one
place we have disclosed in another, that it may be understood by
your wisdom.[26]

The quotation is taken from the *De occulta philosophia* of Heinrich
Cornelius Agrippa von Nettesheim (1486–1535), a Renaissance philosopher of the occult whose book dealt with magic, numerology, and
the power of sacred names. In my view, Eco's citation of this passage
is a completely ironic invitation to his model reader to become
bogged down in the very kinds of paranoid interpretation Eco's book
attacks. As Bloom suggests, "the *Sefirot* fascinate because they suggest
an immutable knowledge of a final reality that stands behind our
world of appearances."[27] It is precisely this fatal fascination for an
immutable, final reality that Eco attacked in *The Name of the Rose* and
which he continues to reject in *Foucault's Pendulum*.

The references to such critics as Bloom, Derrida, or Foucault, a
recent critical reading of the novel reminds us, point to the fact that
Eco's second novel "participates in the genre of academic novels
practiced during the late 1970s and throughout the 1980s by British
authors David Lodge and Malcolm Bradbury . . . labeled *critifictional*,"
novels which provide both fictional accounts of academic life and
polemics directed against various schools of literary theory, especially
deconstructionists.[28] In *Foucault's Pendulum* this relatively contemporary genre popular among academic readers merges with the detective
novel genre so appealing to the general public, since the entire
narrative of Eco's second novel suggests that there is an enormous

[26] *Foucault's Pendulum*, p. i; *Il pendolo di Foucault*, p. 5.

[27] Bloom, *Kabbalah and Criticism*, p. 28. For a very different interpretation of these Sefirot
which are accepted as a true narrative pattern, see Cristina Degli-Esposti, "The Poetics
of Hermeticism in Umberto Eco's *Il pendolo di Foucault*,' *Forum Italicum* 25, no. 2 (1991),
190.

[28] Norma Bouchard, "*Critifictional* Epistemes in Contemporary Literature: The Case of
Foucault's Pendulum," *Comparative Literature Studies* 32, no. 4 (1995), 50.

cosmic plot organized by some very sinister groups of individuals that has existed for some centuries – a kind of cosmic *whodunit*. By joining two normally separate narrative genres, Eco once again hopes to bridge the gap between two very different kinds of audience. As with the model reader he envisioned for *The Name of the Rose*, Eco has assumed a model reader for his second novel who is as comfortable among diabolical conspirators, literary theorists, and occult philosophers as he or she is with literary policemen and fictional private investigators.

One of the aspects of *Foucault's Pendulum* that the novel shares with many of the *critifictional* novels of recent publication (particularly those by David Lodge), is its humorous portrait of publishing houses, universities, and academics in general. The three main characters in the novel – Casaubon, Belbo, and Diotallevi – all work for the Garamond Press, supposedly a serious publishing house which houses another less serious and far more lucrative publishing operation, the Manutius Press, which is a vanity press for Self Financing Authors (SFAs). The cynical manner in which the three men and their publisher manipulate the hapless SFAs in order to squeeze money out of them for their useless and usually unreadable manuscripts speaks volumes about a certain atmosphere within the publishing industry that Eco knows very well from first-hand experience. The humor is bittersweet when one realizes that Claude Garamond (1499–1562) and Aldo Manuzio or Manutius (1450–1515) are among the heroic early pioneers of European printing: Garamond invented the elegant type still employed today by the world's best publishers; Manutius established the famous Venetian printing press identified by the colophon of anchor and dolphin (still employed by Doubleday Anchor Books), and Manutius was a pioneer in creating editions of the classics in small, affordable formats. The owner of the Garamond Press, named after a mysterious Mr. Garamond, is an unsavory figure who eventually is revealed to be one of the Diabolicals responsible for the death of Belbo and the pursuit of Casaubon.

Eco's portrait of work inside the Garamond publishing firm, his discussion of Casaubon's research, and his description of Belbo's computer also provide him with occasions for comic relief. The discussions within the Garamond firm about an educational reform involving a School of Comparative Irrelevance produce a list of useless or ridiculous courses offered by a number of departments. The Department of Tetrapyloctomy (the art of splitting a hair four ways) would serve an introductory function to inculcate a sense of irrelevance in the students. Possible courses here would include Potiosection (the art of slicing soup); Pylocatabasis (the art of being saved by a hair); or Mechanical Avunculogratulation (how to build machines for greeting uncles). The Department of Adynata or Impossibilia would instruct students to understand the reasons for a thing's absurdity by studying empirical impossibilities. Here, the student might follow seminars on Urban Planning for Gypsies, Morse Syntax, the History of Eastern Island Painting, the Phonetics of the Silent Film, or Crowd Psychology in the Sahara. Another important academic unit would be the Department of Oxymoronics, or self-contradictions. Here, typical courses would include Nomadic Urban Planning for Gypsies, Tradition in Revolution, and Democratic Oligarchy.[29]

Belbo's theory of the four kinds of people in the world is an example of the sense of humor Eco usually reserved for his occasional essays in such collections as *Misreadings* or *How to Travel with a Salmon & Other Essays*. According to Belbo, the world may be divided into four groups: cretins, fools, morons, and lunatics. Cretins are not worthy of discussion (examples are people who hit themselves in the face with ice cream cones or enter a revolving door the wrong way). Fools are more interesting, for they put their foot in their mouth (they ask how one's wife is just after she has left her husband). Belbo's best example of a fool is Joachim Murat reviewing troops returning from Martinique: Murat asks an obviously black soldier "Are you a negro?" and when the man replies in the affirmative, Murat responds: "Good,

---

[29] *Foucault's Pendulum*, pp. 74–75; *Il pendolo di Foucault*, pp. 66–68.

good, carry on!"[30] Morons, on the other hand, never make a mistake but mix up their reasoning. Their thought runs in the following pattern: all dogs are pets; all dogs bark; cats are pets; therefore cats bark. Morons are tricky and may even win Nobel prizes, and as Belbo says, the entire history of logic represents an attempt to define an acceptable idea of moronism. Lunatics are morons without a logic behind their thinking, even the kind of false syllogism that concludes cats bark. Lunatics believe everything proves everything else, everything is connected. Lunatics, in other words, believe that *tout se tient*, and according to Belbo, they always bring up the subject of the Knights Templar.

Lunatics are thus at the focal point of *Foucault's Pendulum*, and Eco considers any textual interpretation based upon the concept of universal connectedness as bordering on the insane or the paranoid. As Casaubon, Diotallevi, and Belbo discuss the strange theories of those who are obsessed with the Knights Templar (Causabon's thesis topic), they devise an elaborate parody of the interpretative paranoia of the various diabolicals, what they call "The Plan." This Plan is born after a meeting with a Colonel Ardenti, an old fascist officer who believes that the Templars had a plot to conquer the world. After their order was destroyed by the King of France in 1307, Ardenti believes the Templars went underground, and his attention is focused upon the city of Provins (a site with a maze of underground caves, perfect – according to Ardenti – for a group plotting to take over the world). Visiting Provins, Ardenti meets the daughter of a man named Ingolf (another believer in the Templars as conspirators), and in Ingolf's library Ardenti discovers several interesting documents, including one written in old French but missing some crucial letters:

a la ... Saint Jean
36 p charrete de fein

---

[30] This discussion may be found in *Foucault's Pendulum*, pp. 63–67 ; *Il pendolo di Foucault*, pp. 58–60. I have supplied English translations for the story about Murat, which is in French even in the English version of the novel.

6 . . . *entiers avec saiel*

p . . . *les blancs mantiax*

r . . . *s* . . . *chevaliers de Pruins pour la* . . . *j.nc*

6 *foix 6 en 6 places*

chascune foix 20 a . . . *120 a* . . .

iceste est l'ordonation

al donjon le premiers

it li secunz joste iceus qui . . . *pans*

it al refuge

it a Nostre Dame de l'altre part de l'iau

it a l'ostel des popelicans

it a la pierre

3 foix 6 avant la feste . . . *la Grant Pute.*[31]

Ardenti's translation of this puzzling document reads as follows:

THE (NIGHT OF) SAINT JOHN

36 (YEARS) P(OST) HAY WAIN

6 (MESSAGES) INTACT WITH SEAL

F(OR THE KNIGHTS WITH) THE WHITE CLOAKS [TEMPLARS]

R(ELAP)S(I) OF PROVINS FOR (VAIN)JANCE [REVENGE]

6 TIMES 6 IN SIX PLACES

EACH TIME 20 Y(EARS MAKES) 120 Y(EARS)

THIS IS THE PLAN

THE FIRST GO TO THE CASTLE

IT(ERUM) [AGAIN AFTER 120 YEARS] THE SECOND JOIN THOSE
  (OF THE) BREAD

AGAIN TO THE REFUGE

AGAIN TO OUR LADY BEYOND THE RIVER

AGAIN TO THE HOSTEL OF THE POPELICANS

AGAIN TO THE STONE

3 TIMES 6 [666] BEFORE THE FEAST (OF THE) GREAT WHORE.

Beginning with this intriguing document, the three friends at Garamond launch an elaborate parody of the various conspiracy theories

---

[31] This passage, as well as the English translation of the old French documents, is found
in *Foucault's Pendulum*, pp. 135–36; *Il pendolo di Foucault*, pp. 111–12.

that are held by the numerous crackpot authors they encounter among the Self Financing Authors who frequent the Manutius Press. These Diabolicals, as they are called, have similar ideas concerning not only the Templars but also Freemasons, Rosicrucians, the Jesuits, the Jews, the Nazis, the search for the Grail, the existence of telluric currents that can control the world, and so forth – all of which reflect the paranoid brand of textual interpretation Eco discusses in his theoretical works. The mega-conspiracy they construct with the assistance of Abulafia constitutes an amalgamation of all possible conspiracies, and "The Plan" concentrates upon making "sense" out of Ingolf's document by spinning out every conceivable connection between one conspiracy theory and another. Thus, Ingolf's document can be read to mean that the Templars had planned to meet every 120 years in six different locations, and when these meetings were missed due to various simple events (such as the reform of the calendar), various groups of conspirators spend the next several centuries attempting to contact each other to return to the originally planned encounters.

Needless to say, Casaubon, Belbo, and Diotallevi are extremely amused with the cleverness of their imaginary construction, since it is arranged in such a way that the interconnectedness of their material explains everything from the Crusades to the Holocaust. As Diotallevi puts it: "Not bad, not bad at all . . . To arrive at the truth through the painstaking reconstruction of a false text."[32] The governing principle of their creation rests upon a point of view best expressed by Belbo:

> Any fact becomes important when it's connected to another. The connection changes the perspective; it leads you to think that every detail of the world, every voice, every word written or spoken has more than its literal meaning, that it tells us of a Secret. The rule is simple: Suspect, only suspect. You can read subtexts even in a traffic sign that says "No littering."[33]

[32] *Foucault's Pendulum*, p. 459; *Il pendolo di Foucault*, p. 362.
[33] *Foucault's Pendulum*, pp. 377–78; *Il pendolo di Foucault*, p. 300.

To prove his point, Belbo then proceeds to demonstrate how a driver's manual can be interpreted to represent the Tree of the Sefirot: the ten parts of the engine equal the ten Sefirot!

In constructing "The Plan," the three intellectuals have forgotten a basic axiom of social behavior: things perceived as real (such as their elaborate meta-conspiracy) are real in their consequences. The Diabolicals of every description, upon hearing of this plan, naturally assume that there is a "Truth" behind it that only the three men possess, and they determine to learn the "Truth" from the three friends. Diotallevi dies of cancer and is therefore beyond their reach, but Belbo meets his death literally bound to Foucault's pendulum in Paris, refusing to reveal the "secret" of the plan to the frenzied Diabolicals, and as the novel concludes, Casaubon awaits their arrival to interrogate him as well in Belbo's home in Piedmont. As he waits, he summarizes the "rules" of their Plan:

> Rule One: Concepts are connected by analogy . . . Rule Two says
> that if tout se tient in the end, the connecting works . . . Rule Three:
> The connections must not be original. They must have been made
> before, and the more often the better, by others. Only then do the
> crossings seem true, because they are obvious . . . But if you invent a
> plan and others carry it out, it's as if the Plan exists. At that point it
> does exist.[34]

Eco's novel presents an intriguing overview of the mishaps that can occur when paranoid reading takes control of interpretation. Yet, as Eco is surely aware (and as Brian McHale has pointed out), this kind of textual interpretation is practiced not just by the lunatic fringe but by "other, thoroughly 'respectable' and mainstream interpretative communities as well."[35] Policemen and intelligence organizations collect information in a paranoid manner, amassing it without necessarily knowing a priori that connections exist between their data. Often, the

---

[34] *Foucault's Pendulum*, p. 618; *Il pendolo di Foucault*, pp. 489–90.
[35] McHale, *Constructing Postmodernism*, p. 169.

most absurd bits of information in espionage, counter-espionage, or simple detective work prove invaluable clues to the solution of a problem. In like manner, professional readers, McHale reminds us – including students, professors, reviewers, and Eco himself – have acquired "paranoid reading skills in response to the challenge of modernist verbal art, through the process of learning how to read modernist texts properly and, by extension, how to read pre-modernist texts modernistically."[36] There is a sinister aspect to Eco's humorous presentation of paranoid interpretation that transcends his parody of academic discourse. Eco identifies the same kind of thinking applied to the practical realm of politics as fascist and racist. Thus, *Foucault's Pendulum* also offers a grotesque caricature of the mentality that Eco will eventually call "Ur-Fascism" in a lecture presented at Columbia University years later.[37]

Casaubon, Diotallevi, and Belbo first treat Ingolf's cryptic text with derision, but as they develop their Plan, their parodic intentions begin to be transformed into belief, as they, too, like the Diabolicals, are mesmerized by the interconnectedness they can posit between any bit of information, following the principle *tout se tient*. Casaubon's girlfriend Lia (the Italian equivalent of Leah) provides what Eco as narrator clearly regards as a non-paranoid, common-sense interpretation of the document. We are first introduced to Lia in chapter thirty-five of the novel, the opening of which is introduced by a citation from Dante's *Purgatorio* xxvii (100–02). This citation represents the key to Lia's function in the novel but a key which requires familiarity with the next two tercets of Dante's poem:

> "If anyone should want to know my name,
> I am called Leah. And I spend all my time
> weaving garlands of flowers with my fair hands,

---

[36] *Ibid.*, p. 170.

[37] See "Ur-Fascism," *The New Review of Books* 42, no. 11 (22 July 1995), 12–15. The lecture forming the basis of this article was delivered at Columbia University on 25 April 1995.

to please me when I stand before my mirror;
my sister Rachel sits all the day long
before her own and never moves away.
She loves to contemplate her lovely eyes;
I love to use my hands to adorn myself:
her joy is in reflection, mine in act."[38]

As any good medievalist or Dante scholar would know, the biblical story of Leah and Rachel (Genesis 29:10–31) was interpreted in the Middle Ages as an allegory for two different ways of finding satisfaction in a Christian life: an active life (Leah's gathering of flowers) or the contemplative life (Rachel's contemplation of herself in the mirror). In Eco's novel, Lia not only produces a child, which will be revealed as the ultimate reality in the entire novel – it will be known as "The Thing" which the narrator juxtaposes to "The Plan" that is merely a figment of a paranoid fantasy. But she also offers the most sensible explanation of Ingolf's document in chapter 106 of the novel. Using both common sense (contacting the tourist agency of Provins), traditional philology (she construes the repetitious word *item* as the standard manner in which medieval merchants made a list), and a bit of historical knowledge found in guide books (Provins was once a major center for the trade of cloth and roses), Lia comes to the extremely reasonable conclusion that Ingolf's mysterious document is, in reality, a laundry list drawn up by a merchant of the period. This merchant is paid in 36 coins for some hay; he delivers some fabric to a street that still exists in the town; he delivers six bunches of roses to six different locations, each costing 20 "deniers" for a total of 120; and the six different locations are still on the town map. Here is her translation of the message:

In Rue Saint Jean:
36 sous for wagons of hay.
Six new lengths of cloth with seal

[38] Dante, *The Divine Comedy – Vol. II: Purgatory*, trans. Mark Musa (New York: Penguin, 1985), p. 293.

into rue des Blancs-Manteaux.

Crusaders' roses to make a jonchée:

six bunches of six in the six following places,

each 20 deniers, making 120 deniers in all.

Here is the order:

the first to the Fort

item the second to those in Porte-aux-Pains

item to the Church of the Refuge

item to the Church of Notre Dame, across the river

item to the old building of the Cathars

item to rue de la Pierre-Ronde

and three bunches of six before the feast, in the whores' street.[39]

It is difficult, indeed almost impossible, for a professionally trained reader not to jump to the kinds of conclusions Casaubon and his friends had first imagined and in which subsequently they have begun to believe. They, like the biblical character Rachel, believe in contemplation, in textual readings that are metatextual readings and which reflect upon themselves rather than derive confirmation from inferential walks outside their imagination. Lia, on the other hand, anchored in the corporeal reality of giving birth, keeps her interpretative feet based solidly upon common sense and believes (like Eco) that the simplest and most economical explanation generally constitutes the best one.[40]

Unfortunately, neither Belbo nor Casaubon can tell the frenzied Diabolicals that there is no Plan. Their paranoid perspective assumes the existence of a secret: to tell them that the secret consists in knowing that there is no secret (a version of the Socratic wisdom that the wise man is he who realizes he is not wise) would destroy the

---

[39] *Foucault's Pendulum*, p. 536; *Il pendolo di Foucault*, p. 421.

[40] Were I a Diabolical critic, I would interpret the Lia/Rachel reference, given its location in a book on *Foucault's* pendulum, as a reference to Michel Foucault's postmodern classic, *The Order of Things: An Archaeology of the Human Sciences*. Foucault's book begins with a discussion of Velàzquez's *Las Meninas*, a painting containing an image reflected in a mirror that Foucault selects as the archetypal example of the effacement of the subject and representational mimesis.

foundation upon which their hermetic semiosis is based. If the Diabolicals had been asked (as Casaubon was when he tried to break into Belbo's Abulafia), "Do you have the password?", they would have been incapable of providing the proper response: "NO."[41]

The various harebrained views that constitute the Diabolicals' distorted perspectives have naturally attracted the lion's share of commentary on *Foucault's Pendulum*, especially since Eco's unflattering portrait of overinterpretation or paranoid interpretation in his second novel also involves a devastating value judgment upon certain contemporary trends in literary theory associated with Jacques Derrida, deconstructionism, and Michel Foucault. Little critical interest, however, has been paid to what Eco undoubtedly intended to be one of the high-points of his novel, the death of Belbo upon the pendulum in Paris and Casaubon's subsequent discovery of what Eco calls the "Key Text," a manuscript that Casaubon examines while he is waiting for the Diabolicals to come for him in the study of Belbo's Uncle Carlo. This manuscript, abandoned or hidden long after Belbo came to the depressing realization that he did not have the talent to be a serious writer (perhaps the ultimate reason Belbo enjoyed the experiments with mechanical writing and Abulafia), provides some explanation of why Belbo stood firm and died rather than reveal the truth to the Diabolicals that there was no Plan. Belbo's manuscript describes events which took place at the end of April 1945, the end of the war and the partisan experience – a defining moment in modern Italian history that gave birth to postwar neo-realist culture.

As a young boy, Belbo had always wanted to play the trumpet, and when the partisans decided upon a grandiose funeral for some of their fallen comrades, Belbo seemed to have found his chance. At the appointed moment, Belbo had played a single, solitary note on the trumpet, holding it for what seemed like eternity. In that moment, fixed forever in the "Key Text" that Belbo abandoned, along with his

[41] *Foucault's Pendulum*, p. 42; *Il pendolo di Foucault*, p. 41.

vocation as a writer, Belbo had come as close as he ever would to a revelation of truth. As Casaubon puts it:

> You spend a life seeking the Opportunity, without realizing that the decisive moment, the moment that justifies birth and death, has already passed. It will not return, but it was – full, dazzling, generous as every revelation. That day, Jacopo Belbo stared into the eyes of Truth. The only truth that was to be granted him. Because – he would learn – truth is brief (afterward it is all commentary). So he tried to arrest the rush of time. He didn't understand. Not as a child. Not as an adolescent when he was writing about it. Not as a man who decided to give up writing about it. I understood it this evening: the author has to die in order for the reader to become aware of his truth.[42]

Casaubon describes this magic moment in Belbo's narrative in mystical terms – as the conclusion of the Great Work discussed by the mystics, as the essence of Malkhut or revelation. Eco's remark that the author must die before his work can have meaning agrees with a famous remark that Pier Paolo Pasolini made on numerous occasions. The passage cited above also represents Eco's homage to the influence of James Joyce, since Belbo's "Key Text" describes an epiphany, a concept that Joyce made famous in *A Portrait of the Artist as a Young Man* and which Eco himself analyzes in an important section of *The Aesthetics of Chaosmos: The Middle Ages of James Joyce*.[43] Readers of *Foucault's Pendulum* have no doubt ignored commentary on the novel's conclusion because, at first glance, it seems curiously out of place in a book that has concerned itself almost entirely with various types of crackpot or paranoid interpretations not only of texts but of the world in general. But Belbo's "Key Text" also becomes

---

[42] *Foucault's Pendulum*, p. 633; *Il pendolo di Foucault*, p. 501.

[43] See *The Aesthetics of Chaosmos*, pp. 23–32, or *Opera aperta*, pp. 250–63, for Eco's discussion of epiphany. Eco sees Joyce's concept of epiphany as being derived not only from the aesthetics of Walter Pater but also from Gabriele d'Annunzio, whose work Joyce knew well and whose novel *Il fuoco* contains a chapter entitled "Epifania del fuoco."

Casaubon's key text as well (and, I believe, that of the model author constructed by this novel, if not the empirical author himself): "But that moment, in which he froze space and time, shooting his Zeno's arrow, had been no symbol, no sign, symptom, allusion, metaphor, or enigma: it was what it was. It did not stand for anything else."[44] Casaubon, too, experiences a similar epiphany during the final two sentences of the novel: "So I might as well stay here, wait, and look at the hill. It's so beautiful."[45]

Eco's conclusion is an extraordinary ending for a novel written by one of the world's authorities on semiotics. It paradoxically praises a moment in which things represent, signify, symbolize, stand for, or allude to nothing but themselves – in short, a state of grace in which there is absolutely no need for semiotics! It would be an edenic moment in which comprehension and apprehension would coincide completely and ideally. Such a conclusion seems perfectly consistent with the lessons both Belbo and Casaubon learn from their disastrous tinkering with paranoid overinterpretation and the various conspiracy theories held by the different Diabolicals. Of course, the model author remains aware that Casaubon's conclusion, so seemingly at odds with the general theory of semiotics (not to mention the entire career of the empirical author, the man Umberto Eco) itself represents the model author's interpretation of Casaubon's interpretation. As such, it constitutes yet another step in the process of unlimited semiosis. Earlier in his academic career, Umberto Eco fervently pursued the discipline of semiotics as a means of ferreting out not one truth but many different truths coexisting in our sublunary condition. The discipline of semiotics had been presented as an appropriate philosophical response to mankind's perennial epistemological questions. In *The Name of the Rose*, however, Eco followed Wittgenstein's dictum, turning to fictional narration presumably when the important truths he wished to discuss could not

---

[44] *Foucault's Pendulum*, p. 633; *Il pendolo di Foucault*, p. 502.
[45] *Foucault's Pendulum*, p. 641; *Il pendolo di Foucault*, p. 509.

be adequately treated by philosophical means. At the conclusion of *Foucault's Pendulum*, Eco continues what is in actuality an exaltation of the philosophical potential of fiction. Now, however, the fact that the human condition cannot avoid interpretation or the search for meaning within a jungle of confusing, often contradictory signs, represents a fundamentally tragic state to which we, like the author, are eternally condemned.

seven

§

Inferential strolls and narrative shipwrecks: *Six walks* and *The Island of the Day Before*

Although Eco's entire literary career has been marked by a vast production of works, making it difficult for his critics or intellectual biographers even to keep abreast of what he has written, Eco was unusually prolific after the appearance of *Foucault's Pendulum*. In 1992, the long-awaited sequel to the popular *Diario minimo* appeared – *Il secondo diario minimo* – which received a partial English translation as *How to Travel with a Salmon & Other Essays*.[1] On October 2, 1992, Eco received an unusual honor – induction into the celebrated Collège de France in Paris. His inaugural lecture there was entitled "La quête d'une langue parfaite dans l'histoire de la culture europénne" (The Quest for a Perfect Language in the History of European Culture), which later formed the nucleus of another learned study of the "confusion of Babel." This work, *La ricerca della lingua perfetta*, appeared in 1993 and was translated two years later as *The Search for the*

---

[1] The original Italian edition contains a number of items not reproduced in the English translation. These include the previously mentioned *Filosofi in libertà*, as well as many extraordinary word puzzles, anagrams, and goliardic jokes Eco and his university colleagues have invented while at local taverns in Bologna. One example, that of the game of the "ircocervo," will suffice. An "ircocervo" is a mythical animal, half goat and half deer, and therefore a natural impossible in the real world. This game consists of successfully forming a punning response to an artificial name composed, like the "ircocervo," of two different names or titles. Thus, "Stanley Rubik – Doctor Cube, I presume?"; "Clark Kant – A Critique of Pure Cryptonite"; "Woody Alien – Starwar Memories."

Perfect Language.[2] And in 1992–93 Eco delivered the prestigious Charles Eliot Norton Lectures at Harvard University. They were published first in English in the following year and in Italian shortly thereafter.[3] After the publication of *Foucault's Pendulum*, Eco had jokingly confessed to an interviewer that he composed his second novel only to prove to skeptics that he was not a flash-in-the-pan writer and that he was, indeed, capable of writing more than a single fictional work: "To write a third novel," Eco mused, "is the same as writing thirty novels, it no longer means anything."[4] Nevertheless, as if to contradict his own statement, in the fall of 1994 Eco brought out a third major work of imaginative fiction, *L'isola del giorno prima* (*The Island of the Day Before*),[5] marking a period of furious publication activity spanning less than a decade since the publication of his second novel.

Nothing Eco has ever written is completely without interest, but some readers may judge a few of his latest publications to be mildly disappointing. They may reach such a conclusion because Eco's previous intellectual developments were far more dramatic, and his readers have naturally come to expect major shifts, even leaps, in his thinking from one methodology to another, from one subject to another, from one genre to another. After three novels and a number of major essays on the interpretation of fiction, Eco's interests have now come to focus primarily upon literature and literary theory informed by semiotic principles and less upon pure semiotic theory itself. A good example of this more narrowly defined but sharpened

---

[2] Rome: Laterza, 1993; Oxford: Basil Blackwell, 1995. The book appeared in a new series called "The Making of Europe," which publishes books by five different European presses in five languages (English, German, French, Spanish, and Italian). The series treats central themes in the history of the European peoples and their cultures.

[3] Umberto Eco, *Six Walks in the Fictional Woods* (Cambridge: Harvard University Press, 1994); translated as *Sei passeggiate nei boschi narrativi: Harvard University, Norton Lectures 1992–1993* (Milan: Bompiani, 1994).

[4] Thomas Stauder, "Un colloquio con Umberto Eco su *Il pendolo di Foucault*," *Il lettore di provincia* 21, 75 (1989), 11 (author's translation).

[5] Milan: Bompiani, 1994; New York: Harcourt Brace & Company, 1995, translated by William Weaver.

perspective is *The Search for the Perfect Language*, Eco's study of Europe's quest for an explanation of what occurred when Adam created names for the animals and the objects on earth shortly after the Creation, as well as what transpired after the Tower of Babel sowed linguistic confusion among the world's peoples. Eco himself defined its subject-matter as the history of ideas rather than linguistics or semiotics, but it should not be forgotten that one of Eco's most interesting semiotic essays concerned edenic language and the process of inventing names in the Garden of Eden.[6] Thus, semiotic theory has not been completely abandoned in this *tour de force* of erudition that guides the reader on a whirlwind tour of Europe's most arcane documents on language. Some of the territory Eco covers has obvious links to earlier writings, such as his treatments of linguistic theory linked to cabbalistic writers or semioticians, or his discussions of the art of memory in works by Ramon Lull. We also detect behind the learned footnotes and intricate argumentation the personality of the tolerant, inquisitive, and broad-minded author that has always made Eco's work so appealing. This stance of cultural openness is apparent in Eco's belief that European culture arose "as a reflection on the destiny of a multilingual civilization"; rather than establish a single, unified language as the lingua franca of the Old World, Eco believes a united Europe should respect linguistic differences and create a "community of peoples with an increased ability to receive the spirit, to taste or savour the aroma of different dialects":

> Polyglot Europe will not be a continent where individuals converse fluently in all the other languages; in the best of cases, it could be a continent where differences of language are no longer barriers to communication, where people can meet each other and speak together, each in his or her own tongue, understanding, as best they can, the speech of others. In this way, even those who never learn to speak another language fluently could still participate in its particular genius, catching a glimpse of the particular cultural universe that

---

[6] *The Search for the Perfect Language*, p. 5; *La ricerca della lingua perfetta*, p. 10.

every individual expresses each time he or she speaks the language of
his or her ancestors and his or her own tradition.[7]

Believing fervently in a united but culturally diversified Europe, Eco
ultimately hopes for the same kind of miracle that occurs in the New
Testament when, at Pentecost, the gift of tongues was received by the
apostles. Reading the Bible closely, however, Eco notes that St. Paul
describes the Pentecost in Corinthians 1:12–13 as a gift of *glossolalia* –
the ability to express oneself in an ecstatic language that can be
understood by everyone as if it were his or her native speech – while
in the Acts of the Apostles 2, Pentecost is described as the gift of
speaking in *other* tongues, which is not *glossolalia* but rather *xenoglossia*
(a form of polyglottism or a mystic kind of simultaneous translation).[8]
Ultimately, therefore, Eco's erudition serves as the basis for an
extremely engaged political and cultural position on European unity
through linguistic diversity. *The Search for the Perfect Language* is an
exhaustively researched, learned, and informative academic book. Yet
it cannot be termed a new departure in his thought and is, instead, an
admirable example of traditional scholarship informed by semiotic
theory that is practiced by an intellectual at the top of his form.

The most demanding reader may also conclude that when compared with the subtle irony and the eclectic intellectual acrobatism of
the first *Diario minimo*, the sequel collection fails to engage the reader
in the same fashion. The majority of these essays, particularly those
selected for English translation, come from the "Bustina di Minerva"
column Eco has written since 1985 for *L'Espresso*, the left-of-center
weekly news magazine that vies with *Panorama* in Italy for a large
audience of educated middle-class readers. They display the sense of
humor always associated with their author, but there is a subtle shift
of emphasis in these essays. When Eco wrote *Diario minimo*, he was a
moderately well-known intellectual identified with counter-culture
ideas, such as the "open work," and his satirical barbs were almost

---

[7] *The Search for the Perfect Language*, pp. 18, 350–51; *La ricerca della lingua perfetta*, pp. 25, 377.
[8] *The Search for the Perfect Language*, p. 351; *La ricerca della lingua perfetta*, p. 377.

always directed at the most important intellectual trends of the period – the Frankfurt school, the new anthropology, literary movements such as the French New Novel, and so forth. In short, Eco's subject-matter, even when mercilessly parodied, was always considered to be of more moment than the author of the parody. In the sequel to *Diario minimo*, the emphasis has shifted to focus upon Eco himself – now a world-famous, best-selling novelist. In a sense, by virtue of the fact that the bulk of the material contained in the sequel volume comes from a weekly magazine column, Eco has become the embodiment of what Italians often call a "tuttologo" – a person who knows something about everything. Very few contemporary writers can match Eco's erudition or humor in their fictional creations, but there is something intrinsically less sympathetic about a nearly omniscient essayist who discusses himself frequently (the case in so many of the brief columns from *Il secondo diario minimo*). Omniscient narrators in a fictional framework are far more amusing. The task of providing a witty essay every week for a widely circulated news magazine seems to have taken its toll on Eco in this second collection, and the rhetorical formula employed in most of the essays ("how to . . .") sometimes seems slightly repetitious.

The structure of Eco's "how to . . ." essays follows a generally simple pattern. The author presents a dilemma-like situation or a paradoxical proposition with an apparently simple answer or situation. He then reveals hidden absurdities in the obvious answer or evaluation of the situation he has described. For example, in one of the best of these essays (the argument of which Eco repeats shortly thereafter in *Six Walks*) the author discusses "How to Recognize a Porn Movie." The obvious definition of an X-rated film – that it contains explicit sex scenes – is first considered but rejected as insufficient. Instead, Eco declares paradoxically that it is the calculation of how much time is wasted in such a movie that defines its pornographic character: "to put it simply, crudely, in porn movies, before you can see a healthy screw you have to put up with a documentary that could be sponsored by the Traffic Bureau."[9] Such scenes of normal activity within a film devoted to purely sexual activities, Eco believes, are absolutely essential for a pornographic film, since the audience could not endure a work completely given over to the amorous couplings of the actors and needs some narrative breathing room to accept the sex scenes (which are infrequent and interrupt interminable scenes of normalcy) as "real." The idea, employed in Eco's weekly column to arouse a knowing smile from his mass audience, is later inserted in a far more serious discussion in *Six Walks* of the distinction between "lingering" in a narrative situation when one reads, on the one hand, and hurrying through the story to arrive at its conclusion, on the other.[10] This particular essay is one of Eco's best efforts in his second collection and seems not to reflect the formulaic writing that mars some of these brief pieces. It is a pity that the English translation does not contain the admittedly difficult collections of word games that the Italian edition of *Il secondo diario minimo* reprints, since they are fascinating. However, most of them are simply untranslatable. They do reveal a most sympathetic side of Eco's personality – the goliardic and genial drinking companion in a Bologna tavern matching wits with his university colleagues, writers, and friends.

While Eco's popular essays may sometimes be weakened by their formulaic, repetitive quality (no doubt caused by his frequent editorial deadlines), the same kinds of flaws cannot be found in Eco's *Six Walks in the Fictional Woods*. Instead, Eco's skill as a master critic is here everywhere apparent in this beautiful little collection based upon Eco's Harvard Norton Lectures. The quality of this work is not dependent upon its complete originality. On the contrary, the ideas expressed in *Six Walks*, for the most part, have already been outlined in *The Reader in the Story* or its partial English translation, *The Role of*

---

[9] *How To Travel with a Salmon*, p. 224; *Il secondo diario minimo*, p. 131 (the original Italian essay was written in 1989).

[10] See *Six Walks*, pp. 61–62; *Sei passeggiate*, pp. 76–77.

the Reader. We may remember that the central concept from his earlier narrative theory was Eco's definition of the model reader, his belief that an "author" was nothing but a textual strategy activating the model reader, and the view that reading consists of making a certain number of semiotic abductions which require the reader to move outside the text from time to time during "inferential walks" that gather intertextual support for understanding what is being read. Subsequently, in *Interpretation and Overinterpretation*, Eco outlined his views on the intention of the author, the intention of the reader, and the intention of the text, rejecting making the empirical author of any work a privileged interpreter of his creation but admitting that the empirical author may become a potential model reader offering possible explanations for the work's meaning, a position opposed to the deconstructionists' view that texts can be considered as author-less and capable of unlimited interpretation.

In *Six Walks*, Eco does not retract or modify the theories about narrative developed in these earlier works. Instead, he broadens his previous discussions and enriches his earlier definitions with concrete analyses of various narrative problems. He provides satisfying and entertaining close readings of examples taken from his own novels, as well as from other classic narratives, such as Nerval's *Sylvie*, Poe's short stories, *The Three Musketeers* by Dumas, and Ian Fleming's James Bond novels. Before presenting his discussion of how a reader may wander in a fictional wood, Eco evokes the spirits of two earlier Norton lecturers – Jorge Luis Borges and Italo Calvino. In *The Name of the Rose*, Eco had employed the metaphor of the labyrinthine library and the suggestive name of its evil librarian as an homage to the postmodernist influence of Borges. Here, the very metaphor at the basis of his Norton Lectures, the narrative wood, owes its existence to his Argentine model:

> To use a metaphor devised by Jorge Luis Borges (another spirit who is very much present in these talks and who gave his own Norton lectures twenty-five years ago), a wood is a garden of forking paths.

Even when there are no well-trodden paths in a wood, everyone can trace his or her own path, deciding to go to the left or to the right of a certain tree and making a choice at every tree encountered. In a narrative text, the reader is forced to make choices all the time . . . there are cases in which the author wants sadistically to show us that we are not Stanley but Livingstone, and that we are doomed to get lost in the woods by continuing to make the wrong choices.[11]

If the book's dominant metaphor owes a debt to Borges, one of the most important literary influences upon his fictional works, the tone of *Six Walks* bears witness to the benevolent influence of Italo Calvino. Calvino's Norton lectures were intended to be delivered during 1985–86 but were published posthumously after Calvino's death prevented them from being heard in Cambridge. Perhaps Calvino's greatest literary achievement, these *Lezioni americane: Sei proposte per il prossimo millennio* (*Six Memos for the Next Millennium*, 1988) avoid almost entirely the pompous, pretentious, and jargon-filled academic prose typical of too much contemporary scholarship – there is no discussion of "textual paradigms," "master discourses," "hegemony," "paradigm shifts," or "the social construction of gender." Instead, Calvino concentrates upon six indispensable *literary* values in five completed essays and one projected essay he was unable to write, six values reflecting "things that only literature can give us, by means specific to it."[12] In the essay on "Lightness," Calvino evokes the myth of Perseus and the Medusa (as well as a story about the medieval Italian poet, Guido Calvacanti, in Boccaccio's *Decameron*), to argue that the poet should rise above the weight of the world in his vision and that such a poetic vision should deal with reality only obliquely. In "Quickness," Calvino focuses upon a number of examples, including that of Galileo Galilei's prose. Calvino approvingly

---

[11] *Six Walks*, pp. 6, 7; *Sei passeggiate*, pp. 7, 8.

[12] Italo Calvino, *Six Memos for the Next Millennium*, trans. Patrick Creagh (Cambridge: Harvard University Press, 1988), p. 1; or in *Lezioni americane: Sei proposte per il prossimo millennio* (Milan: Garzanti, 1988), p. 1.

cites Galileo on quickness in narration. The Florentine astronomer once wrote that "discoursing is like coursing, not like carrying, and one Barbary courser can go faster than a hundred Frieslands."[13] An essay on "Exactitude" praises the role of great literature in pursuing precision and clarity of language. Here, Calvino seems to be echoing the feelings of many contemporary readers who believe literary criticism has lost touch with this crucial aspect of literature. He defines literature as "the Promised Land in which language becomes what it really ought to be" and argues that the distressing lost of form and aesthetic values in the contemporary world can only be opposed by a single weapon, imaginative literature written with precision and exactitude.[14] A chapter on "Visibility" emphasizes the primacy of the visual imagination over the verbal fantasy in his own later fiction and praises the role of comic books in his intellectual formation (a testament to the importance of popular culture that parallels Eco's own interest in the comics). The fifth section of the work, on "Multiplicity," reads like a poetics of the Oulipo group (to which Calvino belonged and which has had an important formative influence upon Eco), with praise of such authors as Carlo Emilio Gadda, Georges Perec, Borges and (implicitly) Calvino himself for providing contemporary audiences with what he calls an "open" encyclopedia or the "ultra-completed book," an only apparent logical contradiction that seeks both to "exhaust knowledge of the world by enclosing it in a circle" and to allow unexamined possibilities by providing for "an intentional loophole left for incompleteness."[15] Calvino's notion of an open encyclopedia of meaning(s) is similar to the concept of encyclopedia Eco outlines in his *Semiotica e filosofia del linguaggio* (*Semiotics and the Philosophy of Language*, 1984).[16] Calvino never completed the last

---

[13] *Six Memos*, p. 43; *Lezioni americane*, p. 43.

[14] *Six Memos*, pp. 56, 57; *Lezioni americane*, pp. 58, 59.

[15] *Six Memos*, pp. 116, 120; *Lezioni americane*, pp. 113, 118.

[16] *Semiotica e filosofia del linguaggio*; or *Semiotics and the Philosophy of Language* – especially the second chapter entitled "Dizionario versus enciclopedia" (pp. 55–140) or in English "Dictionary v. Encyclopedia" (pp. 46–86).

essay on "Consistency," or at least a manuscript of it has yet to be unearthed.

Much contemporary literary theory employs literature as a spring-board for discussions of highly charged ideological questions concerning class, gender, race, colonialism, power, and the like. All literature, both the great masterpieces and the less great pulp-fictional works, can certainly be read as a reflection of these problems. But race, class, gender, and power are not specifically *literary* topics, and they most certainly are not *aesthetic* categories. That is to say, they are not grounded upon a concern with the *literary-ness* of a work of imaginative literature. Calvino's discussion of the inherently *literary* qualities of literature in his Norton Lectures thus flies in the face of much contemporary literary theory. Eco's *Six Walks* represents a concrete response to Calvino's earlier Norton Lectures, and it is this relationship that explains, at least in part, Eco's particular poetics of reading in his own series of lectures.

Eco himself emphasizes the fact that his major book on narrative theory – *The Reader in the Story* (partially translated as *The Role of the Reader*) – appeared in the same year as Calvino's seminal novel *Se una notte d'inverno un viaggiatore* (*If On a Winter's Night a Traveler*, 1979), a work of fiction preoccupied with the role of the reader, just as Eco's collection of essays had been engaged in the question of reader response. Eco and Calvino had even exchanged their books with warm personal dedications when they first appeared in Italy. In homage to Calvino – both Calvino's fiction treating the role of the reader and Calvino's later Norton Lectures that sought to define the preeminently literary qualities of imaginative fiction – Eco begins his lectures with a reference to Calvino's second essay, on "Quickness," and devotes a third chapter to its contrary quality, "Lingering" (a particular trait of literature to which Calvino had already drawn attention).

Eco's ideas here expand upon several key theories from *The Reader in the Story*, particularly the identification of a model author (as opposed to an empirical author or the narrator of a story) with "style."[17] But Eco believes that the voice of this model author is expressed through a series of instructions given to the reader. They must be followed if the empirical reader wishes to become the model author's model reader. In the second chapter of *Six Walks* ("The Woods of Loisy"), almost entirely devoted to the treatment of narrative time and voice in Nerval's *Sylvie*, Eco makes clearer what kind of fictional wood interests him. In real life, he asserts, a person can walk through a wood in two ways, The first way is to try various routes so as to get out of the wood as fast as possible, seeking a preordained destination. The second and more complex way is to walk so as to discover the nature of the forest and the reasons why some routes are open and others are blocked. The same is true for any intelligent reader of fiction:

> Any such text is addressed, above all, to a model reader of the first level, who wants to know, quite rightly, how the story ends (whether Ahab will manage to capture the whale, or whether Leopold Bloom will meet Stephen Daedalus after coming across him a few times on the sixteenth of June 1904). But every text is also addressed to a model reader of the second level, who wonders what sort of reader that story would like him or her to become and who wants to discover precisely how the model author goes about serving as a guide for the reader. In order to know how a story ends, it is usually enough to read it once. In contrast, to identify the model author the text has to be read many times, and certain stories endlessly. Only when empirical readers have discovered the model author, and have understood (or merely begun to understand) what it wanted from them, will they become full-fledged model readers.[18]

Here, without explicitly stating that he is doing so, Eco embraces

---

[17] *Six Walks*, p. 15; *Sei passeggiate*, p. 18.

[18] *Six Walks*, p. 27; *Sei passeggiate*, pp. 33–34. For a treatment of critical rereading, see Mattei Calinescu, *Rereading* (New Haven: Yale University Press, 1993), which discusses the "inferential walks" Eco discusses in his earlier essays.

Calvino's praise of imaginative literature as a source of aesthetic pleasure first and foremost. This exaltation of the pleasurable function of literature in *Six Walks* is even more explicit in another passage in the fourth lecture, "Possible Woods," where Eco declares that "fictional worlds are parasites of the real world" and that "everything that the text doesn't name or describe explicitly as different from what exists in the real world must be understood as corresponding to the laws and conditions of the real world."[19] Eco believes this particular parasitical relationship between the "real" and the "fictional" world stands as the foundation of all fiction, for it underlies the particular pleasure we derive from reading, actually a form of pleasurable play:

> But any walk within fictional worlds has the same function as a child's play. Children play with puppets, toy horses, or kites in order to get acquainted with the physical laws of the universe and with the actions that someday they will really perform. Likewise, to read fiction means to play a game by which we give sense to the immensity of things that happened, are happening, or will happen in the actual world. By reading narrative, we escape the anxiety that attacks us when we try to something true about the world. This is the consoling function of narrative – the reason people tell stories, and have told stories from the beginning of time. And it has always been the paramount function of myth: to find a shape, a form, in the turmoil of human experience.[20]

Eco repeats this definition of literature as preeminently pleasurable once again in the concluding lecture, "Fictional Protocols," where he declares that fiction is to adult experience as play is to children's experience, since fiction allows us limitlessly to employ our faculties for perceiving the world and for reconstructing the past, and it is through the pleasurable activity of fiction that adults structure our past and present experience.[21]

[19] *Six Walks*, p. 83; *Sei passeggiate*, p. 101.
[20] *Six Walks*, p. 87; *Sei passeggiate*, p. 107.
[21] *Six Walks*, p. 131; *Sei passeggiate*, p. 163.

The fact that literature stands in a parasitical relationship to reality also explains why the pleasure of fiction resides, to a great extent, in what Eco terms "inferential walks." Here, Eco reminds the reader of the short comic stories *Mad* magazine used to run in the 1950s, "Scenes We'd Like to See," offering an example on the facing page wherein a noble Dumas-like swordsman fights his way to rescue the damsel in distress, only to be killed by the villain who wins the girl! Such inferential walks presumed by the model author of the *Mad* stories were imaginary journeys outside the fictional wood established by Hollywood happy endings. They were meant to amuse the reader by frustrating his or her natural tendency to expect a story to terminate in a traditional manner.[22] Eco then concludes: "the readerly process of making predictions constitutes a necessary emotional aspect of reading which brings into play hopes and fears, as well as the tension that derives from our identification with the fate of the characters."[23] Again, aesthetic pleasure is Eco's focus.

Literature's parasitical relationship to reality also moves Eco to celebrate what he calls the "alethic privilege" of fictional worlds in asserting that we read novels "because they give us the comfortable sensation of living in worlds where the notion of truth is indisputable, while the actual world seems to be a more treacherous place."[24] But, as Eco also notes, our notion of truth in the actual world is not so far removed from our conception of truth in the fictional world, since we accept much of the information upon which our lives depend on trust just as we accept much of the fictional information the author provides for us on trust. Yet, in fiction, as Eco notes, "we suspend our disbelief about some things but not others."[25] Rex Stout's character Archie Goodwin, for example, cannot hail a taxi on Fifth Avenue and ask to be taken to Alexanderplatz, since Döblin has associated that particular

[22] *Six Walks*, pp. 50–51; *Sei passeggiate*, pp. 63–64.
[23] *Six Walks*, p. 52; *Sei passeggiate*, p. 63.
[24] *Six Walks*, p. 91; *Sei passeggiate*, p. 111.
[25] *Six Walks*, p. 77; *Sei passeggiate*, p. 94.

street with Berlin; if one reads Tolstoy's *War and Peace* and believes that nineteenth-century Russia was governed by the Communist Party rather than the Czar, it will be difficult for the actual reader to behave like the model reader envisioned by the model author. Returning to the theory he had outlined in both *The Limits of Interpretation* and *Interpretation and Overinterpretation*, Eco notes how these simple truths about fictional narrative underline the fact that interpretation does, in fact, have outer boundaries: "you may infer from texts things they don't explicitly say – and the collaboration of the reader is based on this principle – but you can't make them say the contrary of what they have said."[26] When a reader confronts a text and lacks the necessary erudition to understand it properly, this situation represents a missed opportunity for the actual empirical reader to transform himself or herself into the model reader envisioned by the model author.

But there are also contrary examples, when the model author stumbles and makes a mistake. One amusing example of this kind of error occupies an entire chapter of *Six Walks*, a discussion of how Dumas describes a street known as the rue Servandoni in *The Three Musketeers*. Such a name reflects an impossible situation for a seventeenth-century novel designed to reflect historical verisimilitude, since the street was only dedicated to the Italian architect Giovanni Niccolò Servandoni in 1806. Eco explains that Dumas's model readers were not so sophisticated that they would have recognized his mistake. Of course, Dumas's characters could not possibly have walked down a street called rue Bonaparte, since every single one of his readers, even the most naive, would have realized that Napoleon had lived in a different century. But not even Dumas, the model author, realized that the rue Servandoni was called the rue des Fossoyeurs during the historical period treated by his novel. The model reader of Joyce's *Finnegans Wake*, on the other hand, was conceived by its author as possessing an unlimited encyclopedic competence, even superior to its creator. If the passage containing

[26] *Six Walks*, p. 92; *Sei passeggiate*, p. 112.

Dumas's small, factual error is read by the kind of model reader Joyce envisioned, Eco believes an overinterpretation is almost inevitable. Naming the street with an historically anachronistic name in a novel by James Joyce would not necessarily be a mistake but could actually constitute an allusion, a hint to the careful model reader Joyce hoped to create that every fictional text contains a contradiction because of its attempts to make literature coincide with reality. A Joycean reading of Dumas would thus construe his "mistake" as a metaliterary sign pointing to the fact that every work of literature is a "self-voiding fiction." It would, therefore, constitute a statement about the nature of narrativity itself.[27] Reading Dumas in the same manner in which we read Joyce would be just as ridiculous as reading Joyce as if he were Dumas. Eco's illustrations emphasize a simple truth about literature: the relationship between the real and the fictional world contains the secret to pleasure in the text.

Ultimately, the aesthetic pleasure readers derive from literature emanates from a metaphysical, almost religious source, for Eco believes that fiction makes us feel "more metaphysically comfortable" than reality:

> There is a golden rule that cryptanalysts and code breakers rely on – namely, that every secret message can be deciphered, provided one knows that it is a message. The problem with the actual world is that, since the dawn of time, humans have been wondering whether there is a message and, if so, whether this message makes sense. With fictional universes, we know without a doubt that they do have a message and that an authorial entity stands behind them as creator, as well as within them as a set of reading instructions.[28]

I have stressed Eco's acceptance of the role aesthetic pleasure plays in the reading process and his belief that correctly perceiving as a model reader what a model author has intended to convey represents the maximum degree of fictional pleasure. This position is of

---

[27] Six Walks, pp. 112–13; Sei passeggiate, p. 138.
[28] Six Walks, p. 116; Sei passeggiate, p. 143.

fundamental importance to Eco's evolution as both a literary theorist and a practicing novelist in his third book of fiction. If we recall some of the most interesting of Eco's earlier essays on popular culture from his formative years, it was precisely the "consolatory" function of much of popular culture that Eco questioned most closely, for he felt such a function of popular literature could form an obstacle to free and critical judgment. Eco's discussion of popular culture in such popular myths as that of *Superman* or James Bond or other lesser-known forms of comic strips and popular advertising or songs developed this objection at some length, particularly in Eco's definition of apocalyptic intellectuals.[29] Eco did not originally examine manifestations of popular culture in order to uncover the mechanisms of pleasurable consumption they embodied. On the contrary, he initially viewed the pleasure derived from popular culture as suspicious, for it could lead to unthinking consumption of such products and to a form of cultural brainwashing by popular culture's inherently conservative ideology. Instead, Eco was far more concerned with employing semiotic or pre-semiotic methodology to uncover the underlying ideological foundations of much of popular culture, often revealing its ideology as a defense of the status quo or even concealing reactionary political views. Narrative pleasure was the least of his concerns. Thus Ian Fleming's works were first described in Eco's earlier essays as "the last *avatar* of Kitsch."[30] A key passage from *Casino Royale* describing the death of Le Chiffre by a single bullet in the villain's head, making it appear (in Fleming's words) as if he had suddenly grown another eye, was quoted in Eco's earlier essays on narrative to provide an example of the "Midcult" style practiced by Fleming that Eco analyzed for its rhetorical efficiency, not its ability to produce narrative pleasure in the reader: "The novels of Fleming exploit in exemplary measure that element of foregone play which is typical of the escape machine geared for the entertainment of the

---

[29] See *Apocalypse Postponed*, p. 18; *Apocalittici e integrati*, p. 5.
[30] *The Role of the Reader*, p. 172; *Il superuomo di massa*, p. 184.

masses. . . . Fleming is, in other words, cynically building an effective narrative apparatus."[31] Now in *Six Walks*, after the experience of writing two novels of his own and during the composition of yet a third work of fiction, Eco cites the very same passage from *Casino Royale* in his third lecture, that treating lingering in the fictional woods. His judgment has now changed radically, and it contains a very different evaluation of Fleming's narrative skills. Fleming's descriptive metaphors employed in depicting Le Chiffre's grotesque death are not only placed within a discussion of other classic works, novels by Alessandro Manzoni and Jules Verne, but Eco now believes that this aspect of Fleming's style represents "an example of that *defamiliarization* extolled by the Russian Formalists."[32] This is rare praise indeed for a supposedly reactionary, cold-warrior writer. Eco even makes a detraction of his earlier critique of Fleming's narrative style, the long descriptions of which he had once denounced as designed to persuade his readers that they were reading highbrow literature, since popular readers, in his earlier view, were convinced that highbrow literature contained long digressions and descriptive passages. Eco once believed Fleming gave these readers such passages in an attempt to cover up his own lowbrow, ideological intentions. Now Fleming's ability to switch back and forth between long descriptions of the inessential (such as the design on a package of Player's cigarettes) and sudden, brief descriptions of the most crucial elements of his narrative is praised by comparing Fleming to Alessandro Manzoni: "Manzoni, like the good nineteenth-century romantic novelist that he is, used basically the same strategy as Fleming."[33]

Eco's change of opinion on Ian Fleming represents an important admission that his earlier preoccupation with ideology in Fleming's narrative style simply failed to take into account the fact that the creator of the James Bond myth was an accomplished model author

---

[31] *The Role of the Reader*, p. 161; *Il superuomo di massa*, pp. 168, 169.
[32] *Six Walks*, p. 56; *Sei passeggiate*, p. 70.
[33] *Six Walks*, p. 68; *Sei passeggiate*, p. 84.

from whom any aspiring narrator could learn a great deal. Since the James Bond essay was one of the articles that first established Eco's international reputation, Eco's admission in *Six Walks* that he may well have misread Fleming because of his own ideological agenda in the past reveals Eco as an honest theorist, willing to reconsider positions he has taken years ago and capable of revising his most cherished theoretical ideas when they prove inadequate or mistaken.

Such a reconsideration of the role and function of fictional narrative in *Six Walks* has clearly been guided by Eco's conviction that aesthetic pleasure represents the fundamental purpose of narrative. This conviction was obviously encouraged by Eco's appreciation of Italo Calvino's defense of literature in *Six Memos*. But Eco also came to hold such a view primarily because of his own practice as a novelist. Faced with the elementary problems every writer faces when he or she sets out to create a fictional wood, Eco discovered that Ian Fleming, Alexandre Dumas, Jules Verne, and the many other "popular" novelists so closely identified with bestsellers or "lowbrow" reading were actually far more sophisticated narrators than many literary critics or theorists cared to admit. Some critics of Eco's work will surely argue that Eco's shift of focus from pure semiotic theory addressed to a small circle of specialists in the 1970s (such as *A Theory of Semiotics*) toward a broader interest in literature and literary theory, still informed by key concepts taken from semiotic theory, represents a step backward. More than a step backward, the direction of Eco's career during the last decade might also be construed as an implicit admission of the failure of the grandiose promise of a universal theory of culture semiotics once offered. Such a negative view of Eco's intellectual development would ultimately be founded upon a belief in the primacy of theory over practice. But it is clear from a reading of Eco's works during the last decade that he has given pride of place to fiction over pure philosophy and that his theoretical concerns have become more narrowly focused upon narrative problems that have arisen from his own concrete work as a successful novelist.

Let us now turn to Eco's *The Island of the Day Before*, armed with the knowledge that Eco's third novel has been conceived to emphasize what Roland Barthes called "the pleasure of the text." It would be a gross error of interpretation to assume that Eco's restored faith in the aesthetic pleasure derived from storytelling would return him to the nineteenth-century world of the pulp novel or the historical romance. Nothing could be further from Eco's intentions in his latest fictional creation. In fact, *The Island of the Day Before*, as Norma Bouchard has argued, is very much "an exemplification of Eco's manifold version of the postmodern."[34] Moreover, the author's decision to place his fictional narrative squarely within the era identified by cultural historians as the baroque – the first page of the book refers to the date of 1643 – occurs for very specific theoretical reasons, just as Eco's earlier selection of a particular moment in medieval history within which to construct the plot of *The Name of the Rose* represented a fundamental statement of intellectual purpose, as the author himself explained in his *Preface to "The Name of the Rose."*

Eco has long been fascinated with the baroque period for a variety of reasons, but primarily because of the parallels he sees between our own postmodern age (that of the "open work") and the seventeenth century. In *The Open Work*, his earliest treatise on aesthetics that still remains fundamental to an understanding of his mature thought, Eco contrasts the "static and unquestionable definitiveness of the classical Renaissance form," to a baroque aesthetics that he defines as "dynamic," a reflection of "an indeterminacy of effect" that "never allows a privileged, definitive, frontal view" but, instead, "induces the spectator to shift his position continuously in order to see the work in constantly new aspects, as if it were in a state of perpetual transform-

---

[34] For discussions of Eco's third novel, see: Norma Bouchard's "Umberto Eco's *L'isola del giorno prima*: Postmodern Theory and Fictional Praxis,' *Italica* 72 (1995), 193–208; and Rocco Capozzi's "Metaphors and Intertextuality in Eco's Neo-baroque Narrative Machine: *The Island of the Day Before*," *Rivista di studi italiani* 14, no. 1 (1996), pp. 165–89, which the author allowed me to read in manuscript.

ation."[35] Moreover, Eco goes on to claim that the baroque sensibility also represents an historically unique situation, because it corresponds to a moment in the development of mankind where "man opts out of the canon of authorized responses and finds that he is faced (both in art and in science) by a world in a fluid state which requires corresponding creativity on his part," and therefore baroque poetic treatises attempting to establish the parameters of the marvelous, wit, or metaphor reflect man's new inventive role in culture, where the work of art has become a "potential mystery to be solved, a role to fulfill, a stimulus to quicken his imagination."[36]

Three decades after the composition of *The Open Work*, Eco obviously remains fascinated by the implied parallels between our own postmodern era and the baroque. This was most recently underlined by his foreword to a discussion of postmodern aesthetics defined as "neo-baroque" by his colleague at the University of Bologna, Omar Calabrese.[37] In this brief but revealing essay, Eco draws a clear parallel between his own ideas and Calabrese's, remarking that if he had written *The Open Work* in the 1990s it would be very much like Calabrese's treatise on the neo-baroque.[38] For his part, Calabrese views Eco's first novel as the "prototype" of the neo-baroque aesthetic because of its status as an "enormous fresco of semantic, narrative, and figurative invariables in which everything is quotation, and where the presence of the author survives in the combination and insertion of systems of variables adapted to the different types of model reader envisaged by the novel."[39] Eco's fiction embodies the palimpsest, an aesthetic category that for Calabrese defines the essence of the postmodern; and in turn, Calabrese believes that "the many important cultural phenomena of our time are distinguished by a specific internal

---

[35] *The Open Work*, p. 7; *Opera aperta*, pp. 38–39.

[36] *The Open Work*, p. 7; *Opera aperta*, p. 39.

[37] Omar Calabrese, *Neo-Baroque: A Sign of the Times*, trans. Charles Lambert with a foreword by Umberto Eco (Princeton: Princeton University Press, 1992); the original Italian edition was *L'età neobarocca* (Rome: Laterza, 1987).

[38] Eco, "Foreword," in Calabrese, *Neo-Baroque*, p. viii.   [39] *Neo-Baroque*, p. 45.

'form' that recalls the baroque."[40] Calabrese certainly must have remembered Eco's own observation in his *Postscript to "The Name of the Rose"* that postmodernism might well be the "modern name for mannerism as metahistorical category," an ideal category that could be detected in every artistic era rather than a stylistic mode limited to a single historical period.[41]

The Island of the Day Before continues the narrative practice begun in his first two novels – the creation of an overarching image that metaphorically suggests a complexity of philosophical, semantic, and narrative ideas. In *The Name of the Rose*, the key metaphoric image was the labyrinth of the library in the ancient monastery. In *Foucault's Pendulum*, the dominant images were the gigantic pendulum in a Parisian museum and the traumatic memories of the partisan experience during the war. In *The Island of the Day Before*, Eco imagines a minor Italian nobleman from Piedmont, Roberto della Griva, who is shipwrecked in the South Seas on an almost abandoned ship a mile away from an island to which he cannot repair because he does not know how to swim. Roberto has embarked on an ocean voyage because he is forced to accept Cardinal Mazarin's offer to go on a secret mission. He must investigate a British plot to discover the mystery of measuring longitude, the key to the mastery of the oceans of the world. The narrative moves back and forth from Roberto's abandoned ship, the *Daphne*, to Roberto's account of his life in Europe, beginning with the siege of the city of Casale during the

---

[40] *Ibid.*, pp. 29, 15.

[41] *The Name of the Rose*, p. 530; *Il nome della rosa*, p. 528. As one of our era's most learned medievalists, Eco must surely have encountered a similar view in Ernst Robert Curtius's monumental study, *European Literature and the Latin Middle Ages* (New York: Harper, 1963), which devotes an entire chapter to the concept of mannerism, defining it as "the common denominator for all literary tendencies which are opposed to Classicism, whether they be pre-classical, post-classical, or contemporary with any Classicism" and as a "constant in European literature," the "complementary phenomenon of the Classicism of all periods" (p. 273). Curtius deliberately prefers the term "mannerism" to the term "baroque" but uses the two terms to refer to the same historical period.

Thirty Years War, his obsession with a twin brother named Ferrante, and his encounter with a woman named Lilia in Paris, with whom he has an unrequited love affair and to whom his letters, abandoned on the *Daphne* after his death, are addressed. Thus, as in *The Name of the Rose*, once again Eco's narrative departs from the imagined reconstruction by an anonymous narrator of Roberto's letters to Lilia and of his unfinished novel or "romance." Or, to put it in the simple words Eco employed to open his first novel, "naturally, a manuscript." In this case, Eco's anonymous narrator speculates that the papers written by Roberto were discovered either by Abel Tasman in 1643, who thought they contained important secrets about the method of calculating longitude during his voyages that charted Tasmania and New Zealand; or by Captain Bligh, who might have come upon them in 1789 long after the development of the marine chronometer had made the "secret" of measuring longitude common knowledge, relegating Roberto's papers on the subject to the status of historical curiosities.

Eco bases the entire plot of his novel upon an intriguing but little remembered scientific problem – that of measuring longitude. Until the marine chronometer invented by John Harrison in the eighteenth century came into widespread use, as a genial account of the problem states it dramatically,

> for lack of a practical method of determining longitude, every great captain in the Age of Exploration became lost at sea despite the best available charts and compasses. From Vasco da Gama to Vasco Nez de Balboa, from Ferdinand Magellan to Sir Francis Drake – they all got where they were going willy-nilly, by forces attributed to good luck or the grace of God.[42]

The measurement of longitude concerns the question of time (something not required in measuring the much more accessible lines of

---

[42] Dava Sobel, *Longitude: The True Story of a Lone Genius Who Solves the Greatest Scientific Problem of His Times* (New York: Walker, 1995), p. 6. My discussion of the historical ramifications of this navigational problem is indebted to this book.

latitude, which are measurable by observing the length of the day, the height of the sun, or certain guide stars above the horizon). To know the longitude of a ship at sea, it is also required to know precisely what time it is aboard ship as well as the precise time at the home port or another fixed place of known longitude. Knowing the two times in different places at an identical moment in time allows a navigator to convert the difference in hours into a geographical separation. The earth completes a revolution of 360 degrees in 24 hours; therefore, one hour represents 15 degrees, and these 15 degrees correspond to a distance traveled. The problem is that while 1 degree of longitude equals 4 minutes everywhere, in terms of distance traveled, it can refer to 68 miles at the Equator but almost no distance at all at the Poles. Telling time on board ship until Harrison's marine chronometers were perfected was virtually impossible, due to the fact that temperature changes and the pitching of the deck would completely confound the ordinary technology of the pendulum clock, making the mechanisms run fast or slow or not at all and breaking down under the extreme changes of weather.

Focusing such attention on a scientific problem associated with telling time and measuring physical distance by means of time should alert the careful reader to the obvious fact that time also represents an integral aspect of both writing and reading. A historical problem associated with the difficulty of navigating around the globe in the baroque period thus creates a foundation in Eco's novel for an exploration of a question that has both scientific and literary consequences. So much of modernist literature follows Marcel Proust's search for "lost time," but few narrators before Eco have invented such an ingenious context for the presentation of literary time. The protagonist has been shipwrecked on a boat which is itself apparently located near the 180th meridian. Navigators of the era were obsessed with locating what the Spanish called the "punto fijo" – a "fixed point" where longitude could be calculated with complete accuracy. It is important to bear in mind that this so-called "fixed" location was a conventional term for any location at which the correct longitude could be fixed, not merely one unique place in the world. As Father Caspar (the only other person alive that Roberto eventually discovers on the ship), remarks in his comical language: "To me matters that at this point of the earth there is a line that on this side is the day after and on that side the day before. And not only at midnight but also at seven, at ten, every hour!"[43] As Caspar explains the odd situation to the incredulous Roberto, the two men are standing on a ship that faces the island of the day before (the source of the novel's title), since a day is lost sailing from America toward Asia, when the 180th meridian is crossed, the point at which the world is divided in two sections by this imaginary line of demarcation.[44] In effect, if the two men could cross the line separating the island from the shipwreck upon which they are stranded, they would reach the day before today. Unfortunately, neither of the men can swim. If they could reach the island, they believe they might be capable of fixing the onward rush of time.

Father Caspar Wanderdrossel, a German Jesuit scientist following the fashion of the seventeenth century, provides Eco with the opportunity to satirize the strange combination of erudition and crackpot ideas that constituted the scientific world view of the baroque period. Father Caspar is searching for the answer to the problem of measuring longitude, and to that extent he seems to be the normal kind of scientist we might expect to find engaged in such a task. But he is perhaps even more concerned to discover in the process of locating the

---

[43] *The Island of the Day Before*, p. 266; *L'isola del giorno prima*, p. 247.

[44] In a personal letter to me dated 30 January 1996, commenting on the "fixed point" and its meaning, Eco stressed the fact that the "fixed point" has nothing to do with either the 180th meridian (which is a conventional position calculated *after* longitude can be calculated with accuracy) or with the pendulum of Foucault, which would work equally well at any point on the globe. Thus, the search for the "fixed point" is the search for a method of measurement, not a specific point on the globe. Father Caspar, of course, thinks that the only place in the globe that constitutes a fixed point is the 180th meridian, where the date changes from one side of this imaginary dividing line to the other.

180th meridian a "scientific" proof that the Universal Flood described in the Old Testament actually occurred. According to Caspar's harebrained explanation, since the rains could not have covered the earth in forty days, God must have stood at that meridian, taken water from the previous day (that is, on the left side of the dateline), and poured it onto the other side of the dateline for forty days in a row! Learned men of the seventeenth century, like Father Caspar, could easily combine the most brilliant of scientific or mathematical achievements with what today seem to be ludicrous theories. We should not forget that Sir Isaac Newton, whose physical model of the universe would eventually revolutionize the world Eco depicts, believed not only in the force of gravity but also in alchemy. Newton was also mistaken in having no faith in the marine chronometers of John Harrison, preferring instead an astronomical rather than a mechanical solution to the mystery of measuring longitude. With his portraits of Wanderdrossel and other savants of the age, Eco suggests that there is ultimately no certainty in scientific research, now or in the distant past.

Much of *The Island of the Day Before* can be read, in fact, as the kind of *conte philosophique* one might encounter in the works of Jonathan Swift or French Enlightenment writers such as Voltaire. Father Caspar believes he can establish the location of the 180th meridian by means of two almost familiar instruments. The first, the "Specula Melitensis" or "Maltese Mirror," remains a mysterious tool whose nature is "not clear" according to the narrator's own account of the machine. Caspar had mounted it on a high point on the island before his crew had been murdered there by savages and he had escaped alone to the ship. The second, the "Instrumentum Arcetricum," seems to be identical with the telescopic device invented by Galileo Galilei, who spent his last troubled years in the town of Arcetri near Florence. Galileo had, in fact, worked out an astronomical solution to the problem of longitude based upon the predictable eclipses of the moons of Jupiter, which he had discovered, to produce a series of astronomical tables known as ephemerides. While the moons of Jupiter could be seen only during the evening and then only when skies were not obscured, this method actually became the standard method of figuring longitude on land (not on the ocean, where the solution discovered was eventually mechanical, not astronomical). In 1668, a professor at the University of Bologna, Giovanni Domenico Cassini, produced the most accurate set of tables of ephemerides and was rewarded for his troubles by none other than Louis XIV and his minister Jean Colbert with the post of director of the Royal Observatory in France. Thus Cassini was part of the same world that Eco pictures in his humorous satirical portrait of science in the baroque age. It is also of interest that Galileo himself designed a special navigational helmet through which a sailor was supposed to gaze upon Jupiter's moons, not unlike the strange apparatus that Father Caspar fails to operate properly on board the *Daphne*. Galileo called this instrument a "celatone," and it apparently looked like a brass gas-mask with a telescope attached to one of the eye holes.[45] In spite of the theoretical workability of Galileo's contraption, the practical problems associated with it – the need for clear skies, the fact that the slightest motion could impair observations – rendered unsatisfactory Galileo's attempt to resolve the longitudinal dilemma through astronomy rather than through mechanical clocks.

Eco's descriptions of what seem to us senseless scientific schemes, but which in reality were extremely complicated and intellectually challenging scientific responses to genuine problems, serve a double purpose. They are intrinsically amusing, given their Rube Goldberg designs and workings, all of which Eco delights in inventing or recounting. But, more important, their faulty functioning emphasizes Eco's belief that there is no "system" in scientific method that can explain the sum totality of the universe. The most outlandish scientific theory presented in the novel concerns what is termed the

---

[45] I owe this description of Galileo's solution of the longitudinal problem to Sobel, *Longitude*, pp. 24–27.

"Powder of Sympathy," which Roberto first hears explained in Paris by an Englishman named Monsieur d'Igby, although he had seen something similar demonstrated earlier, before the siege of Casale and its aftermath had driven him away from his Piedmontese home to the capital of France. D'Igby had first demonstrated this intriguing concept by employing *unguentum armarium* or "weapon salve" to cure the wound of a Spanish soldier. He accomplished this not by applying medicine to the wound the man received (as contemporary scientific logic would demand and even baroque common sense required) but to the cloth that had covered the soldier's wound. D'Igby explains the workings of this miraculous cure as deriving from "a conformity or sympathy that connects things among themselves," the word "sympathy" being used to define this mutual attraction.[46]

D'Igby's sympathetic powders are later tested by the mysterious English Doctor Byrd, who is attempting to measure the longitudes by a method based upon D'Igby's ideas. At a fixed location and a fixed time in London, one of Byrd's collaborators applies the unguent to some of the blood from a dog on board the *Amaryllis*, on which both Byrd and Roberto (as Cardinal Mazarin's spy) are traveling. The dog whimpers in pain when this occurs, supposedly indicating the precise time in London. In theory (very eccentric scientific theory, indeed), this would enable Byrd to calculate the longitude, since with the dog's whimper through the theory of the powder of sympathy, he would have the two precise times at different points on the globe necessary to make such calculations. In the fictional world of *The Island of the Day Before*, this theory actually works. Moreover, the wounded dog on board the *Amaryllis* finds a parallel in a practically skinned-alive character named Biscarat who is employed by Roberto's double Ferrante as a human navigational calculator on the *Daphne*.

Most readers unacquainted with the details of the historical development of the solution to the longitudinal problem will doubt-less take this entire theory, and especially the use of wounded dogs, as

---

[46] *The Island of the Day Before*, p. 165; *L'isola del giorno prima*, p. 155.

an outlandish fictional invention on Eco's part. But this "wounded dog theory," as well as the "weapon salve" and the "powder of sympathy" were widely discussed notions during the seventeenth century. They were treated in a pamphlet published in 1658 by an Englishman named Sir Kenelm Digby (whom the French called D'Igby). The inspiration for Eco's character was certainly suggested by this historical figure, but Eco had no need to invent fantastic theories when those actually advanced in the scientific investigations of the seventeenth century were so interesting. As eccentric and as cruel as keeping a dog on board ship with a gaping wound during an entire ocean voyage might seem, Digby's pamphlet rightly commented that treating a poor animal in this fashion was no crueler than forcing seamen to sight latitudes by measuring the height of the sun while staring directly into its glare. This practice was sufficient to blind almost every navigator in one eye until 1595, when the backstaff replaced the old cross-staff or Jacob's staff that forced seamen to lose their sight in search of latitude. Since longitude was an even more vexing problem, and its inaccurate measurement literally a matter of life and death for sailors, even such a silly scheme as the "wounded dog theory" that Eco exploits so skillfully in his novel would seem well worth considering.[47]

Roberto had encountered an equally bizarre scientific contraption before his ocean voyage, the Aristotelian Telescope of Padre Emanuele. Padre Emanuele is obviously modeled after one of the most famous of baroque literary theorists, Emanuele Tesauro (1592–1675), whose important treatise on metaphor and the rhetorical figure of the conceit was entitled *Il cannocchiale aristotelico* (*The Aristotelian Telescope*, 1655). Metaphor represents a trope absolutely essential to any search for similitudes, analogies, and resemblances between the objects of the universe, a grammatical parallel to the theory of the "Powder of Sympathy," a theory, as the narrator

---

[47] See Sobel, *Longitude*, pp. 41–43 for a detailed discussion of the "wounded dog theory" and the Powder of Sympathy.

himself points out, involving "a description of a universe crowded with spirits that unite according to their affinity."[48] Padre Emanuele saw the role of metaphor in precisely this light:

> And this is the office of the supreme Figure of all: Metaphor. If Genius, & therefore Learning, consists in connecting remote Notions & finding Similitude in things dissimilar, then Metaphor, the most acute and farfetched among Tropes, is the only one capable of producing Wonder, which gives birth to Pleasure, as do changes of scene in the theatre. And if the Pleasure produced by Figures derives from learning new things without effort & many things in small volume, then Metaphor, setting our mind to flying betwixt one Genus & another, allows us to discern in a single Word more than one Object.[49]

Norma Bouchard notes that Padre Emanuele's unusual machine represents both a prototype of Abulafia, the computer of *Foucault's Pendulum* (which was paranoically programmed by the novel's protagonists to find connections everywhere, especially where none existed in reality), and a Las Vegas slot-machine (since it connects words and Aristotelian categories to each other by the giration of a drum).[50] Eco's novel thus returns again to the perennially fascinating problem he has discussed so many times before – that of unlimited semiosis. Ultimately, the baroque fascination for affinities and baroque interest in the production of outlandish metaphors parallel the Diabolicals' belief in *Foucault's Pendulum* that "tout se tient," that everything is connected of necessity to everything else.

Eco's encyclopedic tour through the baroque era with his references not only to the scientific discoveries and mistakes of the period (Kepler, Galileo, Digby) but also its keen interest in wit and metaphor (Tesauro, John Donne, Giambattista Marino), as well as baroque

---

[48] *The Island of the Day Before*, p. 171; *L'isola del giorno prima*, p. 160.

[49] *The Island of the Day Before*, p. 90; *L'isola del giorno prima*, pp. 85–86.

[50] "Umberto Eco's *L'isola del giorno prima*: Postmodern Theory and Fictional Praxis," p. 197.

literary figures such as Don Quixote, who are obsessed with reading and misreading literary texts, leads the attentive model reader of this novel to contemporary literary theory. The contemporary "post-modern" obsession with pastiche, parody, and intertextuality sugges-ted by the theoretical works of John Barth, Harold Bloom, Michel Foucault, Gérard Genette, and Eco himself, to mention only a few obvious names in the constellation of important theorists, asserts that writing and reading involve "revisiting" other texts. What is original about Eco's historical perspective is that he demonstrates with his third novel that the baroque period anticipated by several centuries such postmodern notions. In particular, Eco's own debts to such authors as Italo Calvino or the Oulipo group, who often played with the notion of narrative as a combinatory art, can be seen as a continuity with a writer from the seventeenth century, such as Giovanni Battista Mazini (1599–1664), who defined the novel as a "stupendous and glorious machine."[51] In short, as Rocco Capozzi argues, Eco's three novels ultimately treat the same subject, demon-strating how authors often rewrite the same text, either their own works or those of others, over and over again.[52] And in so doing, Eco actually represents a long tradition in Italian literature stretching back to the mid-sixteenth and early seventeenth centuries, not a post-modern innovation that has blossomed forth during the postwar period.

Eco has repeatedly declared, most lucidly in the *Postscript to "The Name of the Rose"*, that contemporary fiction must constitute a dialogue with other writers and other books. In that bestseller, the image of the library as a universal metaphor for writing emphasized

[51] Rocco Capozzi (p. 185) makes this point very well in his "Metaphors and Intertextual-ity,' quoting Mazini and referring to an important work on the subject edited by Marco Santoro entitled *La più stupenda e gloriosa macchina: Il romanzo italiano del secolo XVII* (Naples: SEN, 1981). In his novel *Cretideo* (1637), Mazini declared that the novel represents the most stupendous and glorious machine that the intellect or wit (*ingegno*) has produced and that it even surpasses the epic in this regard.

[52] Capozzi, "Metaphors and Intertextuality," p. 166.

the fact that Eco's first novel was no mere detective tale but was primarily a book about other books and reading in general. *The Island of the Day Before* is far closer in this regard to Eco's first fictional work than to *Foucault's Pendulum*, which had more in common with theories of interpretation than with fiction itself. But each of the three books shares a common atmosphere of conspiracy about the dissemination of information – either the location of Aristotle's lost treatise on comedy; the meaning of a secret document concerning a plot to dominate the world; or the location of the "fixed point" and the secret of measuring longitude. The conspiratorial atmosphere generated by the characters of each work also creates a universal sense that problematic interpretation reigns paramount in the fictional worlds Eco has created in each book, with paranoid interpretation often gaining the upper hand among the villains, while the positive protagonists attempt to discover the "truth," only to realize that meaning involves a far more ambiguous series of problems than they had originally anticipated.

Nowhere is Eco's postmodern conception of the novel any clearer than at the close of *The Island of the Day Before*:

> Finally, if from this story I wanted to produce a novel, I would demonstrate once again that it is impossible to write except by making a palimpsest of a rediscovered manuscript – without ever succeeding in eluding the Anxiety of Influence. Nor could I elude the childish curiosity of the reader, who would want to know if Roberto really wrote the pages on which I have dwelt far too long. In all honesty, I would have to reply that it is not impossible that someone else wrote them, someone who wanted only to pretend to tell the truth. And thus I would lose all the effect of the novel: where, yes, you pretend to tell true things, but you must not admit seriously that you are pretending. I would not even know how to come up with a final event whereby the letters fell into the hands of him who presumably gave them to me, extracting them from a miscellany of other defaced and faded manuscripts. "The author is unknown," I would, however, expect him to say. "The writing is graceful, but as

you see, it is discolored, and the pages are covered with water-stains. As for the contents, from the little I have seen, they are mannered exercises. You know how they wrote in that century. . . . People with no soul."[53]

The image of the palimpsest – usually a vellum or parchment document which has been written upon several times with remnants of earlier and not completely erased writings still visible (the kind of document which has historically been a major means of recovering lost literary works of classical antiquity) – fits Eco's view of each of his fictional works to the letter. His own creation exists in contiguity with the remnants of the entire range of other literary or critical books that have produced it. Even as he discusses the palimpsestic nature of the novel, Eco's anonymous narrator refers to Harold Bloom's important treatment of literary influence and paints an ironic picture of those contemporary readers or theorists who, unlike Eco, fail to realize that much of what passes for originality in the present may be only unconscious repetitions of what uninformed readers and critics consider to be the "mannered exercises" from the past.

The Island of the Day Before embodies an interpretation of intellectual development found in Michel Foucault's *The Order of Things*, a book mentioned earlier in connection with a possible influence upon *Foucault's Pendulum*. In the third chapter of that influential work, one treating Cervantes and Don Quixote, Foucault explains why Don Quixote represents a pivotal character in Western fiction:

> *Don Quixote* is the first modern work of literature, because in it we see the cruel reason of identities and differences make endless sport of signs and similitudes; because in it language breaks off its old kinship with things and enters into that lonely sovereignty from which it will reappear, in its separated state, only as literature; because it marks the point where resemblance enters an age which is, from the point of view of resemblance, one of madness and

[53] *The Island of the Day Before*, pp. 512–13; *L'isola del giorno prima*, p. 473.

imagination. Once similitude and signs are sundered from each other, two experiences can be established and two characters appear face to face. The madman, understood not as one who is sick but as an established and maintained deviant, as an indispensable cultural function, has become in Western experience, the man of primitive resemblances. This character, as he is depicted in the novels or plays of the Baroque age, and as he was gradually institutionalized right up to the advent of nineteenth-century psychiatry, is the man who is *alienated* in *analogy*. He is the disordered player of the Same and the Other. . . . At the other end of the cultural area, but brought close by symmetry, the poet is he who, beneath the named, constantly expected differences, rediscovers the buried kinships between things, their scattered resemblances.[54]

Roberto's literary pedigree certainly includes the ingenious hidalgo from La Mancha, precisely because he lives in a world where the material underpinnings of languages (*les choses*) have been severed from any necessary connection with language itself (*les mots*), to employ the original words of Foucault's French title for *The Order of Things – Les mots et les choses*. The legacy of Cervantes should remind Eco's reader that the baroque era produced one of the greatest metaliterary classics in Western literature. Roberto even falls in love with an idealized peasant woman (Anna Maria Novarese), just as Cervantes's hero falls in love with Dulcinea. As we have come to expect from *The Name of the Rose*, the list of literary works or phenomena employed by Eco in *The Island of the Day Before* seems encyclopedic.[55] Roberto's epistolary love affair with Lilia displays the entire range of Petrarchan conceits (the beloved's lips are rubies, her breasts alabaster, etc.). The relatively erudite reader will recognize a version of Madeleine de Scudéry's *Carte du Tendre*, an allegorical map of the tender sentiments, from her baroque novel *Clélie* (1654–60).

---

[54] Michel Foucault, *The Order of Things: An Archaeology of the Human Sciences* (New York: Vintage, 1971), pp. 48–49.

[55] Previously cited articles by Bouchard and Capozzi provide lengthy discussions of possible literary references in Eco's novel.

Seventeenth-century *Précieux,* whose Parisian salons and cult of periphrasis Eco represents brilliantly in the novel, also appear in comic garb, as does the metaphysical poetry of John Donne and Giambattista Marino (excellent examples of the baroque period style). A number of learned treatises from the period, not only by Galileo and Tesauro but also by such figures as Robert Burton (*Anatomy of Melancholy,* 1621), also emerge from Eco's narrative as keys to how the novel should be read.

Besides texts (scientific or literary) from the baroque era itself, numerous eighteenth- and nineteenth-century literary works inform Eco's novel, or are "revisited" by Eco in interesting and almost always humorous ways. Roberto's situation on a deserted ship opposite a deserted island changes slightly the lonely but perhaps less desperate situation of Daniel Defoe's *Robinson Crusoe* (1719–20). Roberto's Man Friday has been transformed into a German Jesuit scientist, Father Caspar. The political and military situation described in Roberto's Piedmont during his childhood and the siege of Casale certainly recalls Manzoni's description of the wars and the plague in *The Betrothed* (1827), while the anonymous narrator created by Eco who discovers seventeenth-century manuscripts certainly reminds every Italian reader of Italy's first great historical novel. The story of Ferrante's rescue from prison by the King of the Beggars in Paris sends the mindful reader back to Victor Hugo's *The Hunchback of Notre Dame* (1831). In *Six Walks*, Eco had analyzed the works of Alexandre Dumas in great detail, and it thus comes as no surprise that numerous elements of Eco's novel – the siege of Casale, the story of the double Ferrante confined in a prison in an iron mask – seem to be lifted from Dumas's descriptions of the siege of La Rochelle, the machinations of Richelieu and Mazarin against internal opponents and the Kingdom of England, as well as the tale of a mysterious set of royal twins, in both *The Three Musketeers* (1844) and *The Man in the Iron Mask* (1848–50). Robert Louis Stevenson's *The Strange Case of Dr. Jekyll and Mr. Hyde* (1886) has certainly influenced Eco's description of the relationship between Roberto and Ferrante, since Ferrante (like Edward Hyde) reflects the lustful and amoral projection of Roberto's less charitable instincts. Stevenson's *Treasure Island* (1883) may also have contributed something to Eco's creation of the mysterious island on the other side of the dateline.[56]

Twentieth-century writers to whom Eco is indebted might include Italo Calvino, whose *Six Lectures* was a major influence upon Eco's thinking on narrative pleasure during the time *The Island of the Day Before* was written. In particular, the bifurcated figure of Roberto/ Ferrante owes something to Calvino's fantastic tale of *The Cloven Viscount*, where a single figure is literally split into two parts, one good and the other evil. This source from Calvino would have struck Eco as doubly appropriate, since Calvino's works in general, and *The Cloven Viscount* in particular, owe a special debt to Robert Louis Stevenson. Ultimately, behind Eco's third novel (and all his fiction) stands the imposing figure of Jorge Luis Borges, in particular the famous short story from *Ficciones*, "Pierre Menard, Author of Don Quixote" (1939), which specifically speaks of rewriting Cervantes's masterpiece as "a kind of palimpsest."[57]

The Island of the Day Before contains the kind of intertextual references we have come to expect from Umberto Eco's postmodern fiction, but the book represents more than a collection of the literary sources that interested Eco in his recreation of the world of the baroque. Roberto's shipwreck on an abandoned but mysterious ship facing a deserted island also supplies Eco with a metaphor for the love affair that Roberto remembers but which was always unrequited. As the narrator remarks:

> He suffered doubly, because of the Island he did not have and because of the ship that had him – both unattainable, one through its distance, the other through its enigma – and both stood for a beloved

[56] During the 1995–96 academic year at the University of Bologna, Eco's academic lectures focused upon these very two novels by Stevenson.
[57] Jorge Luis Borges, *Borges: A Reader*, p. 102.

who eluded him, blandishing him with promises that he made to himself alone.[58]

It is, in fact, Roberto's unrequited love for Lilia that leads him to pronounce an impassioned speech about the alleged parallel between the "weapon salve" or the Powder of Sympathy and his lady: "that description of a universe crowded with spirits that unite according to their affinity seemed to him an allegory of falling in love."[59]

Roberto's desperate situation moves him to write letters to his lady. Abandoned on the ship facing the island, and struck by the analogy between his geographic location and his anguished position in his unrequited love affair with Lilia, Roberto turns to the only thing that can save him – literature. As Eco's anonymous narrator remarks: "Perhaps this is why Roberto wrote to his Lady. To survive, you must tell stories."[60] This remark might well be taken as the leitmotif of the entire novel, but it is also a subtle restatement of the remark by Ludwig Wittgenstein that Eco printed on the dust-jacket of the original Italian edition of *The Name of the Rose*:

> If he had wanted to advance a thesis, he would have written an essay (like so many others that he has written). If he has written a novel, it is because he has discovered, upon reaching maturity, that those things about which we cannot theorize, we must narrate.[61]

Roberto comes to the same conclusion. He decides to construct a story in the Land of Romances about Ferrante's competition with Roberto and Ferrante's love for Lilia, a tale that would unfold parallel to his own actual world but which would never supposedly intersect with it. Roberto decides to choose fiction over historical fact in a passage that seems taken directly from Eco's arguments in *Six Walks*:

---

[58] *The Island of the Day Before*, p. 68; *L'isola del giorno prima*, p. 65.

[59] *The Island of the Day Before*, p. 171; *L'isola del giorno prima*, p. 160.

[60] *The Island of the Day Before*, p. 207; *L'isola del giorno prima*, p. 194.

[61] For the complete text, see chapter 5.

I must reconstruct the History of those events, finding the causes, the secret motives. But is there anything more uncertain than the Histories we read, wherein if two authors tell of the same battle, such are the incongruities revealed that we are inclined to think they write of two different conflicts? On the other hand, is there anything more certain than a work of fiction, where at the end every Enigma finds its explanation according to the laws of the Realistic? The Romance perhaps tells of things that did not really happen, but they could very well have happened. To explain my misadventures in the form of a Novel means assuring myself that in all the muddle there exists at least one way of untangling the knot, and therefore I am not the victim of a nightmare.[62]

Roberto's story involves an incredible combination of what the modern reader will recognize as bits and pieces from many of the novels discussed earlier as Eco's sources. Roberto imagines that all his problems stem from his hatred for his twin brother Ferrante. In his romance, Ferrante is present at the siege of Casale as Captain Gambero, opposing the French forces for whom Roberto is fighting. He then becomes an agent of Cardinal Richelieu, as well as a double agent for the English, in the search for the "fixed point" and the mysterious secret of measuring longitude. In this fashion, Ferrante manages to ensnare Roberto into the trap set by Colbert and Mazarin that forces him to leave Lilia and sail away from France in search of the "fixed point." Because of his physical similarity to Roberto, it is inevitable that Ferrante becomes Roberto's rival with Lilia, actually possessing her and making her think he is Roberto. Ferrante even sails the *Daphne* into the South Seas to follow Roberto for revenge, and Roberto's romance can only conclude in one way – in a face-to-face showdown between the two twin brothers resulting in Roberto's triumph. Unfortunately, unlike the model reader Eco's work assumes, Roberto has not read Stevenson's tale of Dr. Jekyll and Mr. Hyde and cannot know that Ferrante only represents his evil nature, that he is

---

[62] *The Island of the Day Before*, p. 368; *L'isola del giorno prima*, pp. 340–41.

only a phantom or a literary projection of his own personality. Aroused by his own fictional narrative and convinced that only he can save his beloved Lilia trapped on the island of the day before, Roberto crosses the imaginary line between History and Romance, between Fact and Fiction, and enters the water even though he cannot swim. He thus vanishes from the story. The anonymous narrator concludes the novel with the previously cited quotation on the Anxiety of Influence, ending Eco's recreation of the baroque age and Roberto's bizarre adventure with a metafictional commentary on the necessarily palimpsestic nature of all literature.

It would be impossible for Eco to equal the unparalleled popular success of *The Name of the Rose* with this difficult but rewarding book. Indeed, the author would be amused by any assumption that a writer creates merely to match his previous creations. As Rocco Capozzi has noted, the majority of reviews of the book in Eco's native Italy have been unfavorable or lukewarm, while more positive statements about the value of Eco's third work of imaginative fiction have come primarily from American reviewers, who are more sensitive to postmodernist narrative strategies.[63] Sales figures do not determine either literary value or the long-term success of a book of fiction. In *The Island of the Day Before*, Umberto Eco's primary goal of pleasing his readers – a goal he accepted as the paramount task of the author in his Norton Lectures – requires a model reader beguiled by postmodern intertextuality and one perhaps even more erudite than the model reader implied by *The Name of the Rose* or *Foucault's Pendulum*.

[63] See Capozzi, "Metaphors and Intertextuality," p. 179.

eight

§

Conclusion

Umberto Eco will turn 65 shortly before the time this book appears in print, but there is very little chance that he will retire from active writing and lecturing to a contemplative life. In many ways, he is presently at the height of his creative powers. He has earned almost every important sign of recognition on several continents, as well as international fame as a best-selling author of popular (albeit difficult) novels. Any conclusion about his contribution to the lively intellectual ferment that has characterized postwar Italy and Europe will therefore of necessity be only provisional, since there is little doubt that Eco will continue to write actively for years to come.

Like Fellini, Calvino, Pavarotti, or Armani, Umberto Eco represents one of the very few Italians who enjoys an international reputation and instant name recognition today by the general public. By virtue of his tireless travels and lectures in a variety of languages, Eco has also become something of a cult figure in Italy and abroad, and his fame resounds not only in the ivy-covered halls of academe but also has a general resonance that few contemporary European intellectuals can match in any country outside of Italy.

Within Italy, Eco's early works – those essays and treatises that preceded *The Name of the Rose* – were tremendously influential. They attacked the premises of Crocean aesthetics that had dominated Italian intellectual life for decades even before the war, laid the foundations for a non-Marxist approach to culture which was progressive and original, and justified the study of cultural phenomena that did not limit itself to a notion of "high" culture. *The Open Work* popularized the revolutionary modernist innovations of James Joyce and prepared the way for a number of subsequent theoretical treatments of contemporary postmodern perspectives on culture that have come out of Italy. The very notion of what an intellectual should or could be was influenced by Eco's important distinction between an apocalyptic and an integrated intellectual, and when postwar thinkers sought a new methodology to apply to the humanities, Eco was one of the first important thinkers to popularize semiotics in Italy. His interest in the role of the reader in the process of narrative led him to pioneering works on narrative and, no doubt, tempted him to try his hand at fiction himself. Important editorial tasks performed by Eco for major Italian publishing firms, not to mention key university appointments and a popular weekly column in one of Italy's most widely circulated news magazines, ensured that the impact of Eco's always evolving thought would not be limited to the somewhat obscure halls of Italian universities but would reach a broader public.

With the publication of *The Name of the Rose*, Eco became a superstar of postmodern culture as well as one of its best exponents in both theory and practice. Eco's fictional works aimed to entertain and to please (a traditional goal of literature which Eco would embrace enthusiastically in his Norton Lectures at Harvard University), but, like the masterpieces of other postmodern writers, they also harbored theoretical intentions. The link of theory and practice is most obvious in *The Name of the Rose*, since Eco himself provides a commentary on this connection with *Postscript to "The Name of the Rose"*. But the same witty combination of erudition, theory, and narrative skill can be found in *Foucault's Pendulum*, where the reasoning behind the most ludicrous paranoid plots about controlling the universe reflects the theoretical denial of meaning in literary texts Eco identifies with deconstructionists. It is also evident in *The Island of the Day Before*, where Eco creates a fascinating portrait of the baroque age not dissimilar from that popularized in Michel Foucault's *The Order of Things*, demonstrating in the process that many of the postmodern perspectives too many contemporary critics and theorists believe to be entirely original to our century actually have far more traditional intellectual antecedents in European culture, especially in the seventeenth century.

Umberto Eco's erudition has been mentioned frequently in this study, and along with his sense of humor, Eco's learning constitutes one of his most striking traits. Unlike many of his fellow cultural or literary theorists, who are far too ready to announce to audiences of breathless academics and fawning students that they have discovered completely original perspectives on human culture, Eco's erudition is joined to a refreshing sense of intellectual modesty. Few scholars had the extensive background in medieval studies required to recognize the tantalizing links in methodology between the familiar Scholasticism of St. Thomas Aquinas and the then current intellectual fad in Europe, structuralism. Recognizing the intellectual similarities between such seemingly different phenomena gave Eco insight into the strengths and weaknesses of both methodologies. Within Italy, with its pronounced distaste for anything that smacked of "popular" culture, Eco's learning allowed him a certain amount of license in advocating that not only "high" culture but also "low" or "popular" culture had much to teach us about social behavior and culture.

The felicitous union of erudition, narrative fiction, and postmodern theory in Eco's three novels has almost no equal in the contemporary period in any country. *The Name of the Rose* places the latest semiotic theories within a framework of the always popular detective novel, exploiting the high level of interest in the Middle Ages as a mirror of our own times. *Foucault's Pendulum* capitalizes upon the reading public's enjoyment of diabolical universal plots to take over the world and demonstrates with good natured parody how the logic behind paranoid interpretation has affinities with one of the most influential schools of literary interpretation, deconstruction. And *The Island of the Day Before* creates a fantasy world of postmodern notions of science and culture but places this world back into the distant past of the baroque era, reminding us that there is nothing new under the sun, especially where literary or cultural theory is concerned.

Eco's cultural and literary theory is profoundly eclectic, democratic, and tolerant of difference. His goal has always been to pursue a tentative view of the truth, holding any theoretical position only so long as new information does not alter its usefulness. In this sense, his three novels all argue against any private or secret information and embrace ideas from any and all intellectual and ideological sources that can be useful in advancing a hypothesis of the truth. Even the interest Eco displays in the role of the reader, as well as his notion of diverging paths in the fictional woods, notions central to Eco's discussion of the process of reading and interpretation, emphasize the freedom Eco believes does or should belong to the reader of the text. And his rejection of the deconstructionist argument that there is no fundamental message in a text or an author of it and, therefore, no basic meaning in it arises from both a theoretical position and a ideological one, since accepting such a view of textual exegesis would destroy humanity's only real hope of inching slowly but surely to a clearer perception of our condition. For this reason, Eco's descriptions of the various cabbalistic groups in *Foucault's Pendulum* have humorous affinities with certain intellectual positions held by influential postmodern intellectuals today, and the novel provides not only entertaining parody but also a serious warning. Unlike so many of the theorists of the postmodern period, Umberto Eco has united theory and practice, philosophy and fictional narrative. Eco should be compared to the *philosophes* of the Enlightenment, such as Voltaire or Diderot, for he has made a wide general audience aware of the kinds of problems that are usually reserved for a small group of erudite thinkers or academic theorists. His search for a universal theory of human culture through the methodology of semiotics, the major focus of his work during the 1970s, has now become more narrowly focused upon the theory and practice of fiction, but this has resulted in an enrichment of his writing rather than a theoretical impoverishment. Such a step backward from the grandiose claims once advanced for semiotic theory derives from a continuous maturing process in his writing: the questions posed by theory still fascinate Eco but the manner in which he responds to such problems has evolved. To paraphrase his own words, upon reaching maturity, Eco discovered that there were matters which must be narrated when they could not be resolved by theorizing.

Two small but not insignificant projects Eco completed in 1995 immediately following the publication of *The Island of the Day Before* in Italy tell us a great deal about Eco's intellectual goals. The first is directly connected to the content of Eco's last novel and is the CD-ROM devoted to the seventeenth century: *Il Seicento: Guida multimediale alla storia della civiltà europea diretta da Umberto Eco* (*The Seventeenth Century: Multimedia Guide to the History of European Civilization Directed by Umberto Eco*, 1995).[1] This CD-ROM differs radically from the kinds of encyclopedias typically found on the shelf in American media stores, such as Microsoft's *Encarta* or the reference works that Microsoft has recently produced on topical subjects, such as *Cinemania*. Faithful to his constant belief that information and knowledge represent a powerful democratic force when disseminated widely and openly, Eco's reference disk encourages interaction between the data base and the user, permits the individual production of hypertexts by the user to personalize the use of the CD-ROM, and generally treats the end user of the product as a researcher and collaborator, not a mere consumer. This intriguing product reflects the socially engaged side of Eco's personality, the aspect of his thought and character that believes a free individual must always conduct a "guerrilla war" against corporate, institutional, or governmental entities that attempt to control and

---

[1] Milan: Opera Multimedia, 1995. To date, there is no English version.

channel information or to influence our minds through manipulation of popular culture.

Eco's sense of humor and his interest in postmodern literary games surface in a mystery tale concocted by Eco in collaboration with Giuseppe Pontiggia, Gianni Riotta, and Antonio Tabucchi. Entitled "La maledizione del faraone" (The Pharaoh's Curse, 1995), the story, obviously intended to entertain a large popular audience attracted by melodramatic adventure stories, constitutes a truly "open work" of fiction.[2] Eco produced the first section of the book without collaboration or consultation with the other three writers, introducing the basic mystery plot and the major characters; Pontiggia continued and elaborated upon Eco's original storyline; Riotta followed, introducing complications; and Tabucchi brought the tale to its conclusion, solving the mystery Eco invented. The three writers who elaborated upon Eco's initial contribution were allowed great artistic liberty but no collaboration between any of the four men was permitted.

Eco's three collaborators are not so well known as he but all are considered major figures in contemporary Italian fiction. Two of them have won the same important literary prize (the Premio Strega) that launched Eco's literary career in 1982 with *The Name of the Rose*: Pontiggia for *La grande sera* (*The Great Evening*, 1989) and Tabucchi for *Sostiene Pereira* (*Pereira Maintains*, 1994). Riotta has published two recent novels and is one of the *Corriere della sera*'s New York correspondents. The literary quality of the finished product may leave something to be desired, but "The Pharaoh's Curse" represents a good example of postmodernist fiction in a minor key. Eco's opening episode employs a number of the commonplaces of popular literature (the murder in a closed chamber, a burial vault in Egypt, from the detective story; the usual love triangle from romance; the mummy's curse from gothic or horror fiction). He also invites his collaborators to engage in a literary game by

[2] "La maledizione del faraone," *Sette: Corriere della sera* (weekly supplement to the Milanese daily), nos. 32–36 (1995).

naming characters after figures in their own novels (Pereira from Tabucchi; Graham Ramsey and Antonio Vitali respectively from novels by Riotta and Pontiggia).

Eco's plot places the opening of the story in the tomb of Pharaoh Thamus, known as "The Agraphic" (the enemy of writing). Thamus is a purely fictional pharaoh invented by Plato in his *Phaedo*. The plot moves quickly to Paris in the second part by Pontiggia and is dominated by a detective there named Robert de la Grive (a descendant of the hero of Eco's third novel), who must investigate the sect of followers of Thamus, the "Agraphoids," who have sworn to oppose the spread of writing. In Riotta's third section, the reader discovers that this strange sect of fanatics is made up of women, who believe that the art of writing underlies patriarchy and that without it, the natural form of government will become matriarchy. Their meetings and actions remind the reader of the hooded monks in *The Name of the Rose* or the Diabolicals of *Foucault's Pendulum*. In the conclusion to the story, Tabucchi moves the narrative to Portugal and introduces new characters. His introduction of two new figures – Daveria and Seume from previous novels by Pontiggia and Riotta – represents a violation of the rules of the game established by the four writers before the story was written. But modifying literary conventions and consciously breaking generic rules produce much of the pleasure readers derive from fiction, especially the postmodern variety. Tabucchi takes the game even further as he introduces a third figure – "The Man With the Pipe," Umberto Eco himself – who recounts the conclusion of the tale. Thus Umberto Eco the author is transformed into a Sherlock Holmes figure reminiscent of his own Holmesian literary creation in *The Name of the Rose*, William of Baskerville. The Agraphoids are foiled by a television broadcast that alerts the citizens of Paris to their plot to reestablish a reign of orality, blind faith, and belief in miracles that will replace the democratic era of writing and reading. After informing the tale's characters that the details of the story's conclusion will arrive the next day by fax from Paris, the Man With a Pipe departs for Naples to pay homage to one of the great word-crafters of humanity (Virgil), singing an imaginary Neapolitan song.

"The Pharaoh's Curse" was designed to entertain Italians during their summer vacations and to increase newspaper sales by including a "whodunit" authored by four of contemporary Italy's most famous storytellers. There is little doubt, however, that this parody of the mystery and adventure story set in an Indiana Jones-like Egypt with mummy's curses and mysterious murders embodies many of Umberto Eco's fundamental beliefs. The narrator's preoccupation in his first and perhaps best novel was "to make truth laugh." For Eco, comedy, laughter, and the search for the truth are never in opposition. In fact, he believes the search for truth can as easily be derailed by pedantry and pretentious erudition as by ideological blinders. Eco's taste for parody, pastiche, and ironic "revisitations" of other literary or philosophical texts constitutes an integral part of his complex and intriguing personality. That his personal traits and the demands of postmodern literature or theory have so many points of convergence explains in no small measure why his collected writings offer one of the most imposing monuments to the postmodern sensibility contemporary readers can enjoy.

Bibliography

PRIMARY WORKS

This selected bibliography of Eco's major writings (primarily books) makes no pretense of being comprehensive. An exhaustive listing of Eco's many articles, newspaper columns, and reviews which would include indications of the extensive evolution of his essays over time before their inclusion in books or anthologies would require a separate book itself and is beyond the scope of this study.

1956

Il problema estetico in San Tommaso. Turin: Edizioni di filosofia. 2nd rev. ed. *Il problema estetico in Tommaso d'Aquino.* Milan: Bompiani, 1970. Translation: *The Aesthetics of Thomas Aquinas.* Translated by Hugh Bredin. Cambridge: Harvard University Press, 1988.

1958

Filosofi in libertà. Turin: Taylor.

1959

"Sviluppo dell'estetica medievale." In *Momenti e problemi di storia dell'estetica*, vol. I. Milan: Marzorati. Enlarged Italian ed. *Arte e bellezza nell'estetica medievale.* Milan: Bompiani, 1987. Partial English translation: *Art and Beauty in the Middle Ages.* Translated by Hugh Bredin. New Haven: Yale University Press, 1986.

Bibliography

1962

Opera aperta: forma e indeterminazione nelle poetiche contemporanee. Milan: Mondadori. 2nd. ed., 1967. 3rd. ed., 1971. 4th ed., 1976. Translation (with omissions and revisions) into two separate books in English: (a) *The Open Work*. Translated by Anna Cancogni. Introduction by David Robey. Cambridge: Harvard University Press, 1989; (b) *The Aesthetics of Chaosmos: The Middle Ages of James Joyce*. Translated by Ellen Esrock. Note to the 1989 edition by David Robey. Cambridge: Harvard University Press, 1989.

1963

Diario minimo. Milan: Mondadori. Numerous editions and printings to the present. Partial translation: *Misreadings*. Translated by William Weaver. New York: Harcourt Brace, 1993.

1964

Apocalittici e integrati: comunicazioni di massa e teorie della cultura di massa. Milan: Bompiani. Partial translation: *Apocalypse Postponed*. Edited by Robert Lumley. Bloomington: Indiana University Press, 1994; one section translated as "A Reading of Steve Canyon," trans. Bruce Merry, in Shenna Wagstaff, ed., *Comic Iconoclasm* (London: Institute of Contemporary Arts, 1988), pp. 20–25; one essay translated in *The Open Work* (see 1962a).

1965

Le poetiche di Joyce: dalla "Summa" al "Finnegans Wake". Milan: Bompiani. [Translation: see 1962b]

1967

Appunti per una semiologia delle comunicazioni visive. Milan: Bompiani. [Non-commercial book intended for Eco's students which was expanded to become *La struttura assente* in 1968]

1968

La definizione dell'arte. Milan: Mursia.
La struttura assente. Milan: Bompiani. Partial translation of one essay in *The Open Work* (see 1962a).

Bibliography

1971

Le forme del contenuto. Milan: Bompiani.

Versus: VS – quaderni di studi semiotici, a quarterly review publishing essays in English, French, and Italian on semiotics founded by Eco that continues to appear.

1973

Il beato di Liébana. Milan: Ricci. Partial translation of Eco's introductory essay published as "Waiting for the Millennium" in *FMR* 2 (July 1984), 63–92.

Il costume di casa: evidenze e misteri dell'ideologia italiana. Milan: Bompiani. Partial translation of several essays in *Apocalypse Postponed* (see 1964) and *Travels in Hyperreality* (see 1977).

"Il linguaggio politico." In G. L. Beccaria, ed. *I linguaggi settoriali in Italia*. Milan. Bompiani.

Il segno. Milan: Istituto Editoriale Internazionale.

1975

Trattato di semiotica generale. Milan: Bompiani. Translation: *A Theory of Semiotics*. Bloomington: Indiana University Press, 1976.

1976

Il superuomo di massa: studi sul romanzo popolare. Milan: Cooperativa Scrittori. 2nd rev. ed. Milan: Bompiani, 1978. Partial translation of two essays in *The Role of the Reader* (see 1979).

1977

Come si fa una tesi di laurea. Milan: Bompiani.

Dalla periferia dell'impero. Milan: Bompiani. Partial translation of several essays in *Travels in Hyperreality*. Translated by William Weaver. New York: Harcourt, Brace, Jovanovich, 1986. Partial translation (one essay) in *Apocalypse Postponed* (see 1964).

1978

"Semiotics: A Discipline or an Interdisciplinary Method?". Thomas A. Sebeok, ed. *Sight Sound, and Sense*. Bloomington: Indiana University Press.

Bibliography

1979

Lector in fabula: la cooperazione interpretativa nei testi narrativi. Milan: Bompiani. Partial translation (not actually a complete translation of *Lector in fabula* but, rather, a collection of major essays written between 1959 and 1979, including selections from *Opera aperta*): *The Role of the Reader: Explorations in the Semiotics of Texts.* Bloomington: Indiana University Press.

1980

Il nome della rosa. Milan: Bompiani. Translation: *The Name of the Rose.* Translated by William Weaver. New York: Harcourt Brace Jovanovich, 1983. *The Name of the Rose Including the Author's Postscript.* Translated by William Weaver. New York: Harvest Books, 1994.

1981

"Guessing: From Aristotle to Sherlock Holmes." *Versus* 30 (1981), 3–19.

1983

"A Correspondence with Umberto Eco." In Stefano Rosso, ed. *Boundary 2: A Journal of Postmodern Literature* 12, no. 1 (1983), 1–13.

Raymond Queneau. *Esercizi di stile.* Trans. Umberto Eco. Turin: Einaudi (original French edition of 1947 entitled *Exercises de style*).

"A Guide to the Neo-Television of the 1980s." In *Culture and Conflict in Postwar Italy: Essays on Mass and Popular Culture.* Edited by Zygmunt G. Baranski and Robert Lumley. New York: St. Martin's Press, 1990. English translation of an article in *L'Espresso* (30 January 1983).

Postille al "Nome della rosa". Milan: Bompiani. Translation: *Postscript to "The Name of the Rose".* Translated by William Weaver. San Diego: Harcourt Brace Jovanovich, 1984. Reprinting with the novel: *The Name of the Rose Including the Author's Postscript.* New York: Harvest Books, 1994.

Sette anni di desiderio. Milan: Bompiani. Partial translation of several essays in *Apocalypse Postponed* (see 1964) and *Travels in Hyperreality* (see 1977).

Il segno dei tre. Milan: Bompiani. Translation: *The Sign of Three: Dupin, Holmes, Peirce.* Bloomington: Indiana University Press.

1984

"The Frames of Comic 'Freedom'." In Thomas A. Sebeok, ed. *Carnival!*. Berlin: Mouton, pp. 1–9.

"The Semantics of Metaphor." In Robert E. Innis, ed. *Semiotics: An Introductory Anthology*. Bloomington: Indiana University Press.

Semiotica e filosofia del linguaggio. Turin: Einaudi. Translation: *Semiotics and the Philosophy of Language*. Bloomington: Indiana University Press.

1985

"Innovation and Repetition: Between Modern and Post-Modern Aesthetics." *Daedalus* 1, 14 (1985), 161–84.

"Reflections on *The Name of the Rose*." *Encounter* 64, no. 4 (1985), 7–19.

Sugli specchi e altri saggi. Milan: Bompiani. Partial translation of a section in *Travels in Hyperreality* (see 1977).

1988

"An *Ars Oblivionalis?* Forget It!" *PMLA* 103, no. 3 (1988), 154–61.

"Intentio Lectoris: The State of the Art." In Giovanna Borradori, ed. *Recoding Metaphysics: The New Italian Philosophy*. Evanston: Northwestern University Press. Revised version in *The Limits of Interpretation*.

Meaning and Mental Representations. Edited by Umberto Eco, Marco Santambrogio, and Patrizia Violi. Bloomington: Indiana University Press.

"Il mio piano." Ed. Ferdinando Adornato. *L'Espresso* (9 October 1988), 92–111.

Il pendolo di Foucault. Milan: Bompiani. Translation: *Foucault's Pendulum*. Translated by William Weaver. New York: Harcourt Brace Jovanovich.

1989

La bomba e il generale. Illustrations by Eugenio Carmi. Milan: Bompiani. Translation: *The Bomb and the General*. Translated by William Weaver. San Diego: Harcourt Brace Jovanovich.

"Un colloquio con Umberto Eco su *Il pendolo di Foucault*." *Il lettore di provincia* 21, no. 75 (September 1989), 3–11.

On the Medieval Theory of Signs. Edited by Umberto Eco and Costantino Marmo. Amsterdam: John Benjamins.

"La semiosi ermetica e il 'paradigma del velame'." Introduction to *L'idea deforme: interpretazioni esoteriche di Dante.* Edited by Maria Pia Pozzato. Milan: Bompiani. Pp. 9–37.

Tre cosmonauti. Illustrations by Eugenio Carmi. Milan: Bompiani. Translation: *The Three Astronauts.* Translated by William Weaver. San Diego: Harcourt Brace Jovanovich.

1990

"Interview with Umberto Eco." Michel Viegnes, ed. *L'anello che non tiene* 2, no. 2 (1990), 57–75.

I limiti dell'interpretazione. Milan: Bompiani. Translation: *The Limits of Interpretation.* Bloomington: Indiana University Press.

1992

"Foreword" to Omar Calabrese, *Neo-Baroque: A Sign of the Times.* Trans. Charles Lambert. Princeton: Princeton University Press.

Interpretation and Overinterpretation. With Richard Rorty, Jonathan Culler and Christine Brooke-Rose. Ed. Stefan Collini. Cambridge University Press. Enlarged Italian translation: *Interpretazione e sovrainterpretazione: un dibattito con Richard Rorty, Jonathan Culler e Christine Brooke-Rose.* Ed. Stefan Collini. Milan: Bompiani, 1995.

"The Quest for a Perfect Language (Blackwell Lectures, Oxford, January 1991)." *Versus* no. 61–63 (1992), pp. 9–45. *La quête d'une langue parfaite dans l'histoire de la culture européenne.* Inaugural lecture (2 October 1992) at the Collège de France for the European Chair. Paris: Collége de France. Italian translation of French lecture: *La ricerca della lingua perfetta nella cultura europea.* Milan: Gruppo Editoriale Fabbri, Bompiani, 1993 [Note: this Italian text of the lecture was distributed as an insert in *La Rivista dei libri,* a literary magazine associated with *The New York Review of Books,* and was never sold separately as a book. It should not be confused with the subsequent book of the same Italian title that appeared in 1993 and is listed below].

"Reading My Readers." *Modern Languages Notes* (1992), 819–27.

Il secondo diario minimo. Milan: Bompiani. Partial translation: *How to Travel with a Salmon & Other Essays.* Translated by William Weaver. New York: Harcourt Brace, 1994.

Bibliography

1993

La ricerca della lingua perfetta nella cultura europea. Rome: Laterza. Translation: *The Search for the Perfect Language.* Trans. James Fentress. Oxford: Blackwell Publishers, 1995.

1994

L'isola del giorno prima. Milan: Bompiani. Translation: *The Island of the Day Before.* Trans. William Weaver. New York: Harcourt Brace & Company, 1995.

Six Walks in the Fictional Woods. Cambridge, Harvard University Press. Italian translation: *Sei passeggiate nei boschi narrativi: Harvard University, Norton Lectures 1992–1993.* Milan: Bompiani.

1995

"Foreword" to Piero Camporesi, *Juice of Life: The Symbolic and Magic Significance of Blood.* Trans. Robert R. Barr. New York: Continuum.

"La maledizione del faraone." *Sette: Corriere della sera* (supplement to the Milanese daily), nos. 32–36 (1995). Written with Giuseppe Pontiggia, Gianni Riotta, and Antonio Tabucchi.

Povero Pinocchio: Giochi lingiustici degli studenti al Corso di Comunicazione. Edited by Umberto Eco. Bologna: Comix.

Il Seicento: Guida multimediale alla storia della civiltà europea diretta da Umberto Eco. Milan: Opera Multimedia (a CD-ROM).

"Ur-Fascism." *New York Review of Books,* 42, no. 11 (22 June), 12–15.

SELECTED SECONDARY WORKS

Artigiani, Robert. "Image – Music – Pinball." *Modern Language Notes* 107 (1992), 855–76.

Baranski, Zygmunt and Robert Lumley, eds. *Culture and Conflict in Postwar Italy: Essays on Mass and Popular Culture.* New York: St. Martin's Press, 1990.

Bauco, Luigi and Francesco Millocca. Edited by Luciano Turrini. *Dizionario del pendolo di Foucault.* Ferrara: Gabriele Corbo, 1989.

Bloom, Harold. *Kabbalah and Criticism.* New York: The Seabury Press, 1975.

Bouchard, Norma. "*Critifictional* Epistemes in Contemporary Literature:

The Case of *Foucault's Pendulum.*" *Comparative Literature Studies,* 32, no. 4 (1995), 50–67.

"Umberto Eco's *L'isola del giorno prima*: Postmodern Theory and Fictional Praxis." *Italica* 72, no. 2 (1995), 193–208.

Burgess, Anthony. "Foucault's Pendulum." *The New York Times Review of Books,* 15 October 1989, pp. 1, 22, 24, 26.

Caesar, M. and Peter Hainsworth, eds. *Writers and Society in Contemporary Italy: A Collection of Essays.* New York: St. Martin's Press, 1984.

Calabrese, Oscar. *Neo-Baroque: A Sign of the Times.* Foreword by Umberto Eco. Translated by Charles Lambert. Princeton: Princeton University Press, 1992.

Calinescu, Matei. *Five Faces of Modernity: Modernism, Avant-Garde, Decadence, Kitsch, Postmodernism.* Durham: Duke University Press, 1987.

Rereading. New Haven: Yale University Press, 1993.

Cannon, JoAnn. *Postmodern Italian Fiction: The Crisis of Reason in Calvino, Eco, Sciascia, Malerba.* Rutherford, NJ: Fairleigh Dickinson University Press, 1989.

"The Imaginary Universe of Umberto Eco: A Reading of *Foucault's Pendulum.*" *Modern Fiction Studies* 4 (1992), 895–909.

"Semiotics and Conjecture in *Il nome della rosa.*" *Italian Quarterly* 27, no. 103 (Winter 1986), 39–47.

Capozzi, Rocco. "Eco's Theories and Practice of Interpretation: The Rights of the Text and the (Implied) Presence of the Author." *Signifying Behavior* 1 (1994), 176–200.

"Metaphors and Intertextuality in Eco's Neo-Baroque Narrative Machine: *The Island of the Day Before.*" *Rivista di studi italiani* 14, no. 1 (1996), 165–89.

"Palimpsests and Laughter: The Dialogical Pleasure of Unlimited Intertextuality in *The Name of the Rose.*" *Italica* 66, no. 4 (1989), 412–28.

"*Il pendolo di Foucault*: Kitsch o neo/post-moderno?" *Quaderni d'Italianistica* 11 (1990), 225–37.

"Scriptor et *lector in fabula* ne *Il nome della rosa* di Umberto Eco." *Quaderni d'italianistica* 3, no. 2 (Fall 1982), 219–29.

Caserio, Robert L. "The Name of the Horse: *Hard Times,* Semiotics and the Supernatural." *Novel: A Forum of Fiction* 20, no. 1 (Fall 1986), 5–23.

Cervigni, Dino, ed. *Annali d'italianistica: Italy 1991 – the Modern and the Postmodern.* Volume 9, 1991.

Bibliography

Cipolla, Gaetano. *Labyrinth: Studies on an Archetype.* New York: Legas, 1987.

Coletti, Teresa. *Naming the Rose: Eco, Medieval Signs, and Modern Theory.* Ithaca, NY: Cornell University Press, 1988.

Consoli, Joseph P. "Navigating the Labyrinth: A Bibliographic Essay of Selected Criticism of the Works of Umberto Eco." *Style* 27 (1993), 478–514.

Controneo, Roberto. "Alla ricerca di Eco." *La Rivista dei libri* 2, no. 6 (June 1992), pp. 21–26.

La diffidenza come sistema: Saggio sulla narrativa di Umberto Eco. Milan: Anabasi, 1995.

"La tromba di Eco: dalla *Rosa* al *Pendolo di Foucault*, un'autobiografia per indizi." *La stampa – Tuttolibri* 17 (May 1992), p. 4.

Courtney, Steve. "For Umberto Eco, A Single Layer of Prose Would Never Do." *The Bloomington Herald-Times*, 19 November 1995, p. D9 (rpt. from *The Hartford Courant*).

D'Amico, Masolino. "Medieval Myth. Umberto Eco: *Il nome della rosa*." *The Times Literary Supplement* (9 January, 1981), p. 29.

Degli-Esposti, Cristina. "The Poetics of Hermeticism in Umberto Eco's *Il pendolo di Foucault*." *Forum Italicum* 25, no. 2 (1991), 185–204.

De Lauretis, Teresa. "Gaudy Rose: Eco and Narcissism." *Sub-Stance* 14, no. 2 (1985), 13–29.

"Semiotics, Theory and Social Practice: A Critical History of Italian Semiotics." *Cine-Tracts* 2, no. 1 (1978), 1–14.

Umberto Eco. Florence: La Nuova Italia, 1981.

Docherty, Thomas, ed. *Postmodernism: A Reader.* New York: Columbia University Press, 1993.

Ekblad, Sven. *Studi sui sottofondi strutturali nel "Nome della rosa" di Umberto Eco. Parte I: "La Divina Commedia" di Dante.* Lund: Lund University Press, 1994.

Elam, Dianne. *Romancing the Postmodern.* London: Routledge, 1992.

Federici, Corrado. "Epistemology in Eco's *Il nome della rosa*." *Quaderni d'italianistica* 7, no. 2 (Fall 1986), 183–96.

Fleissner, Robert F. *A Rose by Another Name: A Survey of Literary Flora from Shakespeare to Eco.* West Cornwall, Conn.: Locust Hill Press, 1989.

Frentz, Thomas S. "Resurrecting the Feminine in *The Name of the Rose*." *Pre/Text* 9, no. 3–4 (1988), 124–45.

Ganeri, Margherita. *Il "caso" Eco.* Palermo: Palumbo, 1991.

Bibliography

Giambagli, Anna. "Raymond Queneau, Umberto Eco e gli *Exercises de style*: Linguaggio poetico di creazione e di traduzione." *Equivalences* no. 20 (n.d.), 33–54.

Giovannoli, Renato. *Saggi su "Il nome della rosa"*. Milan: Fabbri, 1985.

Golden, Leon. "Eco's Reconstruction of Aristotle's Theory of Comedy in *The Name of the Rose*." *Classic and Modern Literature* 6, no. 4 (Summer 1986), 239–49.

Gritti, Jules. *Umberto Eco*. Paris: Éditions Universitaires, 1991.

Haft, Adele J., Jane G. White, and Robert J. White, eds. *The Key to "The Name of the Rose"*. Harrington Park, NJ: Ampersand Associates, Inc., 1987.

Haycroft, Howard. *Murder for Pleasure: The Life and Times of the Detective Story*. New York: D. Appleton-Century, 1941.

Haycroft, Howard, ed. *The Art of the Mystery Story: A Collection of Critical Essays*. New York: Biblo and Tannen, 1976 (new edition of 1946 original).

Heide, Herman van der. "On the Contribution of Umberto Eco to Joyce Criticism." *Style* 26 (1992), 327–39.

Hoesterey, Ingeborg, ed. *Zeitgeist in Babel: The Post-Modernist Controversy*. Bloomington: Indiana University Press, 1991.

Holquist, Michael. "Whodunit and Other Questions: Metaphysical Detective Stories in Postwar Fiction." *New Literary History* 3 (1971), 135–56.

Huncheon, Linda. "Eco's Echoes: Ironizing the (Post)Modern." *Diacritics* 22 (1992), 2–16.

Ickert, Klaus and Ursula Schick. *Il segreto della rosa decifrato*. Florence: Salani Editore, 1987 (original German edition Munich: Wilhelm Heyne Verlag, 1986).

Inge, Thomas, ed. *Naming the Rose. Essays on Eco's "The Name of the Rose"*. Foreword by Umberto Eco. Jackson, Miss.: University Press of Mississippi, 1988.

Kelly, Robert. "Castaway." *The New York Times Book Review*, 22 October 1995, pp. 7, 9.

McGrady, Donald. "Eco's Bestiary: The Basilisk and the Weasel." *The Italianist* 12 (1992), 75–82.

McHale, Brian. *Constructing Postmodernism*. London and New York: Routledge, 1992.

Mackey, Luis. "The Name of the Book." *Sub-Stance* 14, no. 2 (1985), 30–39.

Bibliography

Magli, Patrizia, Giovanni Manetti, and Patrizia Violi, eds. *Semiotica: storia, teoria, interpretazione: saggi intorno a Umberto Eco*. Milan: Bompiani, 1992 (with an important Eco bibliography updated to 1992).

Mitgang, Herbert. "Inside Jokes Range from the Knights Templars to Minnie Mouse: *Foucault's Pendulum*." *The New York Times*. 11 October 1989, p. 16.

Most, Glenn W. and William W. Stowe, eds. *The Poetics of Murder: Dectective Fiction & Literary Theory*. San Diego: Harcourt Brace Jovanovich, 1983.

Musca, Giosuè. "La camicia nel nesso: ovvero *Il pendolo di Foucault* di Umberto Eco." *Quaderni medievali* 27 (1989), 104–49.

Nelson, Victoria. "The Hermeticon of Umbertus E." *Raritan* 13 (1993), 87–101.

Norris, David. "Plus c'est la même rose." In Eric Haywood and Cormac O Cuilleanáin, eds. *Italian Storytellers: Essays on Italian Narrative Literature*. Dublin: Irish Academic Press, 1989, pp. 243–53.

O'Mahony, Brendan. "The Name of the Rose: 'Tractatus Contra Zelotes'." In Eric Haywood and Cormac O Cuilleanáin, eds. *Italian Storytellers: Essays on Italian Narrative Literature*. Dublin: Irish Academic Press, 1989, pp. 229–42.

Pansa, Francesca and Anna Vinci. *Effetto Eco*. Preface by Jacques Le Goff. Arricia: Nuova Edizioni del Gallo, 1990.

Parker, Deborah. "The Literature of Appropriation: Eco's Use of Borges in *Il nome della rosa*." *Modern Languages Review* 85 (1990), 842–49.

Pischedda, Bruno. *Come leggere "Il nome della rosa"*. Milan: Mursia, 1994.

Porter, Dennis. *The Pursuit of Crime: Art and Ideology in Detective Fiction*. New Haven: Yale University Press, 1981.

Prince, Gerald. *A Dictionary of Narratology*. Lincoln: University of Nebraska Press, 1987.

Richter, David H. "Eco's Echoes: Semiotic Theory and Detective Practice in *The Name of the Rose*." *Studies in 20th Century Literature* 10, no. 2 (Spring 1986), 213–36.

Robey, David. "Umberto Eco." In Michael Caesar and Peter Hainsworth, eds. *Writers and Society in Contemporary Italy*. New York: St. Martin's, 1984, pp. 63–87.

"Umberto Eco: Theory and Practice in the Analysis of the Media." In Zygmunt G. Baranski and Robert Lumley, eds. *Culture and Conflict in*

Postwar Italy: Essays on Mass and Popular Culture. New York: St. Martin's Press, 1990, pp. 160–77.

Rubino, Carl A. "The Invisible Worm: Ancients and Moderns in *The Name of the Rose.*" *Sub-Stance* 14, no. 2 (1985), 54–63.

"'Oh Language Diabolical and Holy': Notes on the Extravagances of *Foucault's Pendulum.*" *Modern Languages Notes* 107 (1992), 828–39.

Santoro, Liberato. "The Name of the Game the Rose Plays." In Eric Haywood and Cormac O Cuilleanáin, eds. *Italian Storytellers: Essays in Italian Narrative Literature.* Dublin: Irish Academic Press, 1989, pp. 254–62.

Sarup, Madam. *An Introductory Guide to Post-Structuralism and Postmodernism.* Athens: University of Georgia Press, 1989.

Scholes, Robert. *Semiotics and Interpretation.* New Haven: Yale University Press, 1982.

Schulze, Leonard G. "An Ethics of Significance." *Sub-Stance* 14, no. 2 (1985), 87–101.

Stauder, Thomas. "Un colloquio con Umberto Eco su *L'isola del giorno prima.*" *Il lettore di provincia* 26, no. 93 (September 1995), 39–47.

"*Il pendolo di Foucault*: l'autobiografia segreta di Umberto Eco." *Il lettore di provincia* 23, no. 80 (April 1991), 3–21.

Stephens, Walter E. "Ec[h]o in Fabula." *Diacritics* 13, no. 4 (1983), 51–66.

Talamo, Manlio. *I segreti del pendolo: percorsi e giochi intorno a "Il pendolo di Foucault" di Umberto Eco.* Naples: Simone, 1989.

Tani, Stefano. *The Doomed Detective: The Contribution of the Detective Novel to Postmodern American and Italian Fiction.* Carbondale, Ill.: Southern Illinois University Press, 1984.

Vattimo, Gianni. *The End of Modernity: Nihilism and Hermeneutics in Postmodern Culture.* Translated by Jon R. Synder. Baltimore: Johns Hopkins University Press, 1988.

Verene, Donald Phillip. "Philosophical Laughter: Vichian Remarks on Umberto Eco's *The Name of the Rose.*" *New Vico Studies* 2 (1984), 75–81.

Vernon, Victoria. "The Demonics of (True) Belief: Treacherous Texts, Blasphemous Interpretations, and Murderous Readers." *Modern Language Notes* 107 (1992), 840–54.

Viano, Maurizio. "Ancora su *Il pendolo di Foucault.*" *Forum Italicum* 25, no. 1 (1991), 152–61.

Weaver, William. "In Other Words: A Translator's Journal." *The New York Times Book Review*. 19 November 1995, pp. 16–20.

"Pendulum Diary," *Southwest Review* 75 (1992), 150–72.

Williams, Bernard. "The Riddle of Umberto Eco." *The New York Review of Books* 42, 2 (2 February 1995), 33–35.

Wright, Ralph. "Laughter According to Rose: The Theme of Laughter in *The Name of the Rose*." *American Benedictine Review* 37, no. 4 (December 1986), 396–403.

Yeager, Robert F. "Fear of Writing, or Adso and the Poisoned Text." *Sub-Stance* 14, no. 2 (1985), 40–53.

Index

Index

Index

Index

Index

Index